Wannabes, Goths, and Christians

Wannabes, Goths, and Christians

The Boundaries of Sex, Style, and Status

AMY C. WILKINS

THE UNIVERSITY OF CHICAGO PRESS   CHICAGO AND LONDON

AMY C. WILKINS is assistant professor of sociology at the University of Colorado, Boulder.

The University of Chicago Press, Chicago 60637
The University of Chicago Press, Ltd., London
© 2008 by The University of Chicago
All rights reserved. Published 2008
Printed in the United States of America

17 16 15 14 13 12 11 10 09   3 4 5

ISBN-13: 978-0-226-89842-1 (cloth)
ISBN-13: 978-0-226-89843-8 (paper)
ISBN-10: 0-226-89842-3 (cloth)
ISBN-10: 0-226-89843-1 (paper)

Library of Congress Cataloging-in-Publication Data

Wilkins, Amy C.
  Wannabes, Goths, and Christians : the boundaries of sex, style, and status /
Amy C. Wilkins.
    p. cm.
  Includes bibliographical references and index.
  ISBN-13: 978-0-226-89842-1 (cloth : alk. paper)
  ISBN-13: 978-0-226-89843-8 (pbk. : alk. paper)
  ISBN-10: 0-226-89842-3 (cloth : alk. paper)
  ISBN-10: 0-226-89843-1 (pbk. : alk. paper)   1. Young adults—United States—Social
conditions.   2. Young adults—United States—Psychology.   3. Subculture—United
States—Case studies.   4. Identity (Psychology) in youth.   I. Title.
  HQ799.7.W55   2008
  305.2350973′090511—dc22   2007007353

TO MY MOM, ELIZABETH MURPHY, AND MY GRAM, KAY MURPHY (1917–2007)—TWO WOMEN WHO LET ME THROW OUT THE RULES (MOST OF THE TIME)

Contents

Acknowledgments

I vowed to write sparse acknowledgments, but it seems I don't do brevity well. This is my chance to thank the people who made this book happen, and because it was a long haul, there are many to thank. From the start, Robert Zussman encouraged me to think of this project as a book. His confidence that it would, in fact, be a book—and one that people read—pushed me to keep at it when I thought I could never bear to look at it again. Robert was, and is, an outstanding mentor. Among many other things, he taught me his "tricks" for thinking sociologically about my data but let the project be my own. And he is a loyal friend even when I mess up.

This project has taken me through three intellectual homes. At the University of Massachusetts, Naomi Gerstel taught me that I had something to say, changed the direction of my sociological thinking, and taught me to read book acknowledgments. She, Janice Irvine, and Jill McCorkel offered invaluable feedback on the book chapters, some of which I listened to right away and some of which it took me longer to integrate. I appreciate the breadth of knowledge they brought to this project. Before she left UMass, Dee Royster laid the foundation for my thinking about race. I am a different scholar because of her. Joya Misra, who came to UMass near the end of my time there, went out of her way to learn about my work. She has been wonderfully encouraging. Mariana Gerena, Debbie Sicilia, and Javier Flores helped me arrange interviews. Alice Julier suggested, over my groans, University Unity Christians as the third group for the book, eased my transition into motherhood, and provided me with support throughout the process. My writing group—Shawn McGuffey, Hilton Kelley, and Luis Rivera—raised important questions, sharpened my thinking, and provided camaraderie and laughs at a time in which I was either chained to my computer or tethered to a toddler.

This project would not have gotten off the ground without Carlos Figueroa (1973–2006). Carlos facilitated access to my initial Puerto Rican participants, and to Jaclyn, who I introduce in chapter 7, and gave me important insights into the social organization of the local high schools and into the meanings of Puerto Rican culture. He integrated me into his family, and never stopped trying to teach me how to salsa (I am, regrettably, still terrible). His passion, curiosity, and zest for life were infectious.

I have thrived intellectually because of relationships I built in my two years at the University of Missouri-Columbia. Joan Hermsen, Mary Jo Neitz, and Jackie Litt showed me how to be a faculty member rather than a graduate student. Each also expanded my thinking about gender in new directions. Kendra Yoder, Kevin McElmurry, Jill Mahoney, and Jenny Routledge inspired and supported me in different ways. Dave Brunsma read the entire manuscript. The undergraduates at Mizzou were frequently amazing: their energy renewed me. A special thanks to my gender reading group—Brandon Coleman, Jocelyn Diehl, Logan Micheel, Liz Morningstar, Branden Miller, and Kristie Nelson. Estelle ("E") Johnson challenged me to think through the complexities of friendship across the racial border, and reminded me of the importance of local meanings.

I am glad to have finished this project at the University of Colorado. Janet Jacobs, Leslie Irvine, and Mike Radelet, especially, have provided extra help and encouragement. Rajshree Shrestha can solve almost any problem, makes me laugh, and has given me many animated rides home. I started at CU with two fabulous women: Stef Mollborn and Ying Lu. Finally, Liz Morningstar made the transition from Missouri to Colorado with me. Liz is an incomparable TA, an amazing student, and a wonderful friend.

I entered the lives of many people to write this book. I appreciate the generosity, openness, and trust they gave me. I thank especially Beth, Laurie, and Jaclyn, whose pseudonyms I use here for purposes of confidentiality. Each of these women taught me in ways that can't be captured in a book. I was supported financially by a fellowship from the Mount Holyoke College Alumnae Association, and by a Junior Faculty Summer Research Fellowship from the University of Missouri. Both grants gave me time to devote myself fully to this project. Material in two of the chapters in this book was first published in articles. Thanks to *Gender & Society* for allowing me to use that material here. Doug Mitchell and Tim

McGovern, at the University of Chicago Press, took a chance on me, and helped me through the often confusing process of publishing a first book. Rosina Busse has been a thorough and supportive editor. Finally, the anonymous reviewers gave me excellent feedback, encouraging me, especially, to hone my racial analysis further. I hope I have jumped over the bar they set.

Many other scholars have broadened my thinking, challenged my framing, and pushed me to think and write more clearly. Sherryl Kleinman took me under her wing when her plate was already overflowing. She has been an academic guide, an insightful reader, and a wise friend. Mary Ann Clawson, France Winddance Twine, and Krista McQueeney read the manuscript from start to finish. The book is much better because of their insights. Mustafa Emirbayer, Jessica Fields, Doug Hartmann, and Michelle Wolkomir gave me feedback on various chapters. I have benefited from community with these and other young scholars thinking about similar issues, especially Matt Ezzell, Peter Hennen, and Hava Gordon.

Books, of course, are not built out of academic careers but out of lives. Shawn McGuffey, Meg Yardley, and my cousin Karina Murphy are the friends who always understand my interpretation of events, always hold me accountable, and never think what I do is scandalous (even when it is). Shawn and Meg also provide intellectual advice, personal counseling, fashion consults, and babysitting. Neither tires of either talking about sociology or of going dancing. Shawn has provided astute feedback since the very first draft, helping me especially to think through the dynamics of race in each group. Meg read every draft of every chapter, usually within twenty minutes of receiving it. I appreciate not only her excellent feedback and eye for detail, but also her unwavering commitment to the project, especially since she is not herself a sociologist (yet, I say). In many ways, the chapters on the goths are hers too. Shawn, Meg, and Karina all offer me models of how gender can be lived differently. Karina abetted my first experiment with boundary crossing. Since then, neither of us has ever done things quite as we're supposed to. She assures me that she might even read the book—if I give her a free copy.

I was a single mother of a toddler through the early stages of research and writing. This project has only developed fully because of my community of support. In Massachusetts, Debbie Barnes made a second home for my son Liam. Because of her care, I was able to work without worry. Sara Taylor was unfailingly generous with both time and money. Lisa McGahan modeled ways to be a respectful and supportive mother. Kathy Foley and Minh Ly helped me make it through Liam's earliest years. In Missouri, Bob and Gay Gage, Christina Brawner, Scout Merry, and Missy Davis, among others, provided help and support. We have been lucky, also, to have Pat Walker in our lives. She has enriched both our family life and my thinking.

For the most part, my family finds me inexplicable; they love and support me anyway. My dad, John Wilkins, never could figure out what else I could possibly need to do on the book. My brother Jeremy—also an academic—explained to my dad why the book (and first, the dissertation) took so long. Jeremy is among my staunchest academic supporters—especially noteworthy given the little on which he and I agree: I find his enthusiastic support invaluable. He and my sister-in-law, Maureen, stepped in to give me some much needed weekends to myself. My brother Ben took a different path. I admire his resolve to be true to his own commitments, despite the costs. My sister Nori explained to me that "nobody in the [extended] family can figure out what [I] actually DO." Maybe she'll pick a more transparent career.

My son Liam changed everything. He and I have grown together, in pace with this book. To Liam, being "an author in the whole world" (rather than producing work for a family audience) is the coolest thing ever. I hope he too is able to realize this version of coolness. Along the way, we "adopted" (as Liam explains to the many people who can't figure out how a white boy could come to have a Black dad) James Rose. James has moved twice with us in as many years—something for which I do not express enough gratitude. Insightful, brave, humble, and funny, James also has a story to tell. I hope he gets to.

I dedicate this book to two extraordinary women: my mother, Elizabeth Murphy, and my grandmother, Cornelia Murphy. My mother wouldn't let me give up, even at my lowest moments. She taught me to be self-reliant and to mother with a clear sense of myself. She also taught me that people can mess up and still be strong and loved. Once someone told me that I would be just like my grandma when I got older; I can only hope he was right—although I am certain I will never clean a room well enough to suit her. My Gram was a woman of uncommon courage, dignity, and integrity. I am grateful to both women for letting me find my own way—and for sharing with me theirs.

CHAPTER ONE

Introduction: Gender, Race, Class, and Cultural Projects

Hyacinth, who says she chose the name she uses with almost everyone because it represents her "quintessential" self, sews while she talks to me in the postcollege apartment she shares with an assortment of friends, both women and men. She is adjusting a piece of clothing to make it better fit her personal style—a style that revolves around black, nontrendy clothing that she describes as a "dark [and] creative, an aesthetic." Simultaneously involved with several "sweeties," Hyacinth is proud of her ability to manage the complicated scheduling of both time and emotions her relationships entail. She explains, "I really do believe it's possible to love more than one person at a time, and I guess I feel like if you do, why shouldn't you?"

Molly and I meet in a cafeteria in the campus center of a large northeastern university. A sophomore, Molly squeezes our meeting into a busy schedule of classes, University Unity meetings, and Bible studies. Blonde and blue-eyed, Molly is classically pretty and conservatively dressed. She confides that while she was once sexually active, she has now given up both sex and dating. "I used to be like boy crazy," she tells me, "which is something I've been trying to get under God's control cause I don't want to be that way."

Jaclyn searches through her overstuffed closet. She is looking for something for me to wear to the predominantly Black hip-hop club she plans to take me to tonight. I have already endured the pain of eyebrow waxing, and the even greater pain of having my hair twisted into a tight, hip-hop inspired hairstyle. I am impatient. But to Jaclyn, who intends to and will be the center of attention at the club, these elaborate preparations are ordinary. Jaclyn is white, but she has been part of the hip-hop scene and involved with Black and Puerto Rican men since junior high school. "Interracial dating," she explains, "is a lifestyle."

Young white women living within ten miles of each other, Molly, Hyacinth, and Jaclyn occupy different social worlds—in part by choice and in part by circumstance. Hyacinth is a goth. Molly is an evangelical Christian. Jaclyn crosses racial identities, and is labeled a "Puerto Rican wannabe" for doing so. Goths, evangelical Christians, and wannabes look very different and act very differently, yet they are all examples of related identity projects mobilized to solve a range of shared problems. Although their chosen identities may seem inexplicable, they actually make a good deal of sense. The solutions these identities offer mediate a common set of dilemmas facing contemporary young adults.

The young people in this book want to be accepted. This can mean different things, but often means that they want to be cool. At least, it means that they don't want to be invisible or picked on. They want to have friends. They want to see themselves and be seen as authentic, not as fake or "posers." They want to have fun. And they also worry, although not very explicitly, about their futures. Often, these desires are at odds. Goth, evangelical Christianity, and Puerto Rican wannabehood are each ways of fashioning paths through the conflicting demands that prospective adult life imposes on them. Each is a way to manage success and failure, risk and security, membership and personal identity.

Like most contemporary Americans, goths, Christians, and wannabes see themselves as individuals making independent choices and enacting their authentic selves. Yet both their problems and their solutions are anchored to gender, race, and class. Gender, race, and class fashion the constraints and contradictions young people face, but they also provide resources for solving them. The negotiations between constraints and solutions, in turn, shape the cultural meanings local young people give to gender, race, and class.

The analytical call for the intersection of gender, race, and class has been widely sounded (Thornton Dill 1983, Hill Collins 1991, Mohanty 1991). Because no one is ever simply gendered, raced, or classed, the simultaneous examination of all three helps us better make sense of their lives (Anderson 2005). Indeed, as Bettie (2003) argues, the choice not to use an intersectional perspective not only fails to unearth the complexity of sociological phenomenon, but can also lead us to misinterpret them.

Following this approach, I treat goths, Christians, and wannabes as gendered, raced, and classed. Gender, race, and class, however, are not equally salient in these projects. Both the goth and the Christian projects seem to be most obviously about gender; the wannabes' project is most clearly about race. To that end, the goths and the Christians talked little about race. The wannabes talked little about gender. And almost nobody talked about class. In *New Jersey Dreaming*, Ortner (2003) writes about the task of finding class in the stories told by her high school classmates—stories that seemed to be about other things (e.g., space, success) and that never spoke about class directly (see also Kenny 2000). In this project too, I had to look for what was unspoken—for the ways, for example, that race and class distinctions were drawn by people who try to never talk about race.

Gender, race, and class don't just intersect in these projects, they collide. Thus, in pushing against the constraints of gender, for example, young women are often undermined by the constraints of race and class. Sexuality, I argue, is a key place in which this collision occurs. Sexuality is a principal means by which young people claim and repudiate intersected gender, race, and class identities. But it is *also* the key limit on the solutions they enact.

In this book, I explore three subcultures: goth, evangelical Christianity, and Puerto Rican wannabehood. This work is not intended to provide a map of contemporary subcultural options, or to provide an exhaustive account of subcultural nuance. It is also not about *why* youth choose particular subcultural options, although I occasionally explore that question. It is, more precisely, about the ways young people use elements of subcultures to create individual and collective identities, and then how they use those identities to solve problems.

Young people use cultural symbols to establish group membership, to make their lives more tolerable or interesting, and to resist aspects of the mainstream that are constraining or from which they are already excluded. As Willis's (1977) classic study of British working class "lads" demonstrates, a symbol or strategy that provides short-term relief, such as school refusal, can maintain the status quo in the long-term. School refusal allows youth to reject a status hierarchy at which they are less competitive or that perpetuates a white-dominant curriculum, but also denies them preparation for college or professional careers (Bettie 2003). But symbols of resistance and reproduction can also coexist within a subcultural repertoire. In LeBlanc's (1999) study, she finds that punk girls use the masculine punk aesthetic to resist standardized notions of feminine attractiveness, yet their androgynous style does not protect them from sexual assault.

For the young people in this book, subcultures offer cultural tools for the navigation of gendered, raced, and classed identities. In our contemporary imagination, adolescence and young adulthood are developmentally charged periods. They are associated with identity phases purportedly aimed at an eventual settled adult identity. This "identity making [is] public, performative, and often spectacular" (Perry 2002, 10). The developmental model suggests that part of the adolescent imperative is to uncover or resolve who we really are: that is, to find stable, knowable identities. Indeed, goths, Christians, and wannabes all think of their identities in this way. I think about identities as malleable projects that draw on available cultural resources and gain meaning in interaction with others, but I recognize the importance people place on a sense of coherence (Hewitt 1989, Mason-Schrock 1996).

In this book, I consider goth, evangelical Christianity, and Puerto Rican wannabehood as cultural projects—collective, patterned repertoires that give rise to situated strategies. Hochschild (1989, 15) defines a gender strategy as "a plan of action through which a person tries to solve the problems at hand, given the cultural notions of gender at play." I think about strategies similarly. The young people in this book use cultural resources, including gender, race, and class, to craft plans of action. Many of these strategies are deliberate, crafted as a means of achieving something that can be understood: membership, authenticity, status, etc. At the same time, these strategies achieve other things that may not be consciously understood. While some of these strategies may have conscious gender, race, or class agendas, other strategies are effective because their connection to gender, race, or class is unclear. Each case study shows how a set of strategies works.

In thinking about subcultures as projects, I do not mean to imply that young people consciously weigh their options, making rational choices about how different subcultural options will affect them. Instead, I think of the young people in this book as savvy cultural actors, as people who use cultural resources in creative, interesting, sometimes resistant ways to make their own lives more tolerable or more exciting, to push against the limits posed by the expectations of gender, race, and class, or to shore up their positions. But projects often have unintended or unseen effects, and, in the end, each of these projects also constrains its participants. Part of the reason this happens, I argue, is because gender, race, and class are entangled in people's lives in ways that they do not apprehend.

The cases in this book

Former geeks, goths transform themselves into "freaks." They cloak themselves in clothing, makeup, tattoos, and piercings that make them look dark, freaky, and shocking. Their style deliberately and vocally rejects the consumerism they associate with hip-hop. Claiming to be sad or even psychiatrically disordered, they are disenchanted by mainstream expectations of "normal" psychological adjustment. They write dark poetry, read gothic novels, conduct pagan rituals, and engage their fascination with the macabre through an extensive Internet community that also comes together regularly at a dance club. And they have sex in "freaky" ways: they aren't monogamous or strictly heterosexual, they endorse bondage, discipline, and sadomasochism; they have threesomes and group sex.

In contrast, the evangelical Christians are in many ways conventional. University students involved in formal campus Christian organizations, they engage in university-endorsed activities and apply themselves to their classes. They dress in conservative, but not prissy, clothes. They describe themselves as happy and at peace, and try to be tolerant and loving. They hang out in the dorms. But rather than spending their free time partying with other university students, they spend it developing their "relationships" with God—praying, writing in journals, studying the Bible, participating in Christian community. And they do not engage in sexual activity at all, frequently eschewing romantic relationships of any kind.

Puerto Rican wannabes, the local epithet for the pattern of racial crossover Jaclyn enacts, are white young women from various class backgrounds who identify with the local Black and Puerto Rican hip-hop communities. Spectacularly outfitted in hip-hop style, "Puerto Rican" hairstyles, and "Puerto Rican" makeup, they don't look like "normal" white young women. Unlike the stereotype of the suburban hip-hopper, however, these young women don't "do" hip-hop in a superficial way. Instead, they are saturated in the accoutrements of hip-hop culture, aligning not only their physical self-presentations and musical tastes, but also their political, spatial, and, most importantly, heterosexual commitments with poor and working-class Black and Puerto Rican communities. Often this commitment is sealed with the birth of a baby fathered by a Puerto Rican or a Black man. Although white young men also engage in projects of racial crossover, the wannabes' flagrant violation of seemingly all norms for white, middle class feminine decorum makes them more threatening to their peers.[1] Wannabes challenge the delineation of racial boundaries by assumed heritage, using comportment, consumption practices, and sexuality to jockey for authentic membership in a community marked not only by race but also by class.

Thinking about gender, race, and class

In our daily usage, we think of gender, race, and class as natural, unchanging features of people. Often, we also think of them as discrete: one is a girl or Black or middle class, but not always a Black middle-class girl. But sociologists understand that gender, race, and class are much more complex than this popular formulation. Not only are people always gendered, raced, *and* classed, but these features are also malleable and contentious at both the macro and micro levels.

Gender, race, and class emerge out of shifting historical, political, and economic processes (Omi and Winant 1986, Laqueur 1990, Nagel 1996), but they are also enacted through everyday actions and interactions that create the ongoing illusion that gender, race, and class are real, knowable categories (Butler 1990, West and Zimmerman 1987, West and Fenstermaker 1995). These actions and interactions shape the specific contours and contents of these categories. In this sense, gender, race, and class are things that we *do,* rather than things that we *have.* They are *performed,* but these performances are not a free-for-all; instead, they draw on and remake existing cultural ideas about gender, race, and class—cultural ideas that are tightly bound up with structural conditions.

There are two senses in which gender, race, and class are performed. On one hand, they create a largely invisible set of competencies and way of viewing the world that seems natural, like common sense (Bourdieu 1984). In this sense, people perform gender, race, and class without realizing that they are performing. On the other hand, gender, race, and class expectations can also be learned, so that individuals can use cultural per-

---

1. In contrast, Perry (2002) found that in a mixed-race, urban high school, boys' projects of racial crossover were more problematized than girls'. Girls, she writes, were seen as more likely to base their cross-racial relationships on friendships. In this study, I found something quite different.

formances to claim category membership (Garfinkel 1969, Bettie 2003). The performative element of gender, race, and class mean that they are potentially at risk; because they can be lost, people engage—consciously but more often unconsciously—in attempts to fortify them (e.g., Connell 1987, Pascoe 2005). Writing about class, Ortner (2003, 14) describes these efforts as "projects"—"something that is always being made or kept or defended, feared or desired."

Boundaries are an important tool in gender, race, and class projects because they make clear who is in and who is out (Lamont and Fournier 1992, Lamont 1999). "For individuals, boundaries define who they think they are" (Fuchs Epstein 1992, 234). Boundaries create not only insiders and outsiders, but also hierarchies among groups. In drawing boundaries, groups make claims about the value of their cultural capital (e.g., Lamont 2000). To be effective, symbolic boundaries need to be adaptable—capable of responding to new threats by shifting or by selectively incorporating outsiders (e.g., through "tokenism"). Thus, boundaries are necessarily local and contingent. Accordingly, cultural capital is dynamic and variegated; not only does it vary by region and group, but status groups may also rely on multiple forms of capital, drawing on one form in one context and another in other contexts (Hall, J. 1992, Carter 2003).

Contemporary Gender, Race, and Class Meanings

The advances made by second-wave feminism have ushered in a new era for girls. Women's mass entry into the paid labor force, the erosion of male wages, and the breakdown of the "modern" (male breadwinner / female housewife) domestic bargain have clouded the modern gendered distinction between public and private. These sweeping changes opened the door to vocational possibilities previously off-limits to women, allowing young (white, middle-class) women to imagine an adult life beyond marriage and motherhood, because some women have made significant gains in male-dominated professions. At the same time, girls and women have been accorded more latitude in their leisure pursuits and comportment, a change that often leads to the erroneous conclusion that gender equality has already been achieved.

And yet evidence that things aren't quite equal peeks through. The rise in families headed by single women has not been matched by an overall rise in women's earning power, creating a concentration of poverty among women and children that is exacerbated by a concurrent retreat from social support (Hays 2003). The increasing investment of women in paid labor has been countered by an intensification of both mothering (Hays 1996) and beauty standards (Wolf 1991), and not, overall, by an increasing investment of men in domestic responsibilities. Thus, while young women are taught to expect more equality and personal fulfillment, they also learn to expect greater poverty, more work, and less help (e.g., Sidel 1990).

Girls raised to "have it all" face conflicted messages and overwhelming expectations. They should be ambitious but caring, strong but not mean, thin and pretty but not too worried about their looks, interested in boys but not slutty. They should be prepared to have a career, willingly abandon it in favor of their husbands' career ambitions, and then pick up the economic pieces in case of divorce. In the face of such relentlessly complex messages, popular feminist work like Pipher's best-selling book *Reviving Ophelia* lament girls' loss of self-esteem and lack of "voices." But these changes do not affect all girls in the same ways. As Harris (2004) argues, contemporary girlhood is characterized by two tropes: the "can-do girl" and the "at-risk girl." For "at-risk" girls, new expectations that they be confident and career-oriented increase the grounds on which they can fail.

Transformations in gender relations have been accompanied by equally significant transformations in racial meanings. Prior to the civil rights movement, U.S. society was neatly divided between Black and white. Not only was the color border clear, but so was its hierarchical organization. Black inferiority, and white superiority, were maintained through a combination of social customs, laws, and economic discrimination (Omi and Winant 1986). For groups and individuals who were neither of African descent nor clearly white, acquiring whiteness was the key to integration and future social mobility. These groups attained whiteness by modeling white behavior and achieving economic success (Loewen 1971, Roediger 1991, Brodkin 1999).

By breaking down much of the legal scaffolding for racial discrimination and by shifting public sentiment away from overt racist logic, civil rights did not obliterate racial difference, but instead altered its operation. In a few short years, civil rights legislation opened up the door for Blacks to move into white neighborhoods, to marry white people, and to enter white educational institutions and white jobs (e.g., Patillo-McCoy 1999, Romano 2003). Paving the way for the development of a small Black middle class, these changes narrowed the gap between Black and white on a number of intensely patrolled borders. These changes made the Black-white boundary less absolute, increasing the stakes in new forms of boundary work.

At the same time, the declining political and cultural acceptability of what would come to be vilified as "white supremacy" propelled the need for a new way of talking about the racial line. The emergence of "a kinder, gentler antiblack ideology" (Bobo et al. 1997) takes advantage of a new logic of color blindness, in which it is no longer polite to talk about race directly. Instead, racial distinctions are veiled under the language of "culture." The shift to culture effectively allows whites to "not see" racial power, while blaming Blacks for their continued economic disadvantages (Frankenberg 1993, Bonilla-Silva 2003). Culture is central to contemporary racial politics in two ways: as a means of explaining persistent inequality (e.g., the "culture of poverty") and as a vehicle through which racial difference is performed (Hill Collins 2004).

Moreover, the mass influx of Latino/a and Asian immigrants, the increasing class heterogeneity of "traditional" raced groups, and the increase in the ethnically mixed population complicate the Black-white binary (Gans 1999). Latino/as in general occupy the unstable borderland between Blackness and whiteness. This liminal space is concretized by racial classifications that align Latino/as with either whiteness or Blackness: the categories "non-Hispanic whites" or "non-Hispanic Blacks" imply that being Hispanic modifies one's (white or Black) racial authenticity in important ways (Rodriguez 2000, see also Landale and Oropesa 2002). Among Latino/as, Puerto Rican's relationship to Blackness is distinctive. Puerto Ricans, especially those concentrated in New York City and other areas of the northeast, have the dubious distinction of being poorer than native Blacks (Moore and Pinderhughes 1993). Like Blacks, they suffer from the economic and social problems of concentration in urban ghettoes, including widespread joblessness, poverty, and ill health (Bourgois 1995).

But this closeness to Blacks is also contested through a discourse of authenticity that privileges, as "real," forms of Puerto Rican Island culture associated with Puerto Rico's Spanish heritage, rather than those forms associated with their African or Indian heritage. In this way, some Mainland Puerto Ricans reject their association with Blacks through a politics of nostalgia for a romanticized, harmonious "Spanish" Puerto Rican Island home. Nostalgia and authenticity replicate class differences among Puerto Ricans, as lighter-skinned Puerto Ricans are typically economically privileged on the Island and on the Mainland (Lao 1997, Negrón-Muntaner 1997).

Class is entangled in these changes, but its position is difficult to tease out. Class shapes life chances, providing both material resources and a set of dispositions that, like race and gender, seem innate. Although the image of the self-made man continues to launch dreams of upward mobility, middle-class Americans worry about "falling" in a context in which the gap between rich and poor is growing, and previously stable middle-class families are overspent, worried about job stability, and reliant on two incomes to stay afloat (Ehrenreich 1989, Schor 1998). In this context, cultural capital takes on heightened significance, serving as both a gatekeeper and as a stand-in for economic distinctions.

Although Americans are typically "class aware" (Stuber 2006), class is less available than either race or gender as a category of everyday speech in the U.S. (Ortner 1998). Class is displaced onto race, so that whiteness is equated with middle-classness and Blackness with poverty. The "isomorphism" of race and class positions white, middle-class characteristics as "normal" (e.g., Kenny 2000, Perry 2002), while closing off meaningful cultural space for white working-classness or white poverty. At the same time, the class structure *is* heavily racialized, with Black and Puerto Rican youth much more likely to be concentrated among the poor. Class, like race, provides more than just material advantages: it provides a sense of one's human worth and a sense that one is entitled to be treated with dignity (Sennett and Cobb 1972, Lareau 2003).

Whiteness, cultural cool, and young people

These shifts open up new possibilities for young people, but they also muddy the gender, race, and class terrain on which identities are built, making the task of identity building less clear. Historically, whiteness has provided not only material benefits, but also "psychological wages"—the status and privilege of being folded into the dominant group (Blumer 1958, Roediger 1991). The material and other benefits of whiteness remain intact, but identity politics have eroded the unambiguous psychological superiority of whiteness (Wellman 1997). In combination with the ascendance of Black cultural forms, these changes have encroached on whiteness's previously unshared territory of racial privilege, leading to an increasing perception that whiteness itself is under siege and, simultaneously, that it is culturally vacuous (Wellman 1997, Frankenberg 1993, Perry 2002). Whiteness, once taken for granted, is now a more problematic identity.

The young people in this book, like other urban or near-urban youth, live in an area where whiteness is at once normative and constructed as a problem. Whiteness is taken for granted, used to define "normal" behavior or "normal" people. At the same time, though, the context of identity politics—especially in this vocally political area—means that nonwhiteness is imbued with cultural and moral meaning. To be Black or Puerto Rican is to have a salient, celebrated identity, and to be a member of an oppressed, and therefore potentially morally worthy, group. At the same time, hip-hop is culturally dominant, defining coolness around the performance of an urban style associated with Blacks (and to a lesser degree Puerto Ricans), the poor, and young men. These complicated racial meanings are refracted through a cultural order in which "'white' codifies conformity and goodness and 'Black' codifies nonconformity and badness" (Perry 2002, 59). This symbolic opposition further encodes class with race, since whiteness is an upwardly mobile identity, and Blackness is not.

Schools may provide adult-sanctioned avenues for social success (e.g., athletics), but the majority of white students who don't excel on those terms are left negotiating a murkier, less popular middle ground (Eckert 1989) in which they are positioned between the boredom and safety of preparing for "conventional" socioeconomic mobility and the excitement, danger, and coolness associated with withdrawing from those trajectories. This opposition poses a complex and often paradoxical set of status structures, in which hipness provides more immediate, peer-supported status, while academic and professional orientation provides more long-term, adult-supported status. In her work on racial identities among high school students, Perry (2002) contends that both positions offer prestige. Hipness and mobility, however, are not fully equivalent opposites.

Excluded from the institutional award structure by race or class, young people develop oppositional identities with alternative "badges of dignity"—ways of feeling good about themselves that rely on criteria at which they can be competitive, rather than on institutional criteria at which they are likely to fail (Sennett and Cobb 1972, Willis 1977, Eckert 1989, Fordham 1996). For example, Fordham (1996) argues that Black students associate an academic orientation with "acting white," consolidating racial pride by collectively rejecting the institution of school. Behaviors that seem to "opt out" of mainstream opportunity structures often do so in an effort to salvage dignity and pride even while they reproduce class and race hierarchies. Carter (2005) finds that Black and Latino/a youth slip between school and street identities: they both value education and maintain cultural practices that facilitate their membership in their home communities. These youth are facile in both "dominant" and "nondominant" cultural capital.

Class and race provide more than just material resources. They also provide institutional sanctioning that allows young people who are white and middle-class more latitude in their behavior. Young people who are neither white nor middle-class are more likely to have their behavior interpreted in unfavorable ways. Thus, it is not that cultural symbols have inherent meaning, but rather that symbols take on a particular meaning depending on *who* uses them (Eckert 1989). For example, teachers interpret the disruptive behavior of young Black boys as evidence of their "unsalvageability," while the same behavior from white boys is laughed off or even encouraged with the logic that "boys will be boys" (Ferguson 2000).

These dilemmas are gendered. *Cool* is not only imbued with race and class codes, but is also associated with masculinity (e.g., Maira 2002). Thornton (1996) argues that subcultural hip gains its meaning through its juxtaposition to a feminized, unhip mainstream. This formulation means that masculinities are hipper than femininities. Subcultural gendering is more than symbolic, however. Because the particular components of hipness (sexual bravado, toughness, posturing) are behaviors commonly seen as inherently masculine, women's access to them is both more difficult and more consequential. First, young women are more likely to have their behavior policed by their parents (e.g, through earlier and more stringent curfews, less access to spending money, etc.), and by other authorities. This policing makes it harder and more dangerous for them to participate in hipness (McRobbie 1991, see also Gordon forthcoming). Second, their participation threatens their femininity. Thus, women who take on some characteristics of hipness may not fully engage in all its elements, in an effort to protect their femininity. For example, young Indian American women participating in the hip-hop influenced "desi"[2] culture guard their middle-class-bound Indian womanhood by controlling their sexuality (Maira 2002). As this example demonstrates, hipness threatens women's femininity but, because race and class are always gendered, it also amplifies their race and class risks.

---

2. A collective term used to designate someone who is "'native' to South Asia," used commonly among second-generation youth (Maira 2002).

Sexuality

Sexuality is central to the negotiation of intersected race, class, and gender identities. Like other forms of cultural symbolism, sexuality creates moral boundaries and operates as a mode of both differentiation and hierarchy. But because sex is understood as something you *are,* rather than simply something you *do,* sexuality is an intense symbolic arena. As Gamson and Moon (2004, 53) argue, "managing sexuality is central to developing a sense of personal integrity and autonomy."

Sexuality is a strategic resource that can be used for an array of political, cultural, and personal purposes. In this project, then, I think about sexuality as a set of practices, rather than as either a drive or an identity (Stein 1989). Although young people use practices strategically, they, like other people, are not free to simply choose any sexual practices they desire, but rather pick from a preexisting field of choices that favors certain practices, stigmatizes others, and links sexual practices with particular meanings. As feminists have long argued, sexual practices are inextricable from power relations.

The sexual strategies in this book are primarily heterosexual. Only the goths incorporate homosexual rhetoric and practices into their cultural project, but even they are much more thoroughly heterosexual than not. These projects remind us that heterosexuality is dynamic, incorporating a range of rhetoric and practices with different gender implications.

Heterosexuality is predicated on double standards between women and men, in which women are seen as less naturally interested in sex and more interested in emotions; accordingly, women are expected to exercise sexual restraint and are penalized when they don't (Lees 1993). Despite the death of the marital bargain, in which women could expect a man's financial commitment in exchange for her sexual and emotional commitment, girls and women continue to be held to more stringent standards for sexual comportment than are boys and men. At the same time, this double standard seems to be eroding, as the gender gap in sexual behavior shrinks. Some feminists express concern over these changes, worrying that increased expectations of feminine sexual competence increases the pressure on girls to engage in sexual relations that they wouldn't otherwise choose (Brumberg 1997, Pipher 1994). Other feminists applaud them, arguing that women can find power in overt displays of sexuality that subvert the dominant notions of femininity as sexually passive. Lees (1993, 287) notes, for example: "There is...a sense in which if women take on the word 'slag' as subject rather than object, it is possible to subvert the misogyny embedded in the term." And still others urge caution, noting that "[w]ith the sexual and the sexist as 'closely intertwined' as they are in our culture, it is difficult to assess what is truly freeing and what is subtly undermining of women's long-term health and happiness" (Barton 2002, 600, drawing on Chancer 1998). The centrality of sexuality to sexism makes the task of determining women's sexual agency complex indeed.

For girls and young women, the premarital sexual path is muddy. They no longer have clear guideposts pointing their comportment and attitudes in a single direction.[3] Girls and women respond to these changes in different ways. Strategies of accommodation and/or resistance may emerge in collective rituals and in individual interactions (e.g., Stombler and Padavic 1997). Accordingly, the young women and young men in this book engage in different gendered sexual strategies. Goths most clearly embody the sex-positive model: the goth culture encourages goth women to be sexually proactive and is intolerant of gendered sexual double standards. Puerto Rican wannabes' sexuality violates expectations that white women should only be sexually intimate with white men. In contrast, evangelical Christians—both women and men—are abstinent, and often refrain from dating as well. Because the results of these gendered sexual strategies are surprising and contradictory, each gives us additional insight into the complex relationship between gender and heterosexuality.

This relationship is better understood when race and class are taken seriously. Sexuality is an important means of bounding racial categories. For example, the centrality of the theme of interracial sexuality in white supremacy literature indicates its perception as the leading assault on racial purity (Ferber 1998). In this case, the threat posed by interracial sexuality resides in its implied intimacy. But sexuality can also be used to communicate power and distance, as is demonstrated by the wartime use of systematic rape as an act of ethnic domination. Sexuality inscribes both intimacy and power (Nagel 2003).

Historical studies indicate the importance of sexuality as a mechanism for claiming racial membership in U.S. society. In their transition from Negro to (almost) white, the Mississippi Chinese ended their sexual and

---

3. I am not trying to flatten out the complexity of the sexual expectations in previous generations of youth, but to note that current expectations pose increasingly variant options.

marital involvement with Negro women, cutting off ties with both Negro kin and any Chinese who violated this sexual proscription (Loewen 1971). Similarly, the Irish claim to whiteness depended on sexual separation from Blacks—a separation that was enacted by cutting off sexual relations with Blacks and by bringing their own sexual behavior in line with Anglo standards (Roediger 1991).

Much of the burden for performing racialized sexual purity rests on girls and women. Historically and contemporarily, the assumption of insatiable, exotic sexuality—in contrast to the "pure" sexuality of white women—has been used to justify the degradation of women of color (e.g., Davis 1981, Hill Collins 2004). At the same time, women of color have used their own sexual restraint to position themselves above "loose" white women (Espiritu 2001). By resurrecting the moral superiority of the virginal woman, ethnic communities place much of the responsibility for maintaining the community's sexual integrity on women. Das Gupta (1997) and Espiritu (2001) find that women's ethnic membership as Indians and as Filipinas in the United States is tied to a particular, restrictive performance of gender, enacted through sexual behavior aimed at intra-ethnic familial reproduction and devotion.

Black women have also engaged in a politics of respectability as a way to resist the stereotypes that authorized racial inequality; Black women have hoped that emulating the sexual behavior and decorum of white women would result in respectable treatment (Higginbotham 1993, White 2001). As White (2001) argues, this strategy was at once resistant, challenging pervasive images of Black sexuality and inhumanity, while also functioning as a mechanism of intraracial social control that limited the range of acceptable Black sexual expressions, particularly among women, and that promoted class cleavages among Black people.

Today, Hill Collins (2004) argues, some young Black women position themselves as sexual agents, reclaiming their sexuality in an effort to claim freedom and independence. Others continue to bank on an old politics of respectability through restraint (Schalet, Hunt, and Joe-Laidler 2003). Like contemporary young white women, then, young Black women engage in a range of gendered sexual strategies, but white women do so with fewer costs. Because interpretations of gendered sexual behavior are shaped by racial meanings, white women are able to remake themselves in a way that Black women are not (Solinger 1992, Tolman 1996, Kenny 2000). Despite this racial latitude, concern with respectability cuts across these projects.

The Research and the Setting

I conducted my research in a northeastern college community. The towns
and cities in the area seep into each other; the social circles I investigated
thus cross town borders, flowing between the more affluent, less racially
diverse northern towns where most of this research is centered, and pushing
outward into, and pulling in from, the much poorer, more racially heterogeneous cities in the southern part of the area.

The northern towns in this area feature respected public school systems and thriving cultural calendars. The quaint, bustling downtowns blend
the aromas of patchouli and expensive coffee. Gentrification, rising housing
costs, and a declining visible white working-class culture abet the appearance of widespread affluence. The increasing invisibility of economic
hardship in these towns pushes low-income youth to look to the broader
community for both a model of low-income membership and validation
of their experience of poverty. In contrast, the southern cities are the local
symbols of debilitating poverty, dilapidated infrastructure, and uncontrol-
lable crime. One of the cities is in such an economic crisis that the state
has taken over its purse strings.

The area is renowned for its progressive gender politics. One of the
towns has both a national and a local reputation as a mecca for lesbians and
gay men. While many locals resist this association, it nevertheless fosters
gender identity experiments, and provides a backdrop for youth negotiations
of gender and sexuality.

Face-to-face interactions allow young people to craft their own subcultural stories, and thus provide insight into the themes, decisive moments, and narrative structures that shape who they are. Hearing many
such stories reveals the conventional storyline for each subculture. But
identities are not just narrated, they are also lived, and lived in particular
locations. Thus, while I conducted over eighty formal interviews overall,
I also spent countless hours hanging out in the spaces these young people occupy: clubs and malls, online communities, churches and campus
meetings, and in homes. As I talked to and hung out with young people,
I was not interested in finding out the "truth" about their lives or about
their subcultures. Instead, I was interested in the meanings they brought
to bear on particular symbols and the ways in which they negotiated identity interactions.

This study began when I stumbled across the Puerto Rican wannabe. I
was captivated by the unprecedented derision with which a white middle-

class high school girl described these "other girls." But, although I could get plenty of white youth to talk to me about wannabes, I had a harder time gaining the trust of youth of color, and an almost impossible time getting wannabes themselves to talk to me. Although I perceived myself as young and at least not impossibly unhip, they saw me as "that white lady." I was on the other side of an unnavigable chasm. At first, I used friends of color or my Puerto Rican then-boyfriend to facilitate initial conversations with youth of color. Once I gained access, I had little trouble establishing rapport, and these interviews typically generated more contacts. This strategy filled out my initial project, which explored the perspectives of non-wannabe youth about the wannabes.

I wanted to talk to wannabes themselves. My attempts to use the same networking approach with the wannabes, who were embedded in overlapping social scenes with the youth of color, were repeatedly declined, as were my attempts at direct solicitation. Having been warned that wannabes would "beat me up," I was intimidated by their aggressive demeanor. Like many white middle-class women, I had learned to be "nice" and to "avoid making a scene," and had (and still often have) a hard time with more confrontational communication styles. A fortuitous convergence of personal circumstances allowed me to convince Jaclyn, the wannabe I opened with, to talk to me, but not until she had interrogated every aspect of my study. Our initial conversation, which lasted many hours, opened the door to a multifaceted and extended relationship. Jaclyn recruited me into her scene, taking me with her to clubs, parties, parks, and on personal visits. I met and talked to many of her friends and family members, and to even more of her boyfriends.

Changes in my own life facilitated access to other wannabes. My own unplanned and unwed motherhood, attendant financial problems, and struggles with my son's father splintered the class wall that had fostered the wannabes' distance. Although my son's father is white, he is lower working class, and my relationship with him brought me into a more class and race heterogeneous community. These circumstances facilitated my study, but they did not mean that I ever fully crossed raced class lines. Instead, I was desirable for my middle-class cultural capital, which women in this study called on to navigate their own legal and social service dilemmas.

I added both the goths and the Christians to this project for theoretical reasons. I concluded my first analytical piece on the wannabes lamenting the degree to which wannabes relied on conventional notions of feminine sexual restraint to make their racial claims. I wondered if there was a space in which young women were able to engage in more proactive sexual practices. I chose the goths because they claimed to have undone conventional gendered sexual rules. Goths flaunt gender conventions in the ways in which wannabes flaunt racial conventions. Although I never fit in with the goths, my own attempts to push against the limits of gendered rules for comportment did help win their trust and allowed me to empathize with and make sense of the strengths and limits of their strategies.

Unique among these groups, goths have an extensive Web-based community that enabled my access. A friend of a friend used the Web venue to solicit my initial interviews, and then, invited to join the community myself, I used the Web both to set up interviews and as an extensive source of information in its own right. My entrée into the goths was further facilitated by the friendship I established with Beth, the first goth I interviewed. Because Beth is a well-liked and established member of the local goth community, she became my sponsor in the goth scene. Her friendship made me legitimate, even though other goths knew my research intentions. Beth provided me with ongoing access to information and gossip about the goth scene, even after my formal investigation had tapered off, and she also read countless drafts of my analysis, giving me an ongoing internal check on my work. Although Beth set up a number of my interviews, however, she did not set up all of them. Instead, I used my presences on the Web and at goth events to solicit participants outside of her circles.

The goths' weekly gathering at the Sanctuary—the goth night at a local dance club—situated the study for me, enabling casual conversations, as well as some sort of community participation. At first this piece of the study caused me anxiety, because, while I had a sense of what was expected in the hip-hop clubs I went to with Jaclyn, I had no idea what to expect at a goth club, particularly given goths' adamant distaste for hip-hop clubs. In this way, however, I wasn't much different from most goth initiates, and the experience gave me some insight into the process of "learning goth." My first visit involved many discarded outfits before I finally settled on some black combination. At no point did I expect to "achieve goth," but I also didn't want to insult them by not respecting their aesthetic code.

Many people have asked me why I chose evangelical Christians as the third group in this project. Christians are different from goths and wannabes in critical ways: their subcultural affiliation has an adult counterpart, and is more likely to be endorsed by large sections (though not all) of adult culture. They are not spectacular. They don't elicit mainstream moral panics or cause people to cross the street in fear. Indeed, they don't appear to be pushing any boundaries at all. Wannabes and goths often require elaborate introductions, but most of us know evangelical Christians. I grew up with many of them, and have two cousins who are ardently evangelical. In addition, my brother and sister-in-law, while not Protestant evangelicals, are conservative Catholics. These are everyday people, ordinary to some, endlessly vexing to others. In this way, evangelical Christians are in our everyday lives in a way that wannabes and goths are not. Because they don't seem to challenge mainstream conventions, to many people I have spoken with they are also uninteresting. But this is also why they made theoretical sense. Precisely because they appear to be so conventional, Christians provide a distinct counterpoint to the race-transgressing wannabes and the gender-pushing goths. The Christians are an example of a different way of negotiating the dilemmas of white middle-class young adulthood, and thus expand our understanding of the ways in which race, class, and gender are woven together.

Christians also seemed like an easy group to find. I imagined that their formal structure would enable me to quickly identify possible participants, and that the politeness and helpfulness I associate with Christians would encourage them to talk to me. But evangelical Christians, in reality, turned out to be a much harder group to study than I had imagined. Although they were a visible group, regularly staffing tables in the campus center, for example, and many of them were initially happy to talk to me, our rapport too frequently broke down over issues of faith; or, more specifically, my lack of faith. In her study of fundamentalists, Ammerman (1987) explains that although she did not share the specific faith of the community she was studying, her position as a fellow Christian of some sort accorded her trust and acceptance. In this study, my position as a non-Christian impeded my ability to establish trust. The end of every interview brought with it questions about my own interest in Christ. Uncomfortable with being disingenuous, I explained that I had no interest in spirituality, Christian or otherwise. This response did not elicit any vehement protests, but it did often put an end to their interest in me, making it difficult for me to secure further cooperation or gather follow-up information. The same process occurred when I attended their church.

Nevertheless, several of my respondents liked me well enough to connect me with other Christians. Their "friendliness" did come through for me, and, despite the difference in faith, I was able to establish some common ground, particularly with many of the women. Indeed, I was repeatedly surprised by how likable I found these conventional, unspectacular Christian youth. Although (or because) their stories were, in fact, mundane in many ways, I found myself able to relate to their dilemmas, concerns, and values in a way that I frankly found a bit disconcerting to my own sense of self. In the end, almost all of the student leadership of University Unity, as well as many "rank and file" members, had talked to me at some point.

Unlike both the wannabes and the goths, the evangelical Christians are involved in a formal organization that structures their identities. Because this formal structure was open—its meetings announced on a sign in the campus center—it was easy for me to access. On the other hand, the formality reduced the opportunity to engage in casual talk, as I had with the other two groups. I had to catch casual talk where I could, usually before and after the meeting itself. The meetings, on the other hand, sometimes incorporated slide shows from things like "alternative spring break," opening a small window on their identities in action. Although these organizations are led by nonstudents, adults whose job it is to mentor and mold these students in their acquisition and development of an evangelical identity, they also integrate student speakers and other student-led events. These moments provided opportunities for me to see students engaged in leadership roles and performing their identities in front of their communities.

Locating myself

I undertook this project on the tail end of my own youth. Like the young people in this book, I struggled to make sense of the expectations, opportunities, and limitations posed by my own location as a white middle-class woman. Indeed, I have experimented, sometimes self-consciously and sometimes less so, with many of the strategies used by the people in these different projects. Thus, I have a great deal of empathy for many of them, even while I am frequently critical of their strategies. My criticism of them is often also criticism of myself.

When I began this project, I was in many ways a traditional graduate student, powered by a freshly minted undergraduate degree and a heady combination of middle-class earnestness and naiveté. An undergraduate degree in women's studies armed me with feminist energy, a reasonable understanding of gender, a healthy dose of white middle-class guilt, and a limited comprehension of how race and class actually work.

I began this project with the wannabes, who were fascinating to me because of the level of contempt they inspired from girls who otherwise articulated a well-developed "everyone can do their own thing" attitude. At the time, I had just entered a relationship with a Puerto Rican man. This relationship was attended by a good deal of local scandal among our friends and family, so I could empathize both with the wannabe's particular racial transgression and with their position as spectacles. Yet the young people I spoke with repeatedly distinguished my relationship with Carlos from the relationships in which the wannabes engaged. I didn't understand these distinctions at the time, but eventually began to realize that they turned on my continued performance of middle-classness despite my cross-racial relationship.

Some time into the project, my position changed dramatically. Against the advice of most of my family and mentors, I carried an unintended pregnancy to term and became a single mother. The concern, which more often came from women than from men, was not framed in explicitly moral terms, but in (often angry) concern. Would having a baby sabotage the career that had been carefully laid out for me? Was I squandering the hope and expectations that older women had placed on me? These concerns were exacerbated because I was not married (or partnered), and because the baby's father was a white working-class man who didn't have the money (or inclination) to fund my graduate education.

Becoming a single mother changed my social location in significant and often unexpected ways, propelling me both into a perpetually precarious economic situation and into a different social space. This new space was both symbolic and actual: I moved from a rapidly appreciating condo in a trendy, white middle-class town to a house on a busy corner in a more urban, much less "desirable" area. My neighbors and social networks, with the exception of ongoing contacts with academic friends, became working-class and predominantly Black. It was in this new space that I eventually met the Black working-class man who is now my partner.

As I wrote earlier, single motherhood facilitated my research opportunities with the wannabes, creating a shared set of experiences and bringing me into common places I might not otherwise go—like the local WIC office. Single motherhood brought me closer to the working-class and poor women in this study; not only did we share many of the same daily dilemmas, but we also shared the same stigma (because I could envision a return to the middle class, though, I was never fully like them, a distinction that was not lost on either them or me).

On the other hand, single motherhood was also a mark of my class failure to the goths and especially to the Christians. I never hid my circumstances, both because I viewed my ability to single-handedly parent and finish graduate school as a sign of my competence, and because single motherhood constrained my resources, forcing me to work around the hours of my day care (and to make phone calls with my son chattering in the background or demanding my attention). Inevitably, the Christians in this study were aware that I had a child and that I wasn't married. Single motherhood remains a powerful sign of sexual status.

The organization of the book

Although the wannabes were the first case I investigated, they are the last case in the book. Instead, I begin the book with the goths and the Christians. Although they seem strikingly different, goths and Christians are similar in many ways. Both groups are predominantly white and middle-class, but, in good color-blind fashion, see themselves as tolerant, open, and diverse. Both groups use their particular subcultural practices to position themselves as respectable, responsible, and disciplined people. But they do this differently.

In remaking themselves as freaks, goths navigate a cultural position between coolness and geekines; Christians repudiate coolness altogether by establishing themselves instead as "good." Both strategies, I argue, are ways of being white and middle-class. In both groups, sexuality is central. Goths are sexually experimental, advocating nonmonogamy and gender egalitarianism, while Christians are abstinent. Each of these strategies has different, sometimes unexpected, gender implications. Each strategy, moreover, uses the rhetoric of romance. Their interest in romance makes them more respectable, binding their gender projects to race and class concerns.

Goths and Christians both secure their white middle-classness, but Puerto Rican wannabes reject it. In chapter six, I examine the ways in which the spectacle of the Puerto Rican wannabe is used by non-wannabe youth, both white and nonwhite, to express their own race, class, and gender locations. In particular, I show that while these negotiations expand what it means to be white, and bring into question who in fact counts as white, they do so by bolstering hierarchical gender relations based on the idea that proper female sexuality is restrained.

In chapter seven, I analyze the lives of the wannabes themselves. I take apart the caricature drawn by the youth in the previous chapter by showing how their identity strategy is a logical response to the contradictions and limitations they experience in their own lives. For these women, "wannabehood" solves a range of problems they experience because of their particular race, class, and gender identities. Nevertheless, wannabes all run into the same sets of problems in their negotiation strategies, a problem I attribute in part to the heterosexual focus of their strategy and to the dearth of available racial discourses with which they can make sense of their lives.

CHAPTER TWO

From Geek to Freak

I met Crow[1] for the first time at a crowded coffee shop. Rather than providing a detailed self-description, he had simply told me (via e-mail) that he would be "the cute Goth boi."[2] And indeed, no further description was needed. Even in a coffee shop brimming with eccentrically dressed young adults, Crow stood out. A small, blonde man, he wore tight black pants, a fishnet top, and fingerless gloves.

Crow was boastful, full of a braggadocio that contrasted with his cultivated effeminacy, which is often completed by two small ponytails worn in little-girl-style on top of his otherwise shaved head and a small stuffed animal he takes with him to the club. I am used to having to draw people out, but Crow was eager to talk. After all, he told me, "The joke has been: it makes sense to do an interview. You're going to be a rock star anyway." I wasn't so sure, but I didn't tell him that. Crow describes himself as an "elitist freak," telling me that he'll "probably become a bigger elitist as time goes on and won't associate with anyone without a piercing or tattoo." He's more comfortable, he explains, with "people on the fringe, [who aren't] mainstream, [who aren't] sheep." He proclaims proudly, "yes, I'm a narcissist" and "yes, I'm insane." "I posted in my live journal yesterday all of my personalities. I don't have MPD. I have multiple personality order." Although Crow's appropriation of psychiatric labels may seem playful, I

---

1. All the names in this book are changed. Because many of the goths used creative, alternative names rather than their given names, I did my best to reproduce the spirit of their chosen names.

2. Because Crow and I communicated via e-mail, I am using his spelling of the word boy. Crow's spelling is the equivalent of the use of "grrrrl" for girl, and suggests participation in a young, gender-conscious community; these are issues I examine at length in the next chapter.

got the sense that he took himself and his comments very seriously indeed. Goth may be play, but it is serious play.

I open with Crow because he is both prototypical and unusual among the goths in this study. Among these goths, he most adamantly patrols the boundaries of authenticity, suggesting that those who eventually "grow out of it ... didn't get it" in the first place. Being goth, he told me, is about "being who you are, if you're this way all the time, not just five hours a week, dress the same way all the time, that's who you are." Yet in his extremism he makes explicit, and without irony, many of the elements of the goth scene, not least of which is the idea that being goth is not a phase, but rather the expression of a real, innate self. Like other goths, Crow has obviously spent a lot of time thinking about who he is, describing himself decisively as a freak. And like other goths, he sees his real, freaky goth self as distinct from, and better than, the "mainstream."

Consistent with Crow's self-portrait, goths are widely seen as weird, freaky, and disturbing. This image was propelled into the mainstream imagination by the Columbine massacre, in which the two socially isolated, black trench coat clad shooters were inaccurately described as goth. In Columbine's wake, parents, politicians, and the media have voiced alarm about the alleged pathology, Satanism, and violence of the goth scene. Goths like Crow paint themselves with the same broad strokes, portraying themselves as enigmatic outsiders. And yet they object, not incorrectly, to the Columbine association.

The media portrays goth as satanic, and goths portray themselves as rejecting the mainstream, but I have come to understand goth freakiness as a way of becoming a little more hip. By donning shocking self-presentations, embracing taboo emotional repertoires, and (as I explore in the next chapter) violating mainstream sexual norms, goths do what lots of adolescents and young adults long to do: they scare adults, command social distance from their peers, and create a community in which they get to claim membership, but also get to hang out, develop intimate relationships, and have sex. In these ways, the goth subculture—despite its in-your-face rejection of the mainstream and the Columbine-derivative hysteria—is quite ordinary. The goth strategies, while perhaps particularly innovative, are one means of gaining distance from the sting and isolation of being a geek.

In this chapter I am concerned with how white middle-class youth who self-consciously define themselves against the normal nevertheless sustain their privileged race and class locations. For young people who are unsuccessful at (or uninterested in) high-status performances of whiteness, freakiness is an alternative way to do white, middle-class young adulthood. Goth rejects both conventional performances of white middle-classness and racially transgressive performances. Freakiness thus allows young people who at other times and in other contexts might be isolated as geeks to gain social visibility, community, and a version of hipness, bringing validation and desirability, while keeping the path to socioeconomic success as white middle-class adults uncluttered. Both despite and because of their particular cultural innovations, these goths reproduce their own white middle-classness. For them, goth is a culture of limited liability.

Between geeky and cool

The dilemmas of coolness have long been part of coming of age lore: countless movies portray adolescents and young adults negotiating the social poles of "coolness" and "geekiness." Older adults may recall these negotiations as intense and painful, but they are nonetheless rather easily dismissed as distant from "real" (i.e., adult) concerns. It is a mistake, however, to dismiss the negotiation of coolness as trivial simply because it is an adolescent trope. Indeed, the very ordinariness of these negotiations masks their importance in establishing adult social hierarchies (see Eckert 1989, Bettie 2003).

Coolness, like most everything else, is contested terrain. Local meanings jostle with extralocal meanings. Within the same geographical space, individuals and groups launch competing claims to coolness. Despite this dynamism, cool activates race, class, and gender understandings. These understandings, in part, shape the particular dilemmas faced by goths (as well as other young people, as we will see in later chapters), even while race and class remain invisible to them as both material resources and sources of meaning in their lives.

In the high school and on the street, coolness brings rewards, but those rewards diminish in the context of middle-class adulthood, in which people are measured by their socioeconomic success and competence in more traditional forms of cultural capital.[3] While the components of cool may be variable, they express "resistance to established authorities or conventional customs," and are thus frequently antithetical to the characteristics

3. See Carter 2005 for an analysis of these dynamics among Black and Latino/a youth.

associated with "conventional notions of success" (Milner 2004, 59). Indeed, disdain for such success—to "not give a fuck" (Boyd 1997)—is built into cool. Contemporary cool is embodied most emphatically by the Black male "gangsta," whose style, attitude, and (presumed) relentless pursuit of pleasure make him the symbol of rebellion from the confines of white middle-class restraint. Maira (2002, 58) explains that "hip-hop style connotes a certain image of racialized hypermasculinity that is the ultimate definition of cool." Importantly, then, while the symbol of the "gangsta" is most saliently racialized, he is also gendered and classed.

On the other end of the spectrum, geeks are marked by their overinvestment in adult middle-class values. Geeks are studious, industrious, and often technologically adept. But they are also stylistically and socially inept—and consequently, frequently socially isolated. Geekiness is coded as both white and feminine, even when embodied by youth of color or boys (see also Carter 2005). Social invisibility marks geeks as adolescent failures even while it prepares them for conventional adult success. This anticipated trajectory is captured in (white, middle-class) cultural lore about male high school outcasts who attend reunions to show off their economic success as adults (their finances also, at least in myth, garner them social success in the form of a beautiful woman as a partner).[4]

The relationship between cool and geekiness, then, is inverted in adulthood. The values associated with geekiness gain ascendancy in middle-class adulthood, even while they incur social isolation and even humiliation in adolescence and young adulthood. Negotiating these social poles is a pervasive problem of adolescence—many young adults strategize to avoid the social derision of geekiness while maintaining its long-term benefits. This dilemma is perhaps particularly intense for boys, since the characteristics of whiteness are at odds with a hegemonic masculinity that centers on valiance, adventure, toughness, sexuality, and self-gratification. The goths in my study provide one example of this negotiation. In adopting the goth persona, these young adults employ freakiness as a mediating category between geekiness and cool. Goths use freakiness to contest the terms of cool, especially those that are expressed through white youth adoption of Black urban styles, while simultaneously relying on other elements of cool to navigate their own social positions.

---

4. Cooper (2000) similarly documents an emerging form of "nerd" masculinity among adult men in the Silicon Valley. The men in her study mobilize this masculinity to valorize their career success and to legitimate withdrawal from family caretaking.

For these white middle-class goths, freakiness offers temporary solutions to dilemmas of white middle-class young adulthood. The structural advantages of whiteness stem in part from the construction of whiteness as proper, emotionally and sexually restrained, and prudish: in short, safe, boring, and unhip. And yet this prescription for emotionally and sexually sterile lives may be experienced by white youth as relentless and inauthentic (Gaines 1990). Moreover, whiteness is often seen as culturally vacuous (Perry 2002). As Greg remarks, "The average white kid doesn't have anything else to belong to."

Freakiness resolves these dilemmas. Standing between coolness and geekiness, it borrows elements of each without becoming either. Freakiness is a means of accessing some of the valorized social visibility of cool by carving out a space and image that is exciting, even notorious, without integrating its long-term socioeconomic disadvantages. The transformation from geek to freak moves goths out of the shadows they occupied as geeks. Their outlandishness forces acknowledgment of their existence and gives them social power. While geeks are just losers, freaks must stand for something, even if we cannot figure out what it is.

The local goth scene

By most accounts, the international goth scene emerged in the early 1980s through a melding of elements from the punk and the glam scenes. Goth is thus considered by many a music-based scene,[5] integrating both hard-edged sounds (the "stompy" music of the punk and '80s new wave scenes) and ethereal, orchestral music ("swirly-girlie" music). Accordingly, the music lends itself to dancing styles not found in mainstream clubs; depending on the song's style, dancing is either "stompy" and punk-like, or highly stylized, flowing, and balletic. But being goth implies much more than shared musical tastes; indeed, many of the goths I spoke with commented that they frequently listened to non-goth music. "As a whole, goth for me is about culture (and I'm using 'goth' as a broad umbrella

---

5. In Thornton's analysis of club cultures, "music is the cultural form privileged within youth's subcultural worlds" (1996, 12). While goth is also a music-based scene, music did not emerge as a category of distinction in my interviews. My informants often offered me a list of goth bands, but did not elaborate those descriptions (Jeff did talk about the importance of goth music to him, but his comments were exceptional). Consequently, I do not develop music as an important category in this analysis.

term here, not as a narrow reference to gothic rock, a musical subgenre)," posted one man.

The data for the following two chapters is based on eighteen months of ethnographic research in a local goth scene. I entered the goth scene through a friend of a friend, but my first real contact was with Beth. Beth and I hit it off immediately, and she was able to facilitate my integration into the goth scene, introducing me to the Sanctuary, to the Web Listserv, and to her friends. Largely because of Beth (and perhaps also because of my preexisting although casual friendship with Greg), once I gained initial access to the goth community, I did not find it difficult to legitimize my participation. I spent time at the Sanctuary, at private goth events, and generally hanging out. Indeed, I found myself invited to more events than I could possibly attend. This acceptance was perhaps surprising, given goth hostility to "tourists." But in addition to being validated by Beth, I was viewed, I think, as a sympathetic audience, and even a potential goth recruit. More than one goth suggested that they would covert me yet (this conversion has never manifested, despite my real appreciation for many of the goths I met).

I supplemented participant-observation with seventeen in-depth, open-ended interviews with self-identified goths (ten women and seven men). This scene is small enough that groups of friends are highly interconnected. Every person I interviewed knows, to a greater or lesser degree, everyone else in my sample. In addition, I engaged in numerous casual conversations with the interviewees as well as with other goths.

The third set of data for these chapters emerges from the daily musings, anecdotes, rants, debates, and "flame wars" (arguments) that take place on the Web list, GothNet. My six months of lurking (and some participation) on GothNet yielded reams of data. At the time of my participation, GothNet had approximately eighty members collectively posting up to 150 messages a day. These postings gave me more insight into the ongoing construction and negotiation of goth identities than I could glean from single interviews, as the Web venue was a regular forum for most participants, who used it to engage issues both silly and serious. Moreover, as an intra-goth space, GothNet fosters conversations that might not take place between goths and outsiders or "tourists." Although I announced my presence on the list, my participation did not seem to interrupt the flow of exchanges.

Because I confine my investigation to a local goth scene, I do not intend to make claims about the goth scene writ large. Indeed, my informants themselves considered the local scene to be atypical; mostly, I think, because of its location in a less urban area than other large northeastern cities.[6] The goth scene I investigated is centered in a large college town with a reputation for both liberalism and tolerance. The scene absorbs this political atmosphere, priding itself on its inclusiveness. Many in the group claim overlapping identities as bisexual, polyamorous, BDSM (bondage, discipline, domination and submission, sadism and masochism) participants, and pagans. And yet, it is demographically homogenous: with a few exceptions, local goths are youth or young adults, white, middle-class to upper-middle class, college educated, liberal but not radical, unmarried, and childless. They are technologically adept; if they aren't employed in tech support, then they spend an enormous amount of time online. They are known for their brooding solitude, yet they call each other to task for perceived apathy toward the goth community. Indeed, they are exceptionally social, coming together regularly at the Sanctuary, at parties, and online.

Historical changes in the transition to adulthood shape participation in the goth scene. Later ages of family formation and longer educational stints, combined with declining career opportunities, have pushed back the acquisition of a stable, conservative adult middle-class identity, providing space for middle-class adults to conduct identity experiments well into their twenties (Shanahan 2000). The goths in my study are young adults, attending college or working in short-term or entry-level jobs. Unmarried and primarily childless, they are either supported by their parents or supporting only themselves. The reduced dependence on immediate career formation decreases the risks attached to aesthetic and behavioral experimentation. Untethered by economic dependents, they are able to spend their (or their parents') resources on their own stylistic experiments.

Probably because so many of its participants are college students, the goth subculture in my study is perceived by my informants to be less tightly bounded than many goth communities. These goths confine themselves to the goth community to various degrees. Some, like Crow, eschew associations with people who are not visibly marked as freaks, while others are well integrated into the larger community. On the one hand, goths debate each other's authenticity, laughing at "Tuesday goths" (people who only bring out their goth wear for Tuesday nights at the Sanctuary), while, on

---

6. Yet journalistic treatments of goth from other parts of the country indicate that the ways in which the goths in this study explain themselves are shared with goths in other geographical areas as well.

the other hand, they distance themselves from the goth label, explaining that "it's very goth to deny being goth." Regardless of their location on the scale of goth authenticity, the participants in this study are active participants in the goth scene.

The goth label provides a concrete, definable identity—a shorthand way to convey selfhood. Although the goths I interviewed universally contend that "what it means to be goth" is impossible to pin down, their definitions all sketch out the same elements, suggesting a common understanding of subcultural content.

Goth, they explain, is an aesthetic. Hyacinth says, "It's seeing a set of things as beautiful, things that are darker and frightening to most people." The goth aesthetic is dark, eerie, isolationist. They claim a shared aversion to the sun and concomitant fascination with the macabre: cemeteries, the dark, vampires. The goth aesthetic engulfs tastes in music, movies, and humor, but centers on self-presentation: the body is the principle canvas for goth freakiness. Dramatic makeup on whitened faces, jet black or brightly hued hair, and copious tattoos and body piercings accessorize dark, sumptuous outfits that differ dramatically from the preppy or hip-hop styles worn by many of their peers. Many, but not all, claim that "authentic" goths shouldn't be able to pass as "normals."

The goth aesthetic reflects an attitude of cultivated angst, frequently symbolized by graveyards and vampires. Although most of the goths I met seemed sociable and content, they reject the "fetishize[d] happiness" they associate with the mainstream middle class (Polhemus 1994), describing themselves as inordinately sad, consumed with the morbid, or (as we saw with Crow) psychiatrically disordered.

In addition to freaky clothes and emotional angst, goths express their dissent from the mainstream by developing an alternative sexual milieu. The goth scene cultivates an image of itself as sexually competent and risqué. Their sexual experimentation pushes the bounds of dominant sexual mores. In this chapter, I focus on goth style and emotional culture. In the next chapter, I explore goth sexual culture.

From geek to freak: "I was a goth and didn't know it"

A small woman with long brown hair, Anne's exclusive private-school pedigree is apparent in the way she talks, but not in her physical appearance. She is self-consciously articulate, emitting an air of off-putting pretence, yet she dresses in geeky black clothing. In her first year at an exclusive local college, Anne has only recently discovered the goth scene. She describes herself as a "proto-goth," claiming that although she "has the mental thing down," she's in the process of learning the outward symbols of the goth identity. Still, Anne is clear that she was destined for gothdom. She explains:

> In high school, I made one or two desultory attempts at generally wearing black, varying from the established jeans or khakis. It was frowned upon heavily. No rule against it but the extent it led to ostracization [*sic*] was really unpleasant. Because I was never one of the populars to begin with.

Introduced to the goth scene by friends in the Sci-Fi Society, Anne immediately felt at home at the Sanctuary. She sees her fellow goths as "a bunch of people sitting around with our hands stapled to our foreheads [she throws her arm to her forehead in a 'woe is me' gesture], we're harmless." At the same time, she describes them admiringly as "characters," and as "damn weird." Finding a community of fellow "dorks" in the goth scene, she is able to integrate her geeky interests (sci-fi, computers, etc.) into a more socially validated, more interesting, and more fun identity as a freak:

> When I arrived at [college], I was already the [dorm's] token pagan. . . . I joined the Sci-Fi Society because, hey, I'm just a nerd. . . . I'm not going to be the [dorm's] token freak next year because someone's coming in of the "freak persuasion." Word gets around, oh hey, there's another freak coming in, oh rejoice.

Like Anne, most goths were high school geeks. Zoe suggests that the experience of being a social outcast in high school was both widespread and traumatic: "I've talked to a lot of people—their whole junior high, high school was horrible. They had no friends until college, the Sanctuary." Indeed, almost everyone I spoke with began their tale with an account of social discomfort in high school—of being too smart or too shy, of being picked last for sports teams, of not playing soccer in a town where "if you didn't play soccer, you weren't anyone," of wearing the wrong kind of clothes. Some were picked on, others were simply invisible. Regardless of the specific experience of high school geekiness, finding the goth scene changed everything—not because the ideas were new, but because, as Crow says, finding the goth scene "gave a name to something I was already experiencing."

Crow recalls that:

> As a kid—I haven't figured out why I didn't fit in. I was the same class level
> (middle) as everyone else. I was shy but that was about it. Getting picked on,
> not included, the "last guy picked for ball" concept.... The head of the football
> team was on my case—his personal vendetta.

When he was twelve or thirteen, Crow started hanging out at a popular
public youth spot in a nearby city.

> I got more exposure to things that were already interesting to me, more music,
> more literature. I've gone through adaptations in my style over the years. It's
> always been mostly black, creative. So (finding goth) gave a name to something
> I was already experiencing.

As Crow tells it, finding other goths allowed him to find and develop his
authentic self. But finding goth also allowed him to transform the social
pain of geekiness into an identity with social power, an identity in which
he consciously chooses to be outside the mainstream, rather than having
marginality imposed on him. "As you grow up," he says, "You don't want
to fit in anymore. It becomes a point of pride, like the pink triangle for
the gay community." For Crow, freakiness is a badge of authentic selfhood that he wears with pride. The reactions of outsiders confirm his
freakiness:

> [Wearing] fishnets, arm warmers, and lipstick to the mall, I saw stares, kids run-
> ning back to their moms, double-takes.... When you realize people are staring,
> it does tend to get on your nerves. But it has its advantages. I have nothing to
> lose. Everyone expects you to beat me. I'm the little goth boy in makeup.

By choosing to be freaky, Crow becomes the architect of the social responses around him. Remarkably, his freaky persona both elicits fear of
its own, inspiring kids to run back to their moms, *and* undercuts the threats
posed by the mainstream athletic types who had it out for his pre-goth self.
By setting himself up as a target, he reduces the possible status incurred
by beating him. Thus, Crow's freakiness is a multiply useful strategy for
navigating the social terrain of young adulthood.

As for Crow, the construction of a visibly freaky self substantiates
goth claims to authentic nonconformity and symbolizes their disdain for

"mainstream" opinion. It thus angers and frightens (older) adults and in-validates non-goth peer approval (by denigrating non-freaky styles). This purposeful and collective nonconformity is itself status producing; subcul-tures traditionally disparage the "mainstream" as unhip (Thornton 1996). The deliberate embracing of an alternative presentation of self changes the terms of the competition, so that hipness accrues to the presentation of self most at odds with "mainstream" styles. By turning freakiness into a point of pride, goths establish internal criteria for approval—increasing their chances of success by ranking themselves according to a hierarchy on which they are already near the top.

But the performance of authentic freakiness is much more than just an internal subcultural contest. Goth freakiness becomes a way of inverting the meanings attached to external hierarchies as well. In other words, goths use freakiness as a cover under which they can continue to pursue geeky traits, *and* they reduce the stigma of their practices by reconfiguring them as goth. In these ways, goths use the discourse of "the fringes" to further ac-quire mainstream middle-class cultural capital. In their Listserv exchanges, for example, they instruct each other on computer skills, lambaste people who make computer or grammatical errors, bandy around large words, cite literary and scientific sources, recommend and discuss books, and construct and defend arguments. Thus, in the process of entering and engaging in goth community, of marking and celebrating their marginality, they also use and develop a variety of cultural and technical skills that prepare them for adult roles among the intellectual and/or technical elite.

Like other goths, Jeff was a high school geek. "I was isolated as the 'smart one,'" he says, but in college:

> I thought, I want to go [to a goth club]. There's people there who understand something. I'd never seen it but if it's done correctly it has immense amount of power in it. If you can put your mind at another angle, you can change your point of reference, almost like a fantasy world. [I thought] wouldn't it be better to be there and live it?...It's part of a cycle: realism versus idealism, feeling over reason....So little [value] today is placed on imagination, the capacity to feel is played down.

For Jeff, becoming goth validated his own intellectual interests. But more, it re-spun them as exciting, as part of a historically grounded intellectual trajectory, and as "powerful." In short, it made them not only valid, but better.

Jeff's comments exemplify the ways in which goths reevaluate their prior interests, rename them goth, and describe them as distinct, special, or superior. This process allows them to cloak their culturally dominant intellectual patterns in the mantle of freakiness, buffering the sting of geekiness but also disguising the degree to which they are replicating symbolic boundaries shared by other members of the upper-middle class (see Bourdieu 1984, Lamont 1992).

Ironically, goth is frequently perceived to be a subculture that spirits its participants away from conventional forms of social participation. Yet these goths use their subculture participation to consolidate, not devalue, their cultural capital. For these goths, similar patterns of limited liability inflect their fashion, their emotions, and, as I explore in the next chapter, their sexuality. Each of these strategies combats geekiness through the mobilization of freakiness. Each also becomes a site for thinking about themselves as a better kind of people.

Fashion: shocking but impermanent

Goths tell the world and each other who they are by making their bodies freaky. Goth bodies are cloaked in black, pierced, tattooed, dyed, powdered white. The goth style juxtaposes medieval romanticism with bondage wear; puffy velvet with skin-tight PVC. Goths may sport dog collars and spikes, or fishnets and corsets—all in somber colors: black or blood red. Goth style is dramatic, exaggerated, as Lili says, "over-the-top." It reverses the dominant exhortations to look healthy, natural, or sunny, and to hide one's sexual practices. It exploits unconventional fabrics and cuts, ignores color trends, and revels in gender-blending signs. It thus stretches the carnival, excessive, and taboo into the everyday. Goths portray, and outsiders interpret, this style as a sign of depression or pathology, but it is also fun, as many goths report.

I walked into a local coffee shop one weekday night, looking for the goths who were gathering for a weekly coffee night. Coordinated via Goth-Net, Damian proposed the weekly coffee as a way to ameliorate the purported "apathy" among local goths. This was going to be the inaugural gathering, and I assumed, as they did, that participants would be easy to identify. Still unfamiliar with many members of the local scene, I walked around the coffee shop looking for symbols of goth affiliation: black clothes, brightly dyed hair, perhaps striped knee socks with clunky black shoes. The coffee shop, which took up two narrow, uneven, and poorly lit floors, was filled with white middle-class young adults in a variety of unconventional styles. I was frustrated. I recalled that I used to like this place, but now I found it pretentious. I finally got into line at the coffee counter, assuming no one had showed for the meeting. I was prepared to spend the time catching up on other work. And then I saw him: a man dressed as Dracula on this ordinary midweek night. Dressed in sumptuous black clothing complete with black cape, his face altered with white pancake makeup, darkly lined eyes, and red lipsticked mouth, he stood behind me in line for coffee. He earned surprisingly few glances from the patrons, although I assumed that he got more looks on his trip into the coffee shop. By almost all standards, he looked downright weird—like a freak, as he intended.

Crow emphatically argues that real goths are "this way all the time, not just five hours a week, [goths should] dress the same way all the time, that's who you are," but in practice, goths in this scene are much more variable in their use of freaky self-presentations. They almost all dress dramatically for the club, but some may tone down their freakiness in other settings. When I met Beth for our initial interview in the same coffee shop, she wore a black T-shirt advertising a goth band and baggy black men's-style pants. A red streak ran through her long blonde hair and a small ring decorated her nose. In this ensemble, she looked out of the ordinary but did not shout her "freakiness." I ran into Vanessa, on the other hand, window shopping on a Sunday afternoon; although the weather was cold, she was dressed in a short miniskirt, black fishnet stockings, and had on dark goth makeup topped off with the kind of velvet hat I associate with Halloween wear: her freakiness was proudly on display. This flexibility in the goth look means that outsiders may have a harder time identifying goths than insiders do. Just as I was unable to pick goths out of the unconventional coffee shop crowd, people may also assume that unconventional dressers are goth when they're not, as is the case with one of my current graduate students, whose elaborate black clothes and purple-black hair dye earn her this label from other young adults. As with other subcultures, the ability to discern goth from non-goth is a sign that one is an authentic insider.

Pursuit of the right look takes time, knowledge, and commitment. Because the goth aesthetic is a rejection of the mainstream, it is more difficult to find items with which to build the goth look. Accordingly, goths spend time sewing and dying clothing, using the Web to find clothing and makeup, and discussing purchases and clothing fantasies. "What would you buy if you had a thousand dollars?" one Listserv exchange probed; participants, mostly women, constructed lists that included high-end corsets and theatrical makeup. For me, the goth look provoked anxiety. Although I never intended to pass as goth, I also didn't want to offend by appearing too mainstream. When I asked for advice, I was often told that "anything black would do," or alternatively, that "anything sexy would do." But despite this purported carte blanche, anything black, it turns out, will not do, suggesting an abundance of goth fashion nuance that I never fully absorbed, despite the amount of time I spent combing goth Web sites, discussing clothing with goths, and observing outfits.

What I did absorb, however, was that to do the look right, I would have to spend a considerable amount of money. Hot Topic, the often laughed-at mall store featuring goth clothing,[7] is expensive for a mall shop, and the Web sites featuring goth wear are even more steeply priced. A good corset, often seen as a goth woman's staple, can run well over a hundred dollars. Many goths contended that the scene was open to anyone, however, not seeing the ways in which cost can structure participation. Greg, who is unusual in that his mother is Puerto Rican, was alone in noting the class dimensions of goth style. As he acknowledged, "nonwhite people...may or may not have the money to buy the clothes."[8]

But while cost can limit membership, goth use of fashion to make distinctions is more complex. On the one hand, goths look *freaky*—they deliberately violate mainstream sensibilities.[9] Freakiness provides a kind of social power through its ability to shock. On the other hand, goths describe their look as an *aesthetic,* positioning themselves as a *taste* culture, rather than as rejecting the principle of taste. Indeed, they use the notion of an aesthetic to claim that they have *better* taste, that their sense of beauty is more evolved than that of people who follow other fashions.

In its freakiness, goth style provides goths with visibility and with social power. Freaks are shocking. With pride and amusement, they tell stories about people recoiling when they see them, pulling their children away, or crossing to the other side of the street. They recount reactions to their

7. Beth says, "oh those people who shop [at Hot Topic]. We make fun of them but still shop there."

8. Greg's conflation of race and class bespeaks the difficulties of separating race and class in the goth scene since most goths occupy the privileged side of both axes.

9. See Hebdige (1979) for an extended discussion of the uses of subcultural style to express rejection of mainstream values and sensibilities.

self-presentation: of having their photos snapped—"You know, when they *pretend* to be taking pictures of their kids and just *accidentally* move the camera up and to the left to capture us in film"—of being left to sit by themselves on the Greyhound, of "being able to clear a path to a crowded public bathroom sink just by standing there ... [and] being able to successfully intimidate people I otherwise could not" (woman, GothNet).

To be able to intimidate is a powerful feeling, especially if you have previously been either invisible or the recipient of intimidation. But one can imagine that being visibly shocking also comes with costs. And indeed it does cause fear and concern among adults. For many goths these consequences are part of its appeal: the more shocking a person is, the more subcultural currency in hipness she or he is able to accrue. In both the logics of the subculture and of cool, the more visibly a person rejects the standards of the adult culture, the more status she or he has (e.g., Thornton 1996). Thus, the freakiness of goth style provides a kind of notoriety, toughness, and social distance that makes them less geeky and more hip. By deliberately rejecting mainstream appearance criteria, goths communicate that they *don't care* what other people think—an important element of cultural cool.

But for goths, eliciting shock or derision is deliberate. Thus, while they may describe tiring of the negative public attention, in fact, they could avoid it by moderating their public self-presentations. This is a complicated dilemma, raising issues of both authenticity and social regulation. My concern here is not to fully interrogate these issues, but rather to distinguish between these dilemmas and those faced by people of color and working-class/poor people in public settings. Indeed, the kinds of reactions that the goths describe earlier (and with pride) are the same kinds of reactions incurred by people whose dissidence from the mainstream is not chosen, but imposed. For Black men, in particular, the relentlessness of generating public fear regardless of intentions is a source of ongoing marginalization with enormous social and psychological consequences (e.g., Anderson 1990). Thus, for goths, freaky style provides some of the elements of cool but without the ongoing social and psychological "race and class injuries" (Sennett and Cobb 1972, Beattie 2003) incurred by those for whom such social positioning is not chosen.

Goths can downplay, or even take off, their freakiness when it is socially necessary. Austin dresses in non-goth style when she visits her grandparents. Beth and Zoe describe their decisions to de-goth their appearances for work. A social worker, Beth explains that she doesn't wear goth attire to work so she doesn't alienate people, and Zoe says, "When I got a job as a supervisor, I was dying my hair back to brown. I was afraid I wouldn't be taken seriously with green hair." These changes indicate the possibility of moving in and out of embodied freakiness even while maintaining a primary goth identity. Goth women, more than men, discuss concerns about employment and appearance. Women in general are held to more stringent appearance standards than are men (e.g., Wolf 1991). In addition, goth men are more likely to be employed in behind-the-scenes tech jobs in which they have little interaction with the public, and are thus freer to dress as they wish.

The impermanence of style also enables a transition out of the goth subculture. The freaky style can be shed and left behind, with few ongoing reminders that it was ever affected.[10] While impermanence is a general characteristic of fashion, its benefit is particularly salient for young adults located securely within the white middle class. For these goths, stylistic rebellion is an expected part of the life course. Parental alarm, too, is central to the middle-class adolescent (and young adult) script. Some parents may even support experimentation out of a middle-class belief in the importance of "finding oneself." When Austin became a goth, her mother willingly funded her daughter's acquisition of an expensive new wardrobe.

Beth explains that her parents:

> complained about my clothes but when they realized I was still a productive member of society [they accepted them]...I gothed out when I went to the prom: I wore a short vinyl dress with fishnets and boots, a dog collar. My parents were so cool, they took pictures and put them in an album.

For both Austin and Beth, then, expressing dissidence through freaky clothes did not harm their relationships with their families. Rather, they both remain close to their parents. Beth muses:

> Parents usually don't like [the goth style]; they associate it with devil worship, think it's scary. They're conservative—want their kids to dress a certain way. [Parents] associate [the goth style] with not being successful or doing well in school but when people do well in school, parents are more accepting.

---

10. Tattoos and, to a lesser degree, piercings are obviously more difficult to shed, but are common enough within contemporary popular culture to be adapted to a range of styles.

In the presence of other class signifiers, then, middle-class parents are often able to accept their children's freaky clothes.[11] The idea that adolescent rebellion is developmentally normal, at least for white middle-class youth, aids in the interpretation of goth attire as a developmental phase so long as it is not obviously derailing class reproduction. In addition, race privilege buys white youth more latitude in their appearance in general. Youth of color often use a neat appearance (for example, impeccably ironed clothes) to claim respectability, but white youth do not have to worry about automatic assumptions of disrepute. They can, and often do, dress sloppily (see Conley 2000). Goth style is thus freed from the additional burden of racial stereotypes. As Eckert's (1989) study of "jocks and burnouts" demonstrates, the structural consequences of subcultural strategies emerge not so much out of actual behaviors, but out of how those behaviors are interpreted by sanctioning adults (see also Ferguson 2000). Accordingly, goths are often accorded more generous interpretations of their behavior from institutional gatekeepers than are youth of color.

Goths *do* provoke moral panic. Periodically, a newspaper or magazine article surfaces that paints goth as satanic and/or dangerously antisocial, and alerts parents to "warning signs." These articles typically coexist with more moderate interpretations of goths, indicating more cultural flexibility in the interpretation of white youth subcultures than in those of youth of color. For youth of color, in contrast, hip-hop clothing is often read as a sign of gang affiliation, criminal intent, or de facto delinquency, banned from schools and recreational areas, and seen as a legitimate reason for police intervention (e.g., Brunson and Miller 2006).[12]

The class resources of the goth community both enable and insulate goth style. But more than this, goths transform freakiness into an aesthetic, insisting that their style is a sign of their taste and creativity. This rhetorical strategy tempers the use of freaky shock symbols. By formulating goth style and vision as an aesthetic, goths distance themselves from

---

11. Hyacinth did report a difficult relationship with her parents, but this was unusual, and did not prevent her parents from funding her education at an expensive private college.

12. Even when white middle-class youth are perceived to have serious problems, they are more likely to be treated in the mental health system than in the criminal system (Males 1996; and recall that goths themselves are likely to claim psychiatric diagnostic categories for themselves; I have not, however, heard of any goths who have been hospitalized). I do not want to discount the pain, stigma, and disruption of hospitalization, but it does not create the long-term consequences that the juvenile system does. Youth in the mental health system are not stigmatized and dismissed as lifetime criminals, nor do they acquire a criminal record that haunts them as they try to establish adult lives.

popular notions of "rebellious" youth, and learn to think of themselves as
being more intellectually and emotionally evolved than non-goths.

I met Hyacinth in her apartment, which she shared with three other
young adults. Like many apartments in the area, it was the second floor of
an old house and had an all-season porch that overlooked the street. I sat
across from Hyacinth on the porch at a makeshift sewing table. Hyacinth
explained the goth aesthetic while she altered a piece of clothing to make
it better fit her style. Hyacinth's sewing did not signal either domesticity
or economic strain—it was clear to me that Hyacinth did not view sewing
as a mark of her femininity, and it was also clear to me that she didn't
"have" to sew in order to compensate for inadequate material resources.
As Hyacinth sewed, she appeared industrious, independent, and creative,
and it seemed to me that this was indeed how she viewed the activity.
Moreover, while nervousness or discomfort often motivates people to do
something with their hands while talking with someone, Hyacinth's activity much more thoroughly suggested that she wasn't willing to make too
much time for me, that she would talk to me, sure, but not if it meant she
had to take time out from her more meaningful tasks. Hyacinth's sewing
communicated her significance, not her insecurity.

Like most of the goths I spoke with, Hyacinth's account used her sense
of style to describe her spiritual and emotional evolution. Her account not
only countered prevailing notions of youth as superficial and unreflective,
but also showcased her theoretical and literary knowledge. Hyacinth had
clearly spent a good deal of time thinking and talking about these ideas.
For Hyacinth, as for other goths, style was a medium for the invocation of
her worldview. She says:

> Feminine standards about what is good, valuable, beautiful are more central to
> goth. Nobody drinks beer, talks about scoring. It's more about the emotional . . .
> the way in which women are thought of as valuing the emotional / spiritual / roman-
> tic over the material is very much part of the goth culture. You wouldn't brag
> about how much a lover makes but you might brag about their creativity. Ev-
> eryone is valued for how they create their appearance, how they create selves,
> not their physical body. The role of makeup—it's not supposed to look natural,
> it's art. The goth standard of beauty is more about creativity than a particular
> type. Make your own clothes, wear unusual makeup, not look like everyone else.

Here, Hyacinth claims that the goth aesthetic is creative and individualistic, a form of art, unseduced by mainstream concerns. She embeds

the goth style in a set of familiar values: creativity over materialism, the emotional over the superficial. Hyacinth intends to convey goth difference from the mainstream, but the set of distinctions she draws invoke a non-goth discourse about the value of the *real*, the *authentic*, over the swelling tide of materialism and consumption. Greg, too, suggests that goth style is an authentic presentation of self:

> I never liked the macho aesthetic and prescriptions. I always thought it was kind of cruel. . . . I thought I don't have to be that way, I can be anything. [Goth is] deconstructing expectations people have of you: like you should wear pants and sneakers, not skirts.

The self Greg invokes is not only "real" (by virtue of its rejection of "expectations"), but it is also more moral in that it is not "cruel" or "macho." And Wren: goths "had to have a certain courage to put on costumes. [They] weren't there to show off, like at hip-hop clubs." Wren's comment is multilayered. Most obviously, she sets up a direct comparison between goths and hip-hoppers. By juxtaposing goth "courage" against the desire to show off, she distinguishes both goth style and goth motivation. As Wren said this to me, I thought about the range of outfits goths wear to the Sanctuary—the black goth "uniform," but also the butterfly wings and dramatic makeup, the all-year Halloween wear. I thought about the tall, beautiful white woman I met my first night at the Sanctuary, who was wearing a kimono with chopsticks in her hair. And I thought about the man who was wearing chaps and a thong, and nothing else. (Truth be told, it's hard to get an image like that out of one's head.) Courage, okay, but I couldn't wrap my head around Wren's claim that they weren't showing off. I thought also about hip-hop clubs, where I've spent a lot of time, and the flashy, revealing club clothes that are commonplace there. I wasn't sure if Wren had ever been to a hip-hop club, and when I asked her, she confessed, like many goths, that she hadn't. She wouldn't go to such a place, she explained, because they "disgust" her. Yet the distinction was clear. The irony is that goth outfits are equally, if not more, outlandish than hip-hop outfits, and thus equally subject to the critique that they are intended to garner attention.

Wren's talk about motives is also talk about authenticity. Like Greg's bucking of expectations, Wren's courage allows the real self to be revealed, regardless of consequences. Showing off, in contrast, suggests inauthenticity, as well as the immaturity associated with being fake or desiring attention. Wren's remark, then, proposes that goth style is evidence of their authenticity and maturity.

The comments of both Greg and Wren have a racial subtext as well. For Greg, the rejection of the "cruel, macho aesthetic" is a rejection of the masculinities performed by his mother's Puerto Rican suitors. Wren's comparison to hip-hop clubs denigrates popular cultural forms (both music and style) associated with local Black and Puerto Rican youth.

Goth accounts of the role of the goth aesthetic in their lives are textured. They suggest that their style is desirable not only because of its visual qualities, but because it is an expression of their distinctive characteristics. They use their talk about fashion to demonstrate their sophistication— and not just to me; this talk is too well honed to have been formulated for my benefit, and the same kind of talk animates their Listserv conversations. Indeed, talk about fashion is one way that they pull together as a community on the Listserv. Fashion talk is a medium for communicating their self-reflexivity, their intellectualism, their maturity, their nonmainstream spirituality, and their alternative gender politics (which I discuss in detail in the next chapter). Even while these various positions provide alternatives to the mainstream, they invoke elite cultural ideas about evolved people (and thus social progress).

For goths, then, freaky bodies serve multiple, seemingly contradictory, purposes. On one hand, they usefully create the shock effect that lends power and social visibility to the goth identity. In this way, freakiness is a means of pushing against the limits of racialized and classed assumptions about proper presentations of self. Freakiness creates a white middle-class kind of quasi cool, but without the extensive costs of Black urban cool. This tactic is abetted by the transitory nature of fashion, which, despite debates about authenticity, can be changed for jobs, for parents, or for more conventional white middle-class adult identities.

Goths also use their bodies to articulate goth as a superior taste culture in which goths can express their "courage," "creativity," and "individuality." While they reject the particular *kinds* of clothes worn by other members of their status group, and the materialistic, conformist consumption patterns they imply, they use upper-middle-class language and assumptions to validate their alternative style—and middle-class money to acquire it. Goths argue that their style is in fact more beautiful, more creative, and more innovative than mainstream styles (both conservative, preppy clothes and hip-hop clothes), and thus evidence of their better taste. But the use of style as a distinction is much more complex than the belief that some styles look better than others. Goth style becomes such an effective means of drawing distinctions because it is assumed to speak for the real self: if the goth aesthetic is distinctive, then the goth self must be as well. The importance of the authentic self to goth appears again in their emotional culture.

"Death doesn't bother me": freakiness and goth

Sifting through the myriad of Listserv exchanges one day, I came across a post from someone describing how his scanner could pick up the baby monitor kept in the room of an old woman. He found this amusing, he claimed, and alternated between berating the woman for her nighttime routine, especially her prayers, and speculating amusedly about the possibility of listening to the woman as she died. A flurry of gleeful responses milked this scenario for humor for many days. I found this exchange upsetting,[13] but that was exactly the point. To be goth is to be both unafraid of death and disdainful of conventional emotional standards. In treating both aging and the possible death of an old woman as the subject of humor, this Listserv exchange proved the authenticity of the people who participated.

"There's an aspect of depression," Austin confirms in familiar words, "thinking more darkly, somewhat morbidly, understanding death as part of life." Dark, freaky goth clothes bespeak dark, freaky goth emotions, but goth emotions are performed in other ways as well. She tells me that "in poetry class, I write darker poetry and stuff. [The goth clothing] explain it for people who don't know me."

Goth emotional culture, their fascination with "depression," "darkness," and the "morbid," is as important to freakiness as is goth style. Like style, goth emotions serve a number of purposes. Dark goth emotions authenticate goth membership, proving that freakiness is internal as well as external. And while goth emotions may seem isolating, they abet the creation of community, providing a space in which individuals feel support and affirmation for their taboo psychic experiences. Moreover, emotional darkness makes goths edgy, weaving excitement, drama, and a sense of the illicit into daily patterns that might otherwise seem pallid and monotonous.

---

13. And I know that it made at least one other goth, Beth, uncomfortable as well, indicating variability within the emotional culture.

In turn, this freakiness makes them seem a little scary, and allows them to see themselves as fearless and tough. Goths' social locations protect them from everyday tragedy, while internal controls limit experiments with darkness.

Goth emotional culture dramatizes freakiness. Goths disparage the Columbine association, even while they project an image of themselves as dark and disordered, as Crow's boastful psychiatric self-labeling ("narcissistic," "insane," etc.) reveals. They call themselves crazy, claim depression, talk about body mutilation. They romanticize vampirism, visit graveyards, consume and produce dark media (literature, poetry, music, movies), continually producing and performing their rejection of compulsory happiness.

For goths, the performance of dark emotions means that they have conquered fear, that they are tough and stoic in the face of things that others find frightening. "Death doesn't bother me in a sense," Greg tells me. "If somebody's dead, they're dead, you move on." These emotions add to the social power I described earlier, the eeriness that makes some people back away.[14] More importantly, they allow goths to feel that they are tough, rather than wimpy geeks. Crow, again, illustrates this process well:

> Three things I was really afraid of as a kid: the dark, cemeteries, and needles. As I got older, I found myself hanging out in cemeteries at night. I became more comfortable there than anywhere. Needles were taken care of by tattoos (I have seventeen) and piercings.

Goth men, more than women, told stories like his. Similarly, goth men were more likely to join the banter (discussed at the beginning of this section) about the baby monitor. This difference likely reflects the challenge to masculinity posed by the wimpiness associated with being a geek. But it also suggests that men, more than women, perform this aspect of the goth identity. As you will see below, women *do* embrace goth darkness; the differences in their performances is one of volume (and darkness varies among both men and women). In subcultures, Thornton (1996) argues, more valued performances of identity are equated with masculinity. Masculine subcultural performances define authentic subcultural membership, maintaining men's dominance (see also McRobbie and Garber

---

14. That this doesn't work with all people is made clear by my young adult brother's derisive dismissal of goths as "angsty."

1997, Gordon forthcoming). Recall, too, that men were more likely and able to dress in goth style across settings than women, and that Wren associated goth dress with "courage." Although Wren spoke of outfits worn to the Sanctuary, one can assume that dressing goth in less safe settings is also seen as courageous.[15]

Goth comfort with the macabre bespeaks emotional reserve and implacability in the face of death—a combination that gives a veneer of toughness to people who as geeks were, by definition, not tough. Becoming goth does not make young people tough in conventional terms, however. Instead, goths laud the nonviolence at the Sanctuary as a goth virtue. Hunter's comment is characteristic: "People [bouncers] want to work goth nights. Everyone respects one another. The goth scene doesn't really have anything to prove, or if they do, they don't really tell anybody." In this formulation, nonviolence is a validated demonstration of emotional coolness and self-assurance, inverting its association with passivity.

Rather than providing direct experiences with violence, the goth aesthetic incorporates violent symbols through its fascination with "the darker side of things." The goth self-presentation draws on cultural images associated with the medieval, with the occult, and with sadomasochism. Their aesthetic condenses darkness, danger, and sensuality, allowing goths to replace the corporeal blood of physical fighting with the fantasy blood of vampirism. Yet goths do not have to prove their toughness through physical fights. Like the mythology attached to poor urban Black men, goth men claim not to fear death. Instead, they are fascinated with it, romanticizing graveyards and suicide. Unlike poor urban Black men, however, goth men do not face death as a daily possibility. Furthermore, they do not face the consequences (police involvement and incarceration) of causing death or bodily harm. Goth, then, provides the fearlessness of cool without jeopardizing futures, either through bodily harm or through criminal records.

For Siobhan, goth is defined by its cool emotional response:

For me, a lot of the things I find beautiful in life could be considered goth, finding beauty in those things considered dark or evil. Like if I were to see a pool of blood by candlelight, most people would probably be horrified but I'd

---

15. But recall also Hyacinth's claim that goths value the feminine over the masculine. As I will show in the next chapter, goths see their community as promoting alternative gender norms.

see the different ways light reflected in it. Finding a kinship with Lilith—she was thrown out of the Garden of Eden because she wanted to go out and consort with the demons.

Siobhan's insulated social location enables her transformation of her emotional stoicism into a mark of creativity (her ability to see beauty in something socially marked as frightening). First, Siobhan's economic circumstances mean that she doesn't have to live or spend time in areas in which pools of blood might be more commonly found. Instead, she lives in a small, safe home in a quiet country neighborhood. But more, her race and class locations mean that her comments are interpreted through a lens in which she is assumed to be civilized until proven pathological, rather than pathological until proven civilized. As people of color who have read this chapter have already noted, if Siobhan were Black or Latina, white middle-class adults would likely interpret her remark as evidence of criminality, not creativity.[16]

This, then, is toughness with limited liability. Social distance from ongoing, direct experiences with tragedy and violence, and the cultural latitude accorded white middle-class young people, bound the costs of fascination with darkness. And as Siobhan's comment foreshadows, goths use their romance with darkness to do more than gain toughness; they use it, like their style, to see themselves as creative and evolved, and to claim their emotional authenticity.

By publicly and privately embracing the "darker side of things," goths come to feel that they are internally different, that they are authentically freaky, that their style and intellectual preoccupations (with the occult, vampirism, etc.) are *real,* not put on for a specific (shock) effect. Goths "don't really have anything to prove," Hunter tells me. Using familiar words Austin claims, "It's been my mentality since I was little anyway. I was a goth and didn't know it." Because identities are understood to require coherence and temporal continuity, her words are unsurprising.

Yet the goths' projection of freaky interiority does more than communicate an authentic goth self. It is also a signal of authentic humanity. It conveys that goths are different, yes, but different in that they acknowledge and accept the subterranean emotions buried in all of us. Goths suggest that they are more emotionally authentic than "normals" because they acknowledge and value the "darker side of things." This interpretation

16. Thanks to Shawn McGuffey, Hilton Kelly, and Luis Rivera for this insight.

is informed by a broader cultural lament over the loss of the authentic self. Hochschild (1983) argues that the contemporary mandate for intensive emotion management creates an estrangement from our real selves. The expectations, especially, of middle-class jobs require us to behave in inauthentic ways; thus, the flight attendant acts warm and pleasant even when the passenger has just made her angry. In Hochschild's analysis, the process—the emotion work—of transforming inner anger into outer pleasantness causes us to lose touch with how we *really* feel, and thus our *true* selves. By embracing darkness, goths reject what they see as a (white middle-class) cultural mandate to be light and cheery, to put on a happy face. Unlike the fake happy people, they suggest, they are *real*.

Goths see their dark emotional culture as evidence of their authenticity, even while they self-consciously produce, perform, and manage it. Goth emotional management not only bounds group membership but also limits the more devastating possibilities of exploring darkness. Community norms encourage goths to channel painful feelings toward self-knowledge and not toward social dysfunction. In turn, they describe their community as a space of authentic emotional exploration. It is not, as they explain it, that they learn depression from their fellow goths, but rather that the goth scene validates feelings of depression they already had. In their understanding, the alienated self is the authentic self: to feel pain is normal and healthy; acknowledging one's pain means that one is in touch with who one really is. In this regard, Rory's story is typical:

> I was in the process of going crazy while at [college]—I was on medication, I tried to kill myself, I was an alcoholic, into self-mutilation. There was something refreshing about finding people to talk to [in the goth scene] who when you say you want to die, won't tell you to get meds, lock you up, etc.

Rory found the goth community appealing because other goths recognized, accepted, and shared her depression and alienation. Drawing on popular cultural rhetoric about the importance of not "stuffing" feelings, she suggests that acknowledging one's emotions makes them less destructive. Other goths tell similar stories. Sean recalls that before he became goth, "I was too crazy. I didn't like myself or the world, figured if I was miserable everyone else ought to be too. My primary hobby was just generally being a bastard." Since becoming a goth, he explains, he's no longer like that. And Greg says, "When I was younger I was suicidal a lot. I realized I felt pretty crappy about the expectations placed on me, [I] should just give up on the expectations and do what I want." Lance tells me that when he found the goth scene, he was going through a break up and that the loud, thrashing music appealed to him. He says, "I think [the scene] appeals to people who have gone through hard times."

Internal mechanisms, both structured and unstructured, create a community of shared pain. These channels allow participants to authenticate their gothness through emotional performances, but they also police the boundaries of goth darkness. The live journal forum, in which many goths participate, is one example. Live journals (common among Internet-savvy young people) are online journals that can be read by anyone with Internet access (although sometimes you need a password to get in). Many of the members of the goth community avidly post their own, and consume each other's, journal entries. Hunter explains:

> It's very therapeutic to have people read and understand what you're going through—anger, hate, sorrow, random insanity, life in general. People see parts of my life, it's a way to keep in touch, to keep on top of each other.

Live journals create an ongoing, intense emotional community premised on the value of emotional interiority. The live journal forum encourages goths (and others who participate in it elsewhere) to consider and share their inner lives, to create community through the sharing of their intimate emotions, and to respond to others' emotional selves. By definition, live journals herald the sharing of parts of oneself that are elsewhere considered personal (the notion of a journal implies privacy). This forum uses emotional sharing to continuously reproduce the community by involving goths in serial dramas (see Kenny 2000), by providing individuals with insider information on each other's personal lives, and by constituting the community as an emotionally rich space.

In her ethnography of white middle-class suburban girls, Kenny (2000) identifies rituals of "hysterical story making" and "everyday traumas" as key processes in the production of the "normal" (white middle-class) self. She argues that these everyday, serial events "temporarily [fill] the lack that is normal without truly altering the norm. Living a hypersymbolic and a hypernormal life is not a radical move. It is a productive coping mechanism. It socializes girls into a normal life and makes that life bearable" (106). Goth emotional culture similarly makes goth lives bearable, not just because it provides support for their own internal conflicts, but because it makes their lives less boring, inviting them to spin seductive collective fantasies as well as involving them in the ins and outs of their community's lives.

The emphasis on sharing and introspection exemplified by the live journal allows goths to better patrol community emotional norms by giving participants ongoing access to each other's personal lives. Hunter recalls, "I found the journal of someone I despise, one of those fake people—sweet and caring in the club. I read her journal—[and found out she is] selfish, superficial, uncaring." Live journals are thus also a way of policing authenticity, of weeding out people whose emotions are suspect or who are deemed fake (or inauthentic). Furthermore, while live journal readers may be able to identify with each other's psychic experiences, the content of these journals may be upsetting to some readers. Beth describes reading the live journal of a man with whom she was involved and realizing with dismay how peripheral she was in his emotional life. For Beth, the difficulty wasn't just that she had access to information that was hurtful to her, but also that goth emotional norms dictate that she should be able to take this information in stride. There was no space in the goth community for her to voice her hurt feelings, both because the live journal resides in a nebulous space that is neither clearly private nor clearly public, and because jealousy isn't an acceptable goth emotion.

Siobhan recalls her feelings of jealousy when she discovered that the man she was in love with (and who she was having sex with) was in love with someone else. She bitterly explains that she was "ousted from my social circle for being upset about it." Siobhan's story illustrates the ways in which the goth community penalizes both the display of unmanaged jealousy and the experience of feeling jealous (if it is shared). Goths laud the importance of emotional authenticity, but not all emotions are acceptably goth.

Goth emotional performances demonstrate their internal darkness, but they must also demonstrate certain kinds of emotional control. Lili explains that "in the goth subculture, people can play at different things, and go over the top, and it's okay—to be overly angst, overly hurt. Drama can be a way of interacting and can be entertaining as long as people know it's there." Wren describes the scene's collective angst as:

> an excuse to feel sad, pissed off. Some people who are dark and angry because they are working a shitty job or didn't finish school use it as an excuse to express how they're feeling about life. This is what the world did to me. Those people could hold onto it for a long time if they don't choose to change their lot in life.

And Jeff says,

It's sort of a place where everyone puts on their worst—their anger, their pain. Okay to—sort of a celebration of that. I guess a lot of people I've met there don't really understand that part of themselves. They embrace it, but don't understand it.

These comments, common among goths, indicate community norms for appropriate emotional displays. Although their norms allow for greater expression of alienation than in other arenas, they nevertheless bound goth emotional culture. These displays may be dark, but not too dark. Zoe makes clear both the limits on goth darkness and its performative dimension:

For a bunch of people who glorify being alone, [goths are] awfully social.... Goths brag about being depressed and suicidal but [they're] not really. I have this psychiatric disorder, I'm so manic, so depressed, but not really.

Because they are not already dark, goths are able to experiment with their own dark feelings with minimal fear that they will be darkened by them. But they also guard the duration and intensity of these experiments, reigning in any potential danger by imposing an internal safety valve on themselves and each other. Goths thus remain securely embedded in their race and class identities. In rejecting what they see as the inauthenticity, conformity, and softness of happiness, goths expand the emotional territory of their white middle-class suburban identities, claiming toughness, hipness, and authenticity for themselves. They construct an identity that makes their white middle-class lives more tolerable, more fun, more interesting, more *real,* but nonetheless still white and middle class. They thus reject the presumed monotony and cultural vacuity associated with the white middle class, but don't reject the rest of the package.

Making sense of freakiness

Alternative subcultures, like goth, are sometimes conceptualized as spaces in which outcasts can band together, using their collectivity to gain some control over their lives. The goths are not different in this regard: goth facilitates a transformation from geek to freak that gives goths unprecedented social visibility and allows them to taste some of the benefits of cultural cool. But the process of self-marginalization, as Traber (2001) also argues

about punks, is laden with contradictions, combining "transgression and complicity for reasons the participants themselves overlook" (31).

Goth is fashioned, in some ways, as a rebellion (although probably less so than punk), but it is an inchoate rebellion. Tellingly, when I asked Beth in our first interview what goths were rebelling against, she replied, "I don't know." Similarly, Zoe commented that goths are "rebelling against the mainstream but [we're] not sure why." In many ways, goth seems to be a rebellion against the behavioral constraints of the white middle class: the expectation of restraint in sexuality, self-presentation, and emotions. In other ways, goth seems to be a rebellion against the social hierarchies of adolescence and young adulthood, in which geeks are either invisible or harassed. In both of these rebellions, goths are at least minimally successful. The goth strategy of freakiness is a way for former geeks to renounce humiliation, invisibility, and boredom, while resolving some of the contradictions of white, middle-class expectations.

In transforming from geeks to freaks, goths become a little cooler. They gain social visibility, unflinching toughness, and sexual adventure (as you'll see in the next chapter). They also gain fun, community-endorsed excess, and a sense of the carnival, shocking the sensibilities of the mainstream. In claiming these attributes for themselves, goths rework the terms of cool, linking cool to interests and performances that they enjoy and at which they can be successful. Goths differentiate themselves from the mainstream (i.e., the white middle-class culture of their parents and many of their peers) by positioning themselves as aesthetic, emotional, and sexual nonconformists. But even while goths shock the sensibilities of the mainstream, their race and class futures are secure.

A number of factors, in combination, limit the liability of goth freakiness. Goth freakiness is enacted, in large part, though style and emotions. These strategies share the qualities of being shocking but impermanent. In addition, goths diminish the potential danger of their behavior through community safeguards, and evoke middle-class symbolic boundaries by positioning themselves as a culture of taste. For goths, these strategies work *because,* as white middle-class young adults, they are already given the benefit of the doubt. At the same time, goth facility with dominant cultural capital moderates some of the status costs of their self-presentations. The location of these goths as primarily and securely white and middle-class creates a safety zone that limits the costs of cultural experimentation, making them free to reject *aspects* of the white middle class. In turn, probably unconsciously, they rejuvenate key upper-middle-class assumptions about what makes people and life valuable.

Self-marginalization is an important part of the goth strategy. To be goth is to have been inexplicably marginalized and to have now reclaimed marginalization as a desired status. Importantly, this marginalization is personal and social, but not structural. It is not based on cross-cutting dimensions of race and class, or even gender, inequality. The invocation of marginalization becomes the basis for a kind of identity politics, but an identity politics based on a chosen subcultural affiliation rather than an unchosen structural category. The goth scene abets belief in one's individual worthiness not just because, in good color-blind fashion, goths see themselves as "diverse" and "open to anyone," but because they think of themselves as outside the mainstream. By seeing themselves as marginal, they also see themselves as challenging and resisting the status quo, even while they use many of its terms to defend their project.

Goths draw symbolic boundaries primarily (but not always) against other similarly classed white people, yet the boundaries they draw—their comfort with other freaks like them—impedes the development of meaningful relationships across race or class lines. This process maintains the invisibility of the structural advantages they accrue from their position in the white middle class, allowing them to see themselves through "the lens of entitlement and self-congratulation" (Stuber 2006, 285, 290). The use of a model of identity politics further elides the structural differences between the goths' experiences and those of people who are structurally marginalized. Finally, it legitimates the goth claim to the benefits of an identity politics: sympathy and recognition as a derided group. In the next chapter, we will see that these paradoxes play out in goth sexual strategies as well.

CHAPTER THREE

So Full of Myself as a Chick

My first interaction with goths occurred in graduate school, when I attended a party hosted by Greg. At the time, I prided myself on being unshockable, at least about matters of sexuality, and Greg prided himself on being able to shock me. He succeeded. Although I had expected the tortilla chips and the cheap alcohol, I was not prepared for the open display of fetishism. In particular, I was "freaked out" by the couples attached by collars and leashes and the man who showed me his pierced penis. Delighted by my visible reaction, Greg presented me with my very own man-on-a-leash at my own birthday party a month or so later (I declined).

As I argued in the last chapter, my reaction and Greg's pleasure in it are central features of the goth strategy. By "freaking out," I affirmed goth freakiness. And by being unwilling to participate in goth sexual play, I maintained the distinctiveness of goth culture. By establishing myself as a comparative prude hedged in by normative (i.e., mainstream) sexual rules, I reinforced the sexually adventuresome goth image.

Sexuality is an essential tool in the arsenal of goth freakiness. "If there's such a thing that a goth is supposed to be, a goth should be sexually open," Rory explains. Like fashion and emotions, goths limit the potential costs of their open, freaky sexuality, sheltering their status through protective behaviors and aligning talk (Stokes and Hewitt 1976). Also like style and emotions, they use sexuality to think of themselves as a better kind of people—as emotionally, morally, and politically sophisticated. Unlike fashion and emotions, however, goths explicitly tie their sexual strategies to concerns about gender.

Goth sexuality challenges mainstream gender rules. Women act on their sexual desires without being stigmatized as "sluts." Sexually aggressive men are frowned upon. Men dress in women's clothing, participating in gender-blending play. Sexual desire and behavior is not restricted to heterosexual partners. Women and men are deliberately nonmonogamous, frowning upon the possessiveness and jealousy associated with monogamy. Goth women, and to a lesser extent goth men, identify the goth scene as a neofeminist space. Proud of their ability to upturn mainstream sexual rules, they celebrate their personal and collective emancipation from the gender inequalities that plague other settings. But while goth strategies benefit goth women in a number of ways, their effects are partial and contradictory.

We can better understand the relationship between gender and sexuality if we are also aware of the ways in which sexuality is embedded in race and class concerns. The goth rejection of "vanilla" sex is not just a rejection of conventional gender scripts but also a rejection of presumed white middle-class sexual repression. The popular concept of vanilla sex makes visible the racial dimensions of sexuality, in which white middle-class sexuality is constructed in opposition to the alleged hypersexuality of the race and class "other"—particularly Blacks and the poor and working class (Roediger 1991, Hill Collins 2004). At the same time, goths are able to reject vanilla sex with minimal consequences precisely because their race and class status buy them both privacy and freedom from racialized assumptions of hypersexuality. In rejecting vanilla sex, moreover, goths do not reject all dominant sexual expectations; instead, as I will show, they anchor their alternative sexual practices to concerns about commitment, responsibility, and intimacy. In this way, then, their subculture plays out some of the paradoxes of broader white middle-class culture, in which the valorization of sexual freedom and of sexual responsibility vie for dominance.[1]

As I will show below, they are also hindered by the complexity of the moral identities they attempt to weave. For women, sexual agency is a contradictory gender, race, and class strategy. Women's sexual agency contributes to goth women's sense of themselves as independent women and to the community's collective sense that they are more politically progressive than others. At the same time, progressive gender relations are an often

---

1. Irvine (2002) documents this tension in SIECUS's (Sex Information and Education Council of the United States) struggle for respectability. She writes, "Despite their religious commitments, their admonitions for responsibility and moderation, their rejection of sexual sensationalism, their disavowal of sexual revolution, and their fit with changes afoot in the sexual culture, SIECUS nonetheless became notorious" (32). Hennen (2004, 2005) finds similar tensions between sexual freedom and sexual responsibility within gay subcultures.

invisible means of drawing symbolic race and class boundaries (Hondagneu-Sotelo and Messner 1994, Pyke 1996). In these ways, goth sexuality
is one kind of upper-middle-class sexual style, but it's a style that is never
fully freed from the need to defend itself against charges of immorality.
For goth women, agentic sexuality is simultaneously a strategy of personal
empowerment and a threat to respectability.[2] Accordingly, goth sexual
culture combines its dedication to sexual exploration and women's sexual
agency with a concomitant allegiance to "safer sex" practices and a language of commitment and respect. At first glance, this community probably seems ideal. But it is precisely these "irresolvable tensions" (Irvine
2002, 33) that entangle the goth strategy. Goth sexual safeguards, while
offering many real benefits, also maintain an investment in respectability
that disadvantages goth women.

This chapter is about these contradictions. I begin by describing goth
sexuality, showing the ways in which goths use the scene's expectation of
experimental sexuality to think of themselves as both hip and progressive.
For goths, the notion that they are bending conventional gender scripts is
crucial to their self-identification as progressive. Next, I analyze their alternative gender strategies. I argue that, while goths successfully break
down some sexual double standards, their successes are limited. These
limitations become most clear in their relationships, and arise, in part, out
of their efforts to manage the potential status risks of their unconventional
sexual practices. These techniques, particularly the emphasis on successful romantic relationships, reinscribe the gendered inequalities they claim
to have erased.

Freaky goth sex

At the Sanctuary (the goth dance club), goths adorned in black fetish wear,
leather and PVC, dog collars and leashes, gather weekly. Some men "gender blend," wearing makeup and skirts; the women are dressed in sexy,
clearly feminine outfits. The sidelines of the dance floor are populated by
pairs and groups of people kissing, caressing, sucking on each other's necks.

At parties, goths compete with each other to see who can kiss the most
people while the extended version of "Temple of Love" plays. Attempt-

2. Tanenbaum (1999) documents the ways in which the category "slut" is equated with
class disrepute. As I have already noted, it is also associated with girls and women of color.

ing to up their scores, women kiss men, men kiss men, and women kiss women. "It's no big deal," says Hunter. Hyacinth tells me that her "personal record is twelve." Lance explains that these parties "sped along his breaking," encouraging him to take part in more experimental and open sexual behavior. He recalls with satisfaction a party where "five girls were giving [him] hickies" at once.

People familiar with young adults may not find these stories all that unusual. In many ways, goth sexual experiments are much like other young adult scenes in which participants play around with a range of partners and experiment with both casual and committed emotional and sexual liaisons. But goth experiments push beyond the bounds of most young adult scenes through their endorsement of polyamory (explicit sexual and romantic non-monogamy) and BDSM, through the women's openness about their participation, and through their experimentation with "queer" performances. By adding to the aura of goth freakiness, these sexual projects and their visible accoutrements differentiate goths from "normals" by making goth sexuality more experimental, more interesting, and more fun. Goth sexuality, in turn, makes goths rebellious, desirable, intriguing, and adventuresome.

For people who had previously been isolated as geeks, these are enormous gains. Goth sexuality allows former geeks to replace the attribution of undesirability with the image of the freaky goth "who knows ten million sexual tricks" (GothNet). Jeff makes this explicit:

> Before [the club], I didn't feel unattractive. I didn't feel noticed. I think that's the case for a lot of people. Over time, I got more and more noticed because I got better at it. No one wants to be ugly. . . . I think a lot of people who go there do it for that reason: it's an ego boost.

This is true, I was told, for women as well as for men. Recall from the last chapter Hyacinth's self-assured declaration that "everyone is valued for how they create their appearance, how they create their selves, not their physical body." The emphasis on performance in the goth scene means that people who don't fit mainstream criteria for attractiveness can feel desirable and achieve conventional sexual success.

The structure of the goth scene enables its sexual openness. Most of the goths in this book regularly interact with the non-goth world, but the goth community provides them with an insulated space in which they can conduct cultural experiments that go beyond freaky affectations. Indeed,

the freakiness itself abets the construction of a safe zone, both by deflect-
ing outside focus and by inspiring outsider fear and/or aversion. Goths
are able to use the social distance created by freakiness to experiment
with emotional and sexual intimacy.

The Sanctuary itself provides a temporally and geographically bounded
safe zone in which sexuality can be performed with minimal consequences.
Like other clubs, it provides a venue for arranging sexual liaisons, but it
is also a space in which ordinary behavioral rules are purportedly sus-
pended. Goths describe a separate set of "Sanctuary rules"; Sean tells me,
"If it's at Sanctuary, it doesn't count." And Siobhan explains, "At Sanctuary, you can kiss openly. Because it's Sanctuary and it's a different place.
Big cuddle circles. Everyone is open." Even couples in otherwise monogamous relationships, goths say, can kiss and flirt with other people at the
Sanctuary.

It's not just sexual behavior that matters. Comfort with freaky sexuality, regardless of participation, provides goths with status as hip and tolerant. My own uncool reaction to the bondage at Greg's party was evidence of this. Even though those episodes revealed nothing about Greg's
own participation in sexual bondage, his cool and playful reaction to their
display established him as more sexually sophisticated than me. Hunter
also illustrates the process of sexual hipness by association, by proudly recounting to me his comfort at a "roundtable discussion on B & D" (bondage and discipline). His friend, he reported, "looked at [him] and said,
'Oh, you fit in.'" Freaky goth sexuality adds to the aura of darkness and
danger, moving goths away from geekiness and closer to coolness.

The insularity of the goth scene facilitates sexual experiments, but goths
take their sexuality public as well: they wear their bondage gear to the mall,
for example, or talk about their sexuality in public spaces. Thus, goths perform their sexuality not only to each other, but also to outsiders. Goths'
secure race and class positions, as with style and emotions, limit the liability of these public performances. Goths do not have to worry about raced
and classed sexual stigmas. Their "courage," as Wren described it in the
last chapter, adds to their sense of collective hipness. Progressive gender
relations, as I will show next, are a key piece of this strategy.

So full of myself as a chick

Goth sexual culture provides the satisfaction of desirability, regular sex,
and hipness, but it also does much more. As with fashion and emotions,

goths see their sexual style as evidence that they are distinct, special, and evolved. As Siobhan's and Hyacinth's stories will illustrate, goths see their sexuality as a response to the sexual repression of the dominant culture— a repression that is particularly suffocating to women.

I met Siobhan late in the study, but I had been hearing stories about her since I began the project. In part because of her relationship with Bill, which I discuss later in the chapter, Siobhan was a kind of goth legend. Many goths, although not all, pointed to Siobhan and Bill, who had had a polyamorous, master-slave relationship, as a shining example of success- ful goth sexual culture. I met Siobhan in her home, where she sipped tea sitting cross-legged in sweats, her mane of dark hair falling around her face. Siobhan's coiled energy captivated me. I wanted to accept at face value whatever she said.

Siobhan had been a part of the local goth scene since its inception. Her story—how she became a goth, her involvement in the goth scene— revolves around sex: Siobhan went to an "all girls' private Catholic school by choice." She chose the school, she explains, but she "instantly" ex- perienced problems because of her sexuality, which she describes as too precocious and too public for the school's standards. She was sent to the office for her "inappropriate behavior," she recalls, and "all the girls hated [her] because [she] was friends with the boys." For Siobhan, "not fitting in" has always been about sex. Becoming goth helped her "liberate" her sexual self. She explains:

> When [Sanctuary] opened up, we [Siobhan and Bill] went to the second one.... What marked on me the most was the open sexuality and sensuality of the people. There was a big cross on stage, people being flogged and, um, there was this gorgeous guy with long black hair kissing and caressing people on the cross and I totally wanted to be part of it. I got my first public flogging. Maybe already a part of me that was goth—the open sexuality and confidence being sexual openly.... It's very liberating to be around that kind of thing coming from a repressed background sexually.

As she tells it, Siobhan rebelled from the constraints of Catholic school and from her parents. After high school, "I [ran] away from home.... I wanted to live with my guy friends but my parents wanted me to live at home. A lot of it was young teenage angst. But I'd do it again because it was healthier for me in the long run."

Siobhan's story evokes a cultural current in which sexuality, especially white middle-class or elite sexuality, is seen as in need of liberation from

an unnatural (i.e. puritanical) social repression (e.g., Bourdieu 1984), as
well as a cultural understanding that individuals should pursue their "authentic" desires in the interest of social progress. Siobhan's story refor-
mulates her freaky sexual practices as authentic, socially progressive, and
therefore desirable. In her story, freakiness is a positive sign of her personal liberation and of her connection to her authentic self, rather than a
negative, shameful sign that she is wanton.

Like Siobhan, Hyacinth is a local goth legend. Although she had recently moved to a neighboring city and was no longer in the thick of the
local scene, Hyacinth was now in many ways more visible than Siobhan;
she was an avid participant on GothNet, engaging at length in seemingly
every conversational thread. Hyacinth knew things and had opinions, and
she wasn't afraid to share them. Often, those things were about sex. Like
Siobhan, Hyacinth had a clear sense of herself as sexually empowered.
She advised a younger goth woman on STI testing, signing off by adding
that she always uses two forms of birth control and never, ever has unsafe
sex. She penned an essay advising non-goth men on how to pick up goth
women. She frequently discussed her own polyamorous practices.

Like Siobhan, Hyacinth described years of sexual difference. "I've
been identifying . . . as bi and poly since I was sixteen." In high school, she
says,

> I just really, really didn't fit in. . . . Mainly, I just read a lot of books (science fic-
> tion) with alternative sexualities in them and thought, hey, I could do it like that.
> I was dating this guy, my first lover, and thought, hhhmmm, I'm in love with
> him but I'm in love with this other guy too; I told him I'm going to date both.
> He broke up with me. But the new relationship was an open relationship from
> the outset. . . . When you go into the goth community, poly didn't have to be
> explained.

Hyacinth's story, like Siobhan's, is a story of sexual liberation, tied, in
part, to the goth scene. Like Siobhan, Hyacinth tells her story in a way that
situates her as unwaveringly strong, agentic, and proactive. She suggests
that she has identified, prioritized, and asserted her own needs, despite
the costs, since her first relationship. Hyacinth is clear that her own sexual
proactivity is not the unreflective, pleasure-seeking sexual experimentation often attributed to young people. In contrast to this stereotype, she
uses her sexuality to articulate her self-knowledge, her self-possession, and
her willingness to question conventions. "I'm not going to say there aren't

people who are poly just to have sex," she says, but "I needed to know that if I felt something for someone else I could act on it. I don't actually *need* to be dating more than one at a time" (emphasis mine). For some people, she implies, polyamory may just be a justification for sexual hedonism, but for Hyacinth it is an expression of her personal emancipation.

Gender is not explicit in the stories told by Siobhan and Hyacinth, and yet these are gendered tales. Both Siobhan and Hyacinth reject ideals that restrain white middle-class feminine sexuality. Both use their sexual discoveries to establish themselves as agentic, independent women in control of their personal lives and their social spaces. Siobhan and Hyacinth, as I've said, are well known in the goth scene, but the connections they make between goth, sexuality, and personal empowerment are shared by less visible, more reserved goth women. GothNet is replete with similar assertions: "I'm so full of myself as a chick in general that I don't want people talking to me whose sole purpose is to stick their dick in my cooter." "I'm not interested in making someone's life more exciting when they haven't done anything on their own. I'm not a novelty item." "Treat me like a person first, and then I might start flirting with you." On GothNet, as in their face-to-face interactions, goth women craft themselves as strong, independent, and agentic.[3]

Like Siobhan, goth women root their interpersonal independence in the sexual norms of the local goth scene. For Rory, the scene is a space in which she can be "predatory and female." And for Lili, it engenders the "ability to insist on safer sex." These accounts share a notion not only of goth women as strong and independent but of the goth scene as supportive of women's sexual power. These attributions extend to relationships as well: Hyacinth claims, "From what I've seen, most goth women are feminists; [it] tends to strongly inform their relationships."

Even when they don't use the term feminist, goth women draw on the language of feminism to describe the benefits of being a goth. Specifically, they talk about "choice," "objectification," and "empowerment." These discussions focus almost exclusively on sexuality, rather than on other arenas of feminist complaint like employment or family. In part, this focus is logical given the demographics of the community: many are in college or

3. As I will discuss in later chapters, this is a common language for contemporary young women who have been raised to think they can "have it all." It is a language, however, that it used to remake race and class distinctions (see chapter 6, Bettie 2003, Orr 1997, and Harris 2004).

employed in starter jobs, and most have not married or had children. It is also logical since much of the community's activity takes place within the sexualized space of a dance club.

Sexually active femininity is not, of course, unique to the goth scene. Contemporary young women in a variety of arenas use active sexuality to stake out gender independence. This emphasis on women's emancipated sexuality reflects the substantive turn of postfeminism[4]—what Anna Quindlen has labeled "babe feminism" (1996, 4)—a focus on women's right to active sexuality rather than on broader issues of gender equality. Within this goth community, women's sexual emancipation is the basis for individual and collective moral identities.[5] These moral identities are taken up by men as well as women. Indeed, it is important to the women's identities that the men share (at least discursively) their commitment to alternative gender norms. For both women and men, these norms allow them to think about themselves as more morally, politically, and emotionally advanced than outsiders whose sexual practices are more gender traditional.

"I really, really liked it that nobody tried to grab my butt": Gender dynamics at the Sanctuary

[A]t a regular club, it's fairly common for a guy to come up and grind with random girls... In fact that's one of the reasons I prefer goth clubs to regular clubs (woman, GothNet).

I went [to the Sanctuary the first time], looked around, thought, my God, this is silly. They're all taking themselves so seriously. It's kind of cute but silly. But I really, really liked it that nobody tried to grab my butt (Hyacinth).

Goth clubs "are not like other clubs"—a point goths make repeatedly. But rather than noting, for example, the open displays of bondage and fetishism that distinguish the Sanctuary from most non-goth clubs, these

---

4. Postfeminism is a controversial term. I use it here to refer to the emphasis on individual empowerment and choice found in many writings of the feminist "third wave" (Orr 1997), and adopted by many young women raised in a context in which girls are taught that institutional barriers to equal citizenship have been broken down (Stacey 1990).

5. Kleinman (1996, 5) defines a moral identity as "an identity that people invest with moral significance; our belief in ourselves as good people depends on whether our actions and reactions are consistent with that identity." In Kleinman's study, being "alternative" was a moral identity similar in some ways to the goth's "freakiness."

accounts describe the Sanctuary as a special place because it houses distinctive, more gender-progressive norms of heterosexual interaction. Because they don't objectify women, because they respect the right of women
to define their own sexual desires, because they develop emotionally committed relationships with women, and because they participate in some
queer play, goths portray the scene in general and the men in particular
as more tolerant, more gender progressive, and more evolved than other
men. (They also, as we saw earlier, portray the women as stronger and
more independent than other women.) Goths draw distinctions between
goth men and "meat market men" or "Neanderthals." Greg explains, "In
goth clubs, there's more community. . . . It's not a meat market." Jeff describes the goth scene as "very accepting, very open. People [are] very
respectful. If you go another night,[6] there's more riffraff and whatnot."
And Rory tells me that she would find a local hip-hop club "repulsive." In
these ways, the gendered sexual norms of the goth club are an important
basis for drawing symbolic boundaries around the goth community.

For the goth newcomer, the goth club is a curious space. Like others, I experienced initial surprise at the distinctive dynamics of the goth
dance floor. Dance floors in most (successful) clubs that I had previously
attended are typically packed. Bodies jostle each other for space; women
and men dance together in explicitly sexualized styles; women throw each
other hostile glances at an accidental touch. In contrast, the Sanctuary
dance floor is sparsely populated, partly because the club space is generous given the size of the goth community. But even when well-liked songs
bring bigger crowds to the dance floor, dancers maintain individual space.
Goth men and women alike dance alone, typically using a lot of room.
Often the dance floor seems to be a sea of dance soloists, each performing a stylized and intense ballet-like routine for him- or herself. Unlike
other clubs, where dancing alone brings social death, goths rarely dance
in groups or couples. And in contrast to non-goth clubs where the edges
are lined with men ogling the other (mostly women) dancers, few people
watch the dancers here.

Goths call these different practices "spatial rules" and, unsurprisingly, identify them as a big attraction to women. Like Hyacinth's earlier
comment, many of the women I spoke with told me that the absence of

6. The venue that hosts the goth night originally had a wide repertoire of gimmicks, including Latin night and hip-hop night. It has since changed ownership and is now a gay club
except on goth night.

unsolicited physical contact pulled them back to the Sanctuary even if
they didn't immediately feel at home. Hyacinth elaborates:

> The reason I feel comfortable going to a goth club wearing a black vinyl bra,
> short black vinyl skirt, and fishnets is because the etiquette rules are different
> here. Wearing sexy clothes does not mean that you want to be approached. I've
> heard that from a lot of women: the reason they prefer goth clubs is because
> they feel more comfortable here. The rules are sometimes stated and some-
> times understood. . . . The rules are that strong that if you break them, you're
> ostracized. People won't talk to you. "Oh, him, you don't want to talk to him.
> He tried to touch me last week."

Importantly, goths portray their club behavior as superior not because
it protects women's sexual purity but because it allows women more control over heterosexual interactions. A woman on GothNet posts, "I'm per-
fectly capable of letting people know I'm interested in them, and I don't
need to be pursued persistently. If I like you, I'll let you know. I wonder if most women in our scene are like that?" Hyacinth responded af-
firmatively to the previous woman's query, and later told me that "[goth]
women are more comfortable initiating relationships . . . I think there is a
definite idea within gothic culture that to be a powerful woman who is
able to say yes and no to things is sexy."

The mandate to respect individual spatial boundaries reigns in predatory men, goths say, and thus creates conditions of greater sexual freedom for women. In their telling, the rule about spatial boundaries fundamentally departs from outside norms about heterosexual interactions,
allowing women to exercise more "control" over their sexuality. Alyssa
says, "If a guy dances closely to you, people will come down on him with
a vengeance. They don't say, 'oh, you wore a corset, what did you expect?'"

Like Hyacinth and Alyssa, goths connect club etiquette to the freedom,
in Beth's words, "to dress in a way that's sexy without people assuming
that [they're] there to get laid." The clubbing outfits worn by most goth
women in this scene are highly sexualized. The typical goth woman's club
ensemble fetishizes the whore, combining corsets with short skirts and
fishnet stockings. Goth women use the heterosexual etiquette of the goth
scene to frame their clothing choices in ways that sidestep conventional
interpretations of such dress. For example, a goth man posts on GothNet:
"I think people unfamiliar with this scene assume that just because some

woman is wearing a short vinyl dress and fishnets that she wants to get some from you."

Goth women, then, use the Sanctuary rule about spatial boundaries to look and feel sexy without the risks that come with overtly sexualized self-presentations in other arenas. Most obviously, the goth community spatial norms reduce the incidences of unsolicited physical contact, making sexy self-presentations a physically safer option for women than in mainstream clubs or other contexts.[7] But, in a questionable conceptual move, goth women also interpret the absence (or invisibility) of sexual assault as the absence of sexual objectification. This interpretation allows them to position themselves as the ones in control of their own sexuality. In Austin's words, the goth woman is not "objectified unless that's what [she] wants." This is a tricky claim, but it's also a useful one: it allows goth women to portray themselves as sexually appealing but not easy.

For many goth women, the Sanctuary is an unusual arena in that it validates their particular expressions of sexiness. Many of these women may not be able to access sexual attractiveness in conventional contexts where sexy femininity is defined according to narrow beauty standards that emphasize thin, disciplined bodies. At the Sanctuary, even women with larger bodies wear revealing ensembles involving, for example, the aforementioned corsets and short skirts. This freedom was pointed out to me repeatedly and was confirmed by my own appraisal of the Sanctuary crowd. Zoe says, "It's also true that anyone can go and feel sexy," presenting the Sanctuary as a space in which women of all shapes and sizes are sexually validated.

Moreover, as Lili points out, the goth subculture encourages dramatic interpretations of femininity, adding both to the sense of play and to the ability of a wider range of women to participate. Lili explains that she wasn't successful at high school dances because she didn't know how to do "stereotypically girly," but at the Sanctuary she "can always do over-the-top girly." Goth women (and some men) often accessorize their outfits with butterfly wings or sparkly crowns, dark or glittery makeup, velvet capes, or bondage gear (e.g., dog collars and leashes), creating some variations in the typical outfit I previously described. By mocking popular cultural ideas that white middle-class feminine sexuality should be subtle (e.g., "natural" makeup), goths create an ongoing sense of gender as play.

7. This discussion is not meant to imply that women's dress is responsible for sexual assault in other arenas.

Men's participation adds to this notion. Men regularly wear long skirts and makeup to the club, and sometimes in other settings. Greg, laughing because he spends more time applying makeup than his girlfriend does, tells me, "It's hard enough finding clothes for men that are interesting. I am not going to limit myself to men's clothes. It's fun." And Crow says, "Because you can be an individual, some of the things—rules—aren't there. I own skirts, girls' tank tops. I like women's clothing better." Unlike in other contexts, these young men's use of typically feminine accoutrements doesn't signal a rejection of heterosexuality. Rather, goth women find "androgynous" men especially attractive. "Men in skirts are yummy," posts one goth woman.

These experiments in self-presentation suggest an ongoing parody of conventional heterosexual aesthetic rules. Goths propose that the process of experimenting with femininity is an open one: anyone, woman or man, can participate—"because you can be an individual." Sexy femininity, according to this logic, is a choice. This idea is occasionally made explicit, as in the following woman's post about corsets:

> I believe that in the gothic subculture, this old symbol of female restriction has been turned into an empowering one...not only does the voluptuous figure it projects rebel against many modern standards of beauty, but many women embrace it *because* it emphasizes the sexual power that many goth women start to become acutely aware of. In addition, by taking a symbol of restriction and making a *self-conscious* decision to wear it, it becomes an empowering statement of female *choice* (emphasis in original).

This statement, complicated on many levels, elides any compulsion to take part in the feminine performance. As social constructionists have long noted, all femininity is performance, but performing femininity is not a free choice, as a biologically sexed woman's decision not to perform femininity is socially stigmatized (Butler 1990; Lorber 1994). In the context of the Sanctuary, most women and a minority of men seem to participate in the performance of sexual femininity. In my repeated visits to the Sanctuary, I saw few women (if any) who abstained from this performance—an observation that Beth later confirmed. Thus, while goth women may interpret their sexy apparel as "an empowering statement of female choice," women in the Sanctuary are almost universally mandated to perform a sexualized femininity.

The pervasiveness of women's sexualized feminine presentations indicates that, far from being a choice, they are the expected model for women's ensembles, at least within the club. Goth women's investment in their sexual attractiveness is further suggested by GothNet comments indicating that their appeal extends outside of the goth scene. A woman, for example, responds to a hypothetical "regular" man: "I know that goth girls seem mysterious and special, and like they must know some three million sexual tricks, but in reality, they are no different than regular girls only they will have much less in common with you."

Goths value the Sanctuary because it allows them to play with self-presentations, validates sexual experimentation, and provides an arena for sexual interactions. Goths, especially goth women, present these possibilities as liberating and enjoyable. But underlying these freedoms and choices is the unspoken (and perhaps unseen) absence of choice. Goth women may enjoy sexual dress and sexual play, but their claim to goth membership depends on their participation. As Zoe told me, "As long as you dress sexy [you'll fit in]."

Despite claims that anyone can go and feel sexy, women with larger bodies are not free from criticism. One woman self-disparagingly confesses on GothNet that "I've been known to be sitting on a cozy little chair at Sanctuary and think to myself (or even whisper to a nearby friend) about a passerby 'omigod even if I were half her size I would NEVER try to squeeze my ass into something like that, how embarrassing!'" Zoe, who is lithe and beautiful in a Morticia kind of way, admits, "Some women wear very little—large women. I feel two ways. I think it's good that they can feel sexy, but think they'd look so much more attractive if they wore something else."

I also heard grumbling about some women who liked to walk naked through the Sanctuary. Hunter explained that he didn't feel that nudity was appropriate outside of a strip club. He didn't complain, however, about other outfits that were far too outlandish and revealing for most public venues—such as the chaps and thong ensemble I mentioned in the last chapter. Indeed, outlandish and revealing outfits were central to the goth look. Other women told me that the men had protested about the naked women because they weren't attractive. Despite contentions that women are not objectified or limited by mainstream beauty standards, goth women *are* objects of the critical gazes of both men and women.

Goth women are aware of these ambiguities. Women and a few men occasionally use the Web group venue to engage in feminist debates about beauty and women's bodies. GothNet, for example, hosted an ongoing conversation about women's breasts and whether or not it is ever appropriate to look at them. Participants did not reach a clear consensus on the issue, but many expressed the view that when women wear tight or low-cut tops to the Sanctuary, they invite outsiders to look at them. This debate reveals the complexities of "objectification." One woman wrote:

> I dress for myself, whether that means a short vinyl dress or army pants and a big T-shirt. When it comes to people commenting on my appearance, I have to admit that their attitude and intent are much more likely to determine how I feel about their comments...I believe it's called "objectification."

It makes sense that context shapes the meaning of behaviors. Nonetheless, in cases such as this one, goth women use the framework of the Sanctuary as a woman-friendly space to reinterpret behaviors that they might see as sleazy in other arenas. Reinterpretation, perhaps, is one strategy for reconciling the pleasure these goth women get from sexual attention with their desire to be treated equally as women.

Given the pervasiveness of men's sexual aggression in many other social contexts, the focus on women in these accounts makes sense. But men benefit too. The norms of heterosexual interaction in the Sanctuary do not desexualize the club but rather change the game rules, distributing the labor of the chase between men and women and reducing the risk of sexual rejection for men. Goth men can count on getting sex without the pressures (often lamented by "mainstream" men) of a unilateral chase.

Finally, the norms about spatial boundaries do not always protect women from undesirable advances. During my visits to the Sanctuary, I was occasionally advised by women to avoid certain guys with "sketchy" reputations. Likewise, when Beth arranged an interview with a goth man for me, she warned me not to "hook up with him." The man apparently was only willing to participate in the interview if I were "cute and available." The "loser dance" (described to me independently by Beth, Zoe, and Chad), in which women use a series of gestures to signal their discomfort with an overly aggressive male dance partner to their friends, who then intervene, also indicates an awareness among goth women that goth men may not always respect their sexual space. Eventually, my own visits to the Sanctuary began to expose some of the fissures in the goth accounts.

For example, on one occasion, Greg began sucking on a woman's neck. I sensed that Jamie, the recipient of the neck sucking, was uncomfortable, but no one interfered. When I asked other goths about the incident, I was told that they assumed Jamie, a relative newcomer to the goth scene, wanted Greg to suck on her neck because they knew each other. I also asked Greg about it, and he explained: Jamie had come to the club with Beth, and Greg thought the two women were interested in each other. Sucking on Jamie's neck was a way of "breaking the ice" between Jamie and Beth. Neither Jamie nor Beth perceived it this way, however. Both women told me that they would have rather been left alone, but felt unsure about how to discourage Greg without alienating him. This incident not only illustrates the persistence of unwanted sexual advances, it also reveals the ways in which the norm of sexual openness can undermine women's ability to be proactive about their *lack* of desire—at least with a goth insider.

On another occasion, Beth and I were dancing with a Black man we had brought to the Sanctuary with us. The dancing did not involve physical contact and we were all laughing. In this case, however, someone did intervene, ensuring that our friend was not "bothering us." It is possible that the intervention occurred because our friend was an outsider, and so was presumed not to know goth etiquette. But it is also likely, I suspect (as did Beth), that it happened because he was Black (and thus a double outsider). These examples illustrate that the rule about spatial boundaries can be redefined circumstantially, and, at least in this case, can be influenced by dominant fears of men of color.

Heterosexual relations in the goth scene, then, are much more complicated than the scene's master gender narrative claims. In their eagerness to cast the goth scene in general and the Sanctuary in particular as gender egalitarian spaces, goths don't see, gloss over, and reinterpret evidence of persistent gender inequality in sexual relations. This evidence includes the compulsion for women to dress sexy and to be sexually available, the continued objectification of women as recipients of predatory and critical male and female gazes, and the maintenance of gendered double standards in individual sexual relationships.

Yet goth women's sexual strategies are often successful, even if in limited ways. Negotiating the constricted space between pleasure and oppression, they assert themselves as sexual agents. For most of these goth women, both the master narrative of empowerment and the undercurrents of persistent inequality are probably true at different points in time. As Barton (2002) notes in her study of erotic dancers, what is sexually empowering in the short run may not be empowering in the long term. For goth women, gendered sexual expectations are not fully transformed because of the persistence of sexual double standards, and because goths do not see the broader landscape of gender inequality of which sex is only one part.

Bisexuality

At first glance, goth women seem to have more sexual options than do goth men. While the community positions itself as queer-friendly, and there is indeed diversity in sexual identities, the assumption, as Lili points out, "tend[s] to run toward women being bisexual and men being into women." "Are there any straight women?" Siobhan jokes. Of my interviewees, for example, all but one woman claimed bisexuality (the one exception identified as lesbian; no women identified as straight), while none of the men did. Similarly, in a playful GothNet survey that asked for sexual identification, almost all the women indicated their attraction to both men and women while almost all of the men identified as straight (about half of the approximately eighty GothNet members participated in the survey).

Some of the women responded to questions about their sexual identity with playful rejoinders that indicate an understanding of bisexuality as fun rather than political: "Let's say I'm a people person"; "Sexual"; "I play with all the crayons in the box." Hyacinth makes this idea explicit: "Especially in the goth community, women don't have to answer to the queer community for being primarily involved with men if that's what they want, because it's not really a big deal." More often than not, bisexual goth women are involved with straight men.

The depoliticization of female bisexuality provides cultural support for women's physical experimentation with other women. Because "it's not a big deal," sexual possibilities for women are not constrained by gender in the ways they are in "normal" straight (or lesbian) culture. It does not, however, provide structural support for sustained intimate relationships between women. In the absence of a politicized community of women involved in lesbian relationships, it is easier for bisexual women to meet men, as goth women often lament. Consequently, goth women's relationships with other women are frequently subsidiary to heterosexual relationships. Although some goth women do get involved in enduring relationships with other women, short-lived relationships are normative. Zoe comments, "I know a lot of bisexual girls who just date other girls for a week at a time. . . . Even for my own self, I tend to be in these really long relationships with men and barely ever date women." And Beth notes that "permanent relationships are more likely to be heterosexual—bi girls with boyfriends go looking for girls [for casual sex, rather than long-term relationships]."

The predominance of this arrangement has both benefits and drawbacks for women. The prevalence of women's bisexuality creates an atmosphere in which women who might otherwise practice strict heterosexuality are able to experiment sexually with other women. Moreover, some women (both in and out of the goth scene) are able to use bisexuality to traverse the boundaries of monogamy, as Zoe points out: "I've been in relationships with men who didn't care if I saw other women but I felt like he didn't perceive women as a threat...I can still fall in love with a woman...felt like he didn't take it seriously but I took advantage of it." Women like Zoe are able to maintain the advantages of a central heterosexual relationship while also engaging in sexual play outside the relationship.

Bisexuality enhances their sexual allure. The idea of women being sexually involved with each other is a turn-on to many heterosexual men, as the following quote indicates: "You just hit on the number one reason 'normals' go after goth chicks...and because a lot of them assume we're bisexual and will screw another chick while they look on" (GothNet). Within the goth scene, Siobhan tells me, "It's sexy for women to be bisexual." And Hyacinth notes, "It's definitely an 'in' thing to be young and bi and poly and friendly—to be available." Not only are bisexual goth women understood to be sexually experimental by definition, they are also still heterosexually available, both in terms of their potential sexual behavior and in their physical self-presentations.

But, as Zoe's earlier quote makes clear, while individual women may be able to use bisexuality to push against the constraints of feminine sexuality, this strategy is fragile precisely because it uses the terms of gender hierarchy to garner some sexual space. The predominant construction of bisexuality "that doesn't perceive other women as a threat" is predicated on a sexual double standard that defines sex between women as less "real." Because heterosexual relationships enjoy more structural supports than lesbian relationships, relationships between women are less stable or treated as peripheral—in other words, they *become* less real. Furthermore, the eroticization of women's bisexuality (at least between "properly" feminine women) turns it into a performance or a fantasy for men, and thereby devalues the women's own sexual pleasure. Not unique to the goth scene, this use of bisexuality demonstrates the ways in which seeming gender progress can be harnessed to serve traditional sex/gender hierarchies.

Within the goth scene, bisexuality is gendered in other ways as well. Although none of the men I spoke with claimed a bisexual identity, many of them flirted with bisexuality, distancing themselves from the homophobia that is often attributed to unenlightened, intolerant men, but without ever having to take on the consequences of enacting homosexual desire. Jeff, for example, says, "There are a lot of guys who I have a close kinship to. It's not sexual but we are pretty touchy-feely—we hug, throw our arms around each other's shoulders, I've kissed a bunch of them." He proudly admits to having men in his circle of emotional intimates; still, he calls himself heterosexual. For many goth men like Jeff, intimacy between straight identified men involves not just the sharing of feelings but also what Greg would call "sensual" contact with other men, including kissing, which is a behavior outside of the normative framework for homosocial contact between adult men. Hunter makes a similar claim: "I've kissed men, kissed women, I'm completely straight though, nothing bothers me." Hunter demonstrates tolerance and sexual openness through his comfort with kissing men ("nothing bothers me"), even while he claims that he is "completely straight."

As Hunter illustrates, goth men can use sexualized contact with other men (or at least the discussion of it) to reinforce their image as tolerant, enlightened, experimental, and secure in their own masculinity. Their dance with bisexuality, then, increases their sexual hipness, and possibility their desirability as well, as a comment by Siobhan suggests: "In my group, there are a few men who are out as bisexual. I really admire them. But the more popular men aren't out about it. It's sexy for women to be bisexual but not for men—not as many gay men...are considered manly." Thus, *because* the goth scene is not a space in which gay or even bisexual men are normative, playing with bisexuality can make men seem courageous and authentic. They are willing to explore all of their desires, even if those desires are seen as less manly. The irony, of course, is that their purported courage then increases their manliness. Rory sardonically observes: "Most men in the goth scene—theoretical bisexuality, practice heterosexuality. It's cooler. Chicks dig bisexual guys, makes them sound open-minded. I think you need to actually have at least a crush (to call yourself bisexual)."

This does not work the same way for women. Because bisexuality is considered (in this scene) normative for women, lesbian play among women does not make them seem courageous or individually unconventional (although the assumption of women's bisexuality does make the scene seem collectively unconventional). Indeed, it seems plausible, within this context, that sexual disinterest in women could reduce a woman's coolness or desirability. Siobhan's management of her own bisexual identity suggests this, especially when contrasted to her comment about men's bisexuality:

> I'm not as turned on by women so I can't return their sexual energy as much as they'd like. A lot of women say I'm not bisexual because I'm really into the male form. I like being in relationships with women, but I don't like having sex with them.

The challenges to Siobhan's claim to bisexuality indicate that goth women's bisexuality is expected to go beyond the homosocial sensuality that Jeff and Hunter claim, and that her claim to hipness can be challenged if she doesn't live up to those expectations. For goth men, in contrast, merely talking about homosexual contact demonstrates their hipness. These gender divergent uses of homosocial contact/desire are another source of advantage for goth men vis-à-vis goth women. Goth men are able to use bisexual performance (or just discourse) to gain more of a dividend in terms of both "cool" and heterosexual desirability than are goth women, for whom such behavior is expected.

Goth queer play pushes against important gender barriers. Queer play is risky, opening goths to potential stigma, harassment, or even danger from "normals." Schippers (2002) argues that queer play among otherwise heterosexual women in the alternative hard rock scene challenges normative assumptions about femininity. In her study, the women's queer play was more akin to the goth men's symbolic bisexuality than to the goth women's often more sustained bisexual relationships.

But queer play takes on meaning from its context. The goths in this study experiment with sexuality in a community that is known as a lesbian mecca. For local liberals and even moderates, tolerance for and friendliness with gay and lesbian people is expected. Moreover, the venue that hosts the Sanctuary is, on all other nights, a gay club; club personnel are accustomed to diverse sexualities. In addition, while the costs of being queer continue to be severe, stereotypical components of urban gay culture have gained some cultural cool. Bisexuality is "in"—and not just in the goth scene. When I was in high school, anything other than ordinary heterosexuality was unthinkable, but four years later, things had changed; at least in some places. My brother, a senior in 1994, explained that the girls in his class were all "into being bisexual." In the course of the research for this book, local high schoolers—girls and boys—told me the same thing. One of the high schools in the southern, presumably less gender-progressive, part of the area had even earned the nickname "Bi-tech." And at "regular" clubs, women dance seductively with each other, usually as a heterosexual strategy, while bisexual and lesbian women I know laugh at their "inauthentic" moves.

These changes are double edged. While they indicate a growing acceptability and visibility of lesbian women and gay men, and more elastic gender boundaries, they also smack of cultural appropriation. As a consequence, members of the politically and socially active lesbian and gay community view goth behavior with some suspicion. When Hyacinth explains that goths "don't have to answer to the gay community," she means that they can sidestep the often suffocating identity regulations of gay communities (Esterberg 1997, Stein 1997).[8] Yet, not "answer[ing]" to the gay community" also means not taking on the political and social responsibilities of community membership. In short, goths get the benefits of homoerotic behavior but avoid most of the costs. In this way, they stand on the backs of generations of gay and lesbian activists whose work and pain has wrought the changes that make homoeroticism at all socially rewarding in the first place.

For goths, queer play brings both hipness and a kind of status to the goth community, but it does so through contrast to communities and people who are presumably less queer-friendly. These include other white middle-class communities, such as the Unity Christians featured in the next two chapters, and the almost universally despised Greek (fraternity and sorority) students, but also race and class subordinated people who are assumed to be intolerant of sexual diversity. At the same time, goths gain some safety for their experiments by their distance from the gay community.

Polyamory

Wren and Jeff have been together for five years. They live together and are handfasted—married, according to the pagan community in which

---

8. It is important to note here, as well, that bisexuality is often marginalized in both mainstream and gay and lesbian communities. I am not arguing that bisexuality is an easy life strategy. Many goth women stake out lives as bisexuals, and face consequences for doing so. I am critiquing bisexuality as a community practice.

they both participate. They talk about making their marriage legal. By all accounts, they are a happy couple, deeply in love and respectful of each other. Like many goths, Wren and Jeff are polyamorous: they have chosen to maintain their central relationship while also developing sexual and romantic relationships with other people.

Within this goth scene, sexual openness is most often organized through the practice of polyamory. Although polyamory isn't practiced by all goths, it is nonetheless central to their collective identity; it came up in every discussion of "what it means to be goth," it was standard fare for Web list discussions, and the Web sites of individual goths usually discuss polyamory or include links to polyamory Web sites. Polyamory,[9] which means more than one love, embraces romantic intimacy but rejects sexual exclusivity. According to the polyamory Web site that many goths visit regularly, polyamorous relationships can take on a number of forms. For example, each member of a couple may engage in subsidiary sexual and/or emotional relationships with other people or with the same person. Or a polyamorous person may engage in several equally privileged sexual/emotional relationships. Or three or more people may be simultaneously involved.

Wren and Jeff weren't always polyamorous. When they began their relationship, they were monogamous, but they discovered polyamory in the goth scene and, after much discussion, decided to give it a try. Jeff tells me that polyamory was Wren's idea. He objected on familiar grounds: he didn't want to think about her having sex with other men. But Wren wanted, she explains, to be able to "step out and try some adventures with emotions." She persisted, and Jeff finally decided to give it a try. He was committed to Wren and wanted to make her happy, but he also figured polyamory would let him sow his wild oats. Polyamory, they both claim, has transformed their relationship. Jeff says: "Becoming poly was one of the best things that happened to my relationship with Wren because we deal with our fears; we're open and honest." For Wren and Jeff, polyamory is not only a way to reject conventional sexual expectations but also to develop better relationships. They can sow their wild oats while retaining the benefits of a committed, intimate relationship.

Polyamory is complicated. The scheduling alone requires time and flexibility, but "seriously caring about multiple people" can be, in Greg's

---

9. In the following discussion, I am referring specifically to how polyamory is manifested in this goth scene, not to its practice in the broader polyamorous community; although Sheff's (2005) examination of a polyamorous community contains many of the dynamics I describe here.

words, "way too confusing." Crow said, "I make of it me slamming my head into the wall it's so stressful." Beth's relationship with Jeff illustrates some of the intricacies of polyamorous negotiations. When I first met Beth, she had just begun to date Jeff, and was also friends with Wren. Jeff and Beth took their relationship slowly. They spent time together, talking and going on walks. They kissed but they didn't have sex. At the same time, Beth had also begun seeing Jamie, a woman on the periphery of the goth community. Jamie was used to moving a little faster, and was perplexed and a bit impatient with the time Beth took to initiate sex. But Beth's hands were tied. According to the rules of Jeff and Wren's relationship, Jeff and Beth couldn't have sex (the particular behaviors that constituted sex were not clearly defined) until Beth had been tested for STIs. Jamie too had to be tested for STIs, since Beth would presumably be having sex with her. To Beth, these rules made sense but were a burden that had emotional repercussions on her relationship with Jamie. Both Beth and Jamie went through with the testing, but this was still not enough. Wren also had to "approve" of Beth and be "ready" for Beth and Jeff to have sex. In the end, Beth never had sex with Jeff. Although Beth complied with Jeff's requests, she resented that his relationship with Wren dictated the terms of their relationship, and eventually decided that playing emotional second fiddle was not worth it.

The rules of Jeff and Wren's polyamorous relationship exemplify the ways in which the "freedom" of polyamory can be managed by rules that determine not only sexual contact but also restrict emotional intimacy. For Jeff and Wren, polyamory is not a free-for-all. In practice, their rules allow each partner to maintain control over the pace of the "subsidiary" relationships. Thus, while Jeff and Wren explore outside sexual and emotional interests, these explorations are not spontaneous, but rather managed in a way that maintains the emotional centrality of their "primary" relationship with each other. Indeed, because their rules demand that the concerns of their relationship shape liaisons, they necessarily impede the ability of either partner to engage in a sustained or emotionally rich outside relationship, and thus help stabilize their own dyadic relationship.

In addition, Wren and Jeff's rules preclude spontaneous, "empty" sex. Jeff explains:

> The sexual conversations are there to protect me and [Wren]. We're probably going to have kids someday. We want to be healthy when that happens. We don't feel [condoms are sufficient]. We're putting ourselves in a risky situation.

It's an extra level of comfort to know the person is clean.... It brings a lot of restrictions but it's not something I can throw out lightly.

For Jeff and Wren, concerns about their future are paramount. By incorporating rules, they are able to engage in (at least the fantasy of) sexual and emotional freedom with minimal risk.

Wren and Jeff's rules are consistent with public goth culture, which deplores unprotected sexual behavior. Multiple GothNet exchanges proclaim condom use to be merely a baseline sexual practice. These exchanges encourage simultaneous use of multiple forms of contraception (e.g., the pill and condoms) and routine HIV and other STI screening. One exchange warned a goth woman not to trust her boyfriend's self-recounting of his sexual history.[10] As a whole, these norms guard the boundaries of the goth scene, and individual goths, from the stigmatizing invasion of STIs and from unplanned pregnancies. By following these rules (and because of their exposure to contraceptive information and access to actual birth control, both of which they take for granted), goths are able to participate in sexual experimentation while limiting their physical risk.

Rules like these offer not only physical protection, but also fuse their unconventional arrangement with more conventional concerns. Wren and Jeff, like other goths, use polyamory to declare that they are throwing off the confines of uptight middle-class sexual restrictions while also being more restrained, more respectful, and more emotionally and ethically developed than non-goths. They claim a goth sexuality that has somehow freed adult commitments from their associated boredom, where one can have "adventures in emotions" (and sex) while still retaining a sense of oneself as a loving and committed partner.

In many ways, the prevalence of polyamory is the most unconventional aspect of goth sexual culture, as it rejects the central assumption that real and good relationships are dyadic and sexually monogamous. It is thus not surprising that goths put a significant amount of work into managing the potential costs of polyamory. Vigilance over safer sex practices protects the community physically, but the potential costs to moral standing are perhaps harder to manage. Polyamory implies a long-term commitment

10. The frank exchanges of sexual information on the Web list facilitate greater access to information on sexual health; it is possible, however, for a goth to be *too* frank. One woman was ridiculed for her attempts to stop rumors about her STI status by sending a Web list message that she was STI-free.

to nonmonogamy that is distinct from the sexual experimentation of, say, fraternity and sorority members, in that it is not necessarily time-bounded. Sexual experimentation is assumed to end when a person or couple "settles down," but with polyamory, there is presumably no moment of settling down.[11] In order to maintain respectability, then, goths have to "prove" that they are nonetheless sexually moral people.

To that end, goths emphasize the emotional, rather than the sexual, dimensions of polyamory. Indeed, they make repeated distinctions between polyamory and "hedonism," "sleeping around," and "simple promiscuity." These goths spent a lot of time explaining "true" polyamory to me, and an even larger amount of time, via GothNet, reminding each other. As a forum, GothNet hosted a range of conversations, but discussions of community expectations for polyamory were recurrent. Even goths who don't themselves practice polyamory subscribed to these distinctions.

Goths argue that polyamory is morally superior to "promiscuity" because it entails honesty, respect, and the consistent practice of safe sex. Crow expresses contempt for people "who think they can do whatever they want or [are] just swingers." Beth draws a similar moral line: "I feel a lot of people use it as an excuse to sleep around or be irresponsible. It irritates me because they're taking the [polyamorous] label. I don't want to be associated with people who are irresponsible—whether it be emotionally irresponsible or not using protection." Lance, who is currently in his first polyamorous relationship, says:

> I don't want to say that I don't have a lot of respect for polyamory but a lot of [polyamorous goths] get on my nerves; they take something that could be beautiful and use it for self-justification. In its purest form, it's not about sex, it's about love.... People who don't want to think of themselves as easy people who want the fun part of sleeping around without moral consequences claim polyamory. There are some people who do it for the right reasons.

And Hyacinth:

> If I just wanted to do what I want and be irresponsible, I would just describe myself as single and dating. People are generally shocked that the number of

---

11. Indeed, the understanding that polyamory is not a "phase" is important to goths, as is evidenced by Lance's report of angry reactions when he suggested most goths "would grow out of it."

people I'm with is low and stable. In some ways I feel that what I do has more in common with monogamy than, say, swinging where you just go out and fuck whoever you want. Frequently, it's more of a choice between monogamy with cheating and polyamory. A lot of times people can't keep their hands to themselves and lie to their partners, which, among other things, puts their partners' health at risk, not to mention the huge emotional betrayal. I really do believe it's possible to love more than one person at a time and I guess I feel like if you do, why shouldn't you? I guess. It's not like there's too much love in this world.

Although their practices reject monogamy, goths cleverly use other elements of the dominant cultural landscape to position polyamory as not only morally acceptable, but morally superior. Their talk invokes the values of stability, emotional responsibility, physical caution, and love, but rejects their allegedly hypocritical practice.

In this formulation, polyamory is a recipe for *better* intimate relationships: polyamory allows goths to be more emotionally authentic than does monogamy because it allows them to "react" to their "real" emotional and physical desires. Thus, polyamory becomes an avenue, not to hedonism, but to the achievement of emotional sophistication. It improves emotional intimacy, goths argue, because it entails better communication, greater honesty, and more highly developed trust. Thus, as with their culture of emotional darkness, goths use polyamory to claim emotional distinctiveness.

A closer look at the issue of jealousy, discussed briefly in the last chapter, gives more insight into how this works. Jealousy is a common, expected outcome of the central features—exclusivity, emotional intensity—of contemporary intimate relationships. Goth polyamory rejects the mandate for exclusivity, but does not reject the idea that coupling should be emotionally intense. This combination would seem to stoke jealousy, and thus means that these goths are almost inevitably forced to grapple collectively with the issue of jealousy. As we saw in the last chapter, the goth community doesn't tolerate admissions of jealousy. Goths further distance themselves from the possessiveness, jealousy, and hypocrisy associated with mainstream relationship culture through their ability to achieve individual and collective resolutions to this emotional dilemma.

Polyamory is risky. When I discuss polyamory with my classes, they are almost universally flabbergasted at the notion that anyone would reject monogamy. My own brief, ill-fated, experiment with an "open" relationship still earns scornful comments. Regardless of the intentions of the participants, outsiders assume that nonmonogamy, in any form, is wrong. I bring up these experiences to underscore the intensity and pervasiveness of the American culture of monogamy.

By flagrantly violating this expectation, goths risk moral censure. In part, this can be alleviated by their age—most are not yet expected to have settled down and so their (particularly men's) sexual forays are, in some ways, excused. But age does not solve all their problems. Goths further protect their moral standing, as I have shown, by aligning polyamory with other aspects of conventional sexual culture and by arguing that poly-amory creates better relationships. To this end, they insist that polyamory is about love and not about sex. This strategy makes polyamory more respectable, but it puts an additional burden on intimate relationships, which represent not just individual goths but the entire community.

For goth women, the emphasis on relationships and their assumed moral superiority allay their presentation of themselves as sexually free. At once, they are sexually experimental and emotionally responsible. They are thus able to expand their sexual options while protecting their posi-tions as "good" women. Goth men get similar benefits: sexual adventure packaged with emotional responsibility. But, because of the centrality of sexuality to gender identities, men have more to gain from this combina-tion than do women. Women must navigate the stigma that attaches to sex-ually agentic women, while men gain status from their presumed sexual prowess.

Romance, gender, and goth relationships

Relationships exacerbate the paradoxes in goth sexual strategies. For many goth women, gender discrepancies increase when they enter roman-tic relationships. In this final section, I pull together the pieces of goth sex-ual culture to illustrate the ways in which women are ensnared in unequal relationships with men—despite a rhetoric of women's empowerment and good intentions. The predominantly heterosexual relationships within the goth community often restrict women's sexual freedoms but not men's. Three aspects of goth culture support these double standards, which per-sist despite explicit support for women's sexual agency. First, tolerance for sexual experimentation provides the illusion of progressive gender re-lations. The equation of queerness with "gender play" and the practice of mild gender experiments on the part of (some) men create a sense of de facto gender egalitarianism. Similarly, the tolerance for (in fact, the expectation of) women's bisexuality adds to the sense of gender progress. Because gender progressiveness is a moral identity for goths, they are further invested in not seeing internal contradictions in their tactics. Second, in the goth scene (and elsewhere), women's bisexuality is frequently used to excuse and hide inequality in heterosexual relationships (both individually and collectively) and harnessed to serve men's fantasies. Third, goths mitigate the moral threats of polyamory by tying it to enduring relationships. This strategy reinvigorates the importance of romance, but in an environment in which the putative separation of romance from sexuality leaves romance unrecognized as an arena of gender inequity. By emphasizing sexuality as *the* strategy for women's emancipation, these goths maintain the importance of successful intimacy for women's identities.

Although goths use gender talk to endorse their community's sexual practices, gender is noticeably absent from goth accounts of polyamory: relationship ideals and dilemmas are constructed as gender-neutral phenomenon unlinked to "situated social power" (Wartenberg 1988). Talk about the dynamics of specific intimate relationships, however, paints a different story. Siobhan, introduced earlier in the chapter, had been the "slave" in her much lauded relationship with Bill; when she had her collar on, she had to ask Bill's permission to as much as use the bathroom. A number of goths pointed to Siobhan and Bill's relationship as an example of successful polyamory; Beth and Zoe, however, both confided their misgivings. Zoe explained, "He's dated lots of women but she's only dated one guy. She says it's never worked out but I think he's always protested it."

When I met Siobhan, she and Bill had recently broken up. Like most people who have recently ended a relationship, Siobhan didn't have much good to say about Bill and his treatment of her. But to Siobhan, the problem wasn't that she had been a slave; the problem was that Bill had abused their arrangement, and thus her. She bitterly recalls, "[Bill] was jealous and insecure and didn't want me to date any other men. Women were fine as long as he got a piece of ass too." In her telling, the structural arrangements of heterosexuality are fine, but some individual men (like Bill) are bad. She was, in fact, thrilled with her new man. At the time I had also just gotten out of a bad relationship. "Don't worry," she assured me, "there's a right person out there for you too." The trick for women, then, is to find the right man, not to challenge the gender assumptions embedded in heterosexuality.

Siobhan condemns Bill on individual grounds, but her situation adheres to a common pattern in the goth community in which straight men are involved with bisexual women. In these relationships, as Zoe complains, "There seems to be a double standard—girls in heterosexual relationships can date other women but not other men." The intersection of women's bisexuality with polyamory in these relationships shines a lens on the ways in which the power dynamics of the romantic relationship are gendered, despite the discourse of open and egalitarian negotiation.

Zoe and Beth again both flagged Sean and Lili's seven-year relationship as another example of inequity. Lili, however, explicitly denies that a double standard exists. Instead, she explains "we each have our own set of rules. Mine are harder to put into words. His are based on binary gender rules." Her rules include discouraging Sean's involvement with girls who are "bad news...girls who are going to hurt him." But Beth tells me that, over the years, Lili has frequently complained about individual women that Sean has dated, indicating both that her "rule" is less binding than she portrays it to be and that their polyamorous negotiations are emotionally painful to her. This in turn suggests that Lili relies on a version of what Hochschild (1989) calls "family myths." Like the women in Hochschild's study who convinced themselves that their objectively unequal divisions of domestic labor were in fact equitable, Lili seems to have mentally reconstructed her relationship with Sean so that their imbalanced negotiations appear fair. Or at least that is the strategy she uses with me. In keeping with this portrayal, she adds, "It does get more complicated because I'm bisexual and he's not—we can't be just like 'I can see other girls, he can see other guys.'" Her bisexuality, then, allows the appearance of more equality than actually exists.

In polyamorous relationships, women's bisexuality can be used to circumscribe women's sexuality, as in Lili and Sean's case. Sean's participation in a central committed relationship does not require him to delimit his chosen field of sexual eligibles, but Lili's participation requires her to cut hers in half. Her bisexuality is used as the justification for this imbalance. Her ability to sexually engage other women makes it seem like she is gaining something. The supposition that her sexual freedom is equivalent to Sean's masks the inequity of their arrangement.

In cases like Lili and Sean's relationship, the goth notion that sexual diversity automatically confers gender egalitarianism to the goth scene obscures gender inequity. For example, Rory and Hyacinth argue (in Hyacinth's words) that the "BDSM crossover...gives people the idea that they can make up their own rules about power dynamics." And Lili tells me that queerness creates "different...gender rules," implying that the context of "gender as play" obliterates the gender hierarchies that attach to conventional gender roles.

But it is not sexuality that secures Lili's relative disempowerment; it is her emotional commitment to Sean. Because of her belief in the enduring love of that relationship, Lili does the emotion work (Hochschild 1989) necessary to allow her to stay in it. The pervasiveness of conventional relationship ideals is further evidenced by their on-again, off-again discussions of marriage and by Lili's confession that she engages in fewer and fewer outside relationships at all. Moreover, Rory, Zoe, and Siobhan, all previously polyamorous, told me that they were currently monogamous because they didn't want to hurt their boyfriends. And the woman and man with whom Beth once had a triangular relationship (in which all three participants were romantically and sexually involved with each other) have recently sealed their monogamy with marriage. In all of these examples, the promise of love triumphs over the freedom and choice of goth sexual experimentation.

In her study of adolescent girls' sexuality, Sharon Thompson (1995) concludes, "The greatest danger girls narrated was love. Once in love or set on trying to get in love, even cautious girls said they closed their eyes to sexual and psychological danger" (285). It is the ideology of romance, rather than sexuality, that encourages girls and women to sacrifice for the sake of the relationship. Indoctrinated in the intertwined ideologies that "love conquers all" and that "hetero-relationships are the key to women's happiness" (Phillips 2000), girls and women read romantic relationships as signs of their self-worth and of their identities, and thus risk losing both when they lose a relationship. The idea, moreover, that women are responsible for the maintenance of relationships adds to the pressure women feel to make their romantic alliances endure (Phillips 2000). Thus, because romance continues to be ideologically privileged for women, the emancipatory potential of their sexual agency is limited.

Goths scoff at commercialized romance. Yet they do not develop a critical analysis of the relationship imperative behind notions of romance. Rather, they use polyamory to unpin separate notions of monogamous, vanilla sexuality from notions of "ideal" intimate relationships, suggesting, for example, that a person may be able to be involved simultaneously in more than one romantic relationship or that a person may be able to engage in sexual behavior with someone outside of the romantic dyad without undermining the emotional integrity of that pairing. These assertions attempt to expand the terms of romantic relationships without questioning their basic validity. Indeed, they recharge romance as a morally and emotionally important goal.

Conclusion

Goths use sexuality for multiple purposes. Freaky, active sexuality pushes against the bounds of staid white middle-class stereotypes, challenges gendered restrictions on sexuality, and makes goth more hip. Goth strategies push important sexual boundaries. By imagining the possibility of, and attempting to enact, respectful nonmonogamy, and by endorsing women's right to egalitarian sexual relationships, they challenge central aspects of conventional sexuality. Their queer play too, while limited in its effects, challenges the tight link between gender and heterosexuality, as well as the assumption that men's relationships with each other should be emotionally distant. These are gains that should not be overlooked.

Some goths, however, are more successful at attaining their goals than others. In part, this is because goth sexuality questions many of the tenets of conventional sexual rules, but it does not question all of them. Instead, goths suggest that their sexual norms are more desirable *because* they enable them to live up to some of the expectations of conventional sexual culture *better*. These expectations include relational intimacy and commitment, safer sex practices, and the postponement of childbearing until they are "ready." These seem like reasonable, even noble, values. Dedication to these norms, I have argued, safeguards them from some of the potential fallout of unconventional sexual practices, *and* aligns them with some aspects of conventional sexual morality. In many ways (but not all), it makes them respectable.

In these ways, goths' sexuality attempts to play two sides. On the one hand, goths attempt to release sexuality from the hold of heterosexual monogamy. And they are partially successful: both women and men are able to engage in experimental sexual behavior with a range of sexual partners in and out of relationships. On the other hand, many of their practices, especially polyamory, are perceived as immoral and bizarre by outsiders. Goths know this. In part, their claims to superiority are an effort to mitigate this intolerance by linking polyamory to more conventional sexual norms. Goths differentiate their sexual culture from a culture of "promiscuity" by describing it as less repressed, less hypocritical, and more gender progressive than mainstream sexual practices. This is not sexuality for hedonism's sake, they maintain, but a recipe for better, more honest, more committed intimate relationships.

Fields (2001) finds that parents of lesbian women and gay men manage the stigma of their children's sexual violations by "normalizing" them; to do this, they emphasize the ways in which their lesbian or gay children live up to dominant sexual expectations and distance them from sexual stereotypes. This strategy salvages the respectability of both the parents and their adult children, but it does so by redrawing a distinct line between "normal" and "abnormal" sexuality (see also Hennen 2004, 2005).

Goths' tactics are similar. They expand the terrain of acceptable sexuality, but they also draw a line. This line separates the responsible from the irresponsible, the honest from the dishonest, the promiscuous from the polyamorous. In these ways, they align their unconventional sexual practices with conventional sexual norms. But goths don't want to be "normal." Their strategy depends on seeing themselves, and being seen, as freaks. To them, freaks are more authentic, less conformist, and more interesting. Goths distinguish themselves from "normals" because they engage in, or are at least comfortable with, sexual practices that make many people uncomfortable; because their sexual practices and intimate relationships are more "honest," "open," and "trustworthy," and thus stronger, than conventional relationships; and because they are more gender progressive and sexually tolerant than the mainstream.

Goth strategies attempt to reconfigure the link between gender and sexuality, but they are also linked, much less consciously, to the performance of race and class. As feminists of color have long argued, these cannot be separated (Hill Collins 1991, 2004, Thornton Dill 1983). For goths, race and class are hidden assets, freeing them from the significant costs that come from presumptions that one's sexuality is the cause of not only one's own problems but also the problems of one's entire status group. Moreover, for the white middle class, it is not just sexuality that is assumed to be decent, but also gender relations. In short, the association of improper sexuality and gender relations with people of color and the poor is what buys goths their comparative freedom. For goths, this freedom also comes from their distance from the queer community, whose political work has paved the way for many of the goth strategies, but who are still subject to costly gender and sexual assumptions.[12]

12. Poor people of color and queer people are often played off each other, so that one group's gains come at the expense of the other group (Booth 2000). Goths benefit from their distance from both groups.

Furthermore, the sexual ideals that these goths claim and repudiate operate on a field of power cramped with race and class assumptions. Early, unwed childbearing, a lack of commitment to marriage (interpreted, in turn, as a lack of interest in relational commitment), and sexual promiscuity are denigrated as social problems plaguing the poor and people of color (Luker 1996, Hill Collins 2004, Edin and Kefalas 2005,[13] Fields 2005).[14] The goth strategy remakes these symbolic oppositions, even if unintentionally.

But goth distinctions are not just reactionary. Goths are also proud of the ways in which they violate normative gender and sexual assumptions. Indeed, to them, progressive gender and sexual relations are central to their moral selves. By differentiating themselves from the "Neanderthals" and "meat market men" who populate regular, "repulsive" clubs, goths draw lines against the (white middle-class) frat crowd. In this way, they are not different from other white middle-class college students who disdain the alleged conformity and elitism of the "Chad" and "Tiffany" types. Goth is, fundamentally, an alternative to this performance of white middle-classness. Yet these distinctions cut both ways. Their "progressive" gender relations take on meaning not just from their rejection of "Greek" norms, but from their symbolic opposition to the presumably less enlightened gender relations among the poor and people of color (Pyke 1996, Hondagneu-Sotelo and Messner 1994, White 2001).

Ironically, it is goth investment in these sets of distinctions, in part, that undermines their ability to fully remake gender relations in their scene. Goth sexuality faces limitations precisely because it serves complex, sometimes contradictory, purposes. The goths' strategy is limited, first, by its continued investment in romance, and attendant failure to fully challenge male dominance. By defending their unconventional sexuality as a path to better relationships, goths maintain the importance of enduring relationships to both individual and collective goth identities. The need to make relationships work preserves women's reliance (for personal meaning, for self-esteem, and even for justification of their sexual behaviors) on the sexual relationships they establish. This reliance, in turn, reproduces their

13. Edin and Kefalas argue that poor women share the marital values of the middle class but are less likely to be able to actualize them. Regardless, social assumptions about their sexual morality endure.

14. Again, these sexual stereotypes, except for unwed childbearing, are also applied to gay men and lesbian women.

disempowerment within those relationships by undercutting their ability to demand men's accountability for sexism.

Second, the perception that goth is gender progressive covers up enduring gender inequality in the goth scene. The notion that transformed sexuality is inherently gender egalitarian allows participants to feel morally and politically superior to people who haven't transformed their sexuality and allows participants to justify their own lifestyles on political and moral grounds. Gender progressive moral identities can be as seductive as the sexual gains themselves, and can thus be used to stifle internal or external challenges to sexism. In effect, participants can use their involvement in transformed sexual relations as evidence of their de facto egalitarianism, shielding themselves and their community from further challenges to the configuration of gendered power.

Goth women's struggles show that it is possible for women to create a space in which they are able to access sexuality on more gender egalitarian terms, even while they encounter stumbling blocks to full sexual autonomy. It is not enough, however, to change sexual rules without also addressing inequity in other arenas. At the same time, women's emancipation is limited by collective concerns about respectability and status. Investments in respectability undermine their efforts to transform their sexual relations. These concerns retie women to inequitable arrangements, and thus prop up male dominance.

CHAPTER FOUR

Just Good People

Susan, a nineteen-year-old white university sophomore, doesn't come from a Christian family, but she's been a Christian since her junior year of high school. High school, she explains, was decent, but she didn't really fit in. She describes herself as "on the geeky side," someone who didn't party, play sports, or "wear Abercrombie and Fitch." She was mildly depressed, she says, looking for "it." An online friend convinced her to go to a Christian retreat, where she "learned how Jesus died for our sins— a phrase that everyone's heard so much." As she tells me this, she rolls her eyes, suggesting a world of difference between reciting this cliché and *really* being a Christian. For Susan, "it kinda clicked....I knew I wanted Christ in my life, to have the burden of doing everything for myself lifted from me." But becoming a Christian was a process: "and then I'd pray and then I'd think I didn't do it good enough and so I did it again." Like other Christians, Susan needed to learn to how to be a Christian. In repeating the ritual of the prayer until she felt like she got it right, Susan was learning the daily practices of the Christian identity, but she was learning something else as well—how to connect those practices to a particular way of *feeling*.

Susan's Christian identity didn't really click until college, when she found University Unity. Unity helped Susan stop "floundering," by structuring her Christian identity and by providing a group of supportive friends. Indeed, for Susan, as with other participants, the circle of friends—people "who have the same understanding of the world"—is one of the most important things about Unity. Being a Christian has also given Susan a sense of purpose. Now, Susan says, "I have a reason for everything I do." Her purpose, she says, is God: "God was definitely It." And God gives her "the strength to make decisions that [she'll] wish [she] had made," to "see things in terms of long-term benefits," to "not give in to the easiest way all the time," and to be kind to other people.

Susan's high school problems are in many ways mundane: she didn't quite fit in. It wasn't horrible, but she wasn't happy either. Christianity provided her with a solution; it not only gave her a set of friends, a group in which she did fit in, but it also gave her an explanation for her previous discomfort. Moreover, it gave her moral guideposts, and replaced her previous depression with a "depth of peace and love [she didn't know] was possible before."

Susan's tale resonates with the stories told by Smith and Lundquist Denton (2005) in their study of religious teenagers. Religion, they argue, is good for youth—it provides them with moral grounding, motivation, social and cultural capital, and adult support. It is hard to argue that these are not, in fact, good things. Accordingly, Susan seems like an ideal young woman. She is focused and confident. She is concerned about the future. She cares about other people, going to great lengths not to talk about them or to be arrogant around them. And she is happy. Susan is the kind of young woman who others see, and who sees herself, as "good."

In this chapter, I treat Unity Christian "goodness" like I treated goth "freakiness." Although goodness seems to be an innate quality, it is an identity, one that can be achieved, used to solve social problems, and used to think of oneself as a deserving person. The young people in this chapter use the practices and rhetoric of University Unity Christianity to learn to think of themselves as "good." For them, goodness is both behavioral and emotional. They are diligent, hard-working, self-disciplined, and abstemious, avoiding temptations like drinking and sex. And they are loving, warm, and happy. As Susan's story suggests, goodness solves problems for them; in particular, it provides them with an explanation for their withdrawal from peer status hierarchies while also protecting their social location by foreclosing any behaviors that might derail them. It allows them to feel like especially worthy people by providing a meaning system that not only endorses their practices and feelings, but recasts them as culturally and morally superior.

The Unity Christian identity is less risky than the goth identity. Still, goodness is not a perfect strategy. The expectations of goodness can be, in Carolyn's words, exhausting, entailing relentless vigilance over one's behavior and emotions, and requiring young people to relinquish many of the freedoms and rituals associated with young adulthood. In this way, then, goodness can seem not only a little weird, but also boring.

In this chapter, I argue that Unity Christianity, like the other young adult identities in this book, solves common dilemmas. After situating Unity Christianity in its broader context, I turn to Lucas's and Gretchen's stories to exemplify the ways in which Christianity provides a path through the pain and complexity of youth status hierarchies. This path includes clear expectations about drinking and study habits that allow Unity Christians to see themselves as disciplined people, but it also creates conflicts. Unity Christians are often concerned that they are boring, and that Christianity limits their friendships with non-Christians. Carolyn, a young Korean-American woman for whom Christianity is less central than for others in this book, illustrates both the difficulties of the Unity identity and its complex connection to race and class. Finally, I conclude the chapter by examining Unity emotional culture. Unity Christians think of themselves as good people, in large part, because they are happy and loving. Because this expectation is more stringent for young women than it is for young men, it provides a glimpse into the ways in which Unity Christianity is also a means of navigating gender. In the next chapter, I make gender central by turning to the Unity culture of sexual abstinence.

University Unity

These chapters are based on formal, open-ended interviews with fifteen (nine women, six men) self-identified evangelical Christians, on casual conversations with Unity participants, and with participant-observation at University Unity meetings as well as the home church of most of my participants. I made my initial contact through a non-Christian student, and then recruited the other participants through networks.

The young people in this chapter describe themselves as Christians,[1] rather than invoking a particular denominational affiliation. A few of them came from Catholic families, but the organization in which they participate, and their personal orientation toward Christianity, is conservative Protestant. For them, being Christian means experiencing a conversion moment (being "born again"), having a personal relationship with

---

1. I refer to them as Unity Christians. They don't call themselves this, however; they simply call themselves Christians. I use the term Unity Christian to remind readers that I am speaking of a particular group of young Christians, not about all Christians, and because the identity I describe is organizationally grounded.

Jesus, and making the Bible central in determining daily behavior. More-over, although they often find it personally uncomfortable, they believe that they have an obligation to evangelize. Molly, for example, explains enthusiastically, "The best thing I could do for people was to tell them about this." Because of these characteristics, I describe them as evangelicals. Unlike fundamentalists, they are antiseparatist and do not insist on literal interpretations of the Bible.

Evangelicalism, Christian Smith (2000) argues, stakes its identity on a notion of being "embattled." In contrast to fundamentalists, evangelicals stress "compromise and accommodation," rather than separatism, priding themselves on their ability to maintain a distinct belief system without re-moving themselves from the world (Ammerman 1987). Because it requires vigilance about boundaries, this tension intensifies the commitment to the evangelical identity (Smith 2000). In the context of the northeastern uni-versity community, embattledness is easy to come by. Evangelical Chris-tianity is a distinctive identity in a community whose academic sector is both secular and intellectualist and whose student population has a reputation for its zoo-like behavior.

The political and numerical presence of evangelicals at the national level is the subject of much media and academic commentary. Estimates suggest that a quarter of the U.S. population identify as conservative Pro-testants (Emerson and Smith 2000, Wilcox 2004). In addition, the Christian Right is a lucrative and powerful political force; its values and perspectives shape both local and national policy making. Describing throngs of student participants at Boston-based Christian events, Swidey (2003) argues in the *Boston Globe* magazine that New England college students are begin-ning to embrace the Bible Belt traditions. Despite Swidey's observation, though, evangelicalism is not normative in liberal northeastern universi-ties. The evangelicals in my study, all students at a large, public north-eastern university, are not part of such a swelling wave. In keeping with the notion of embattledness, they describe themselves as a self-conscious minority in a university community without much tolerance for conserva-tive religious traditions. "People think we're in a cult," they laugh; they are self-conscious of their distance from both the university mainstream and often their parents. Susan laments that while "lots of religions are cool at [the university], Christianity isn't."

Accordingly, it is important to remember that evangelicalism is not ho-mogenous. The northeastern context undoubtedly means that Christian-ity is a different kind of identity solution for the youth in this book than it is for young Christians in more welcoming parts of the country. In places where Christianity is culturally dominant as an adolescent or young adult identity choice, I imagine that Christianity ranks higher on local status hierarchies. But in the space in which this study takes place, Unity Christianity is seen as a "weird" choice, not as a normative young adult identity. It is *not* what everybody does. Because of these differences, the University Unity young people in this chapter may be surprising to readers from the Bible Belt.

Evangelical adults are the subject of a wide range of academic work, but little academic attention has been given to evangelical youth. In a rare exception, Smith and Lundquist Denton (2005) argue that U.S. teens are more religious than most people think, but that their religiosity tends to be compartmentalized; that is, religion tends to be confined to their church and family lives, and not a significant factor in their friendships or school experiences. In contrast, the young people in these chapters are the kinds of religious youth who Smith and Denton characterize as "devoted." For them, Christianity is not just one of many identity attributes, but their dominant identity, a master frame that they use to make sense of who they are across situations. They are able to do this because Christianity provides them with an alternative system of meaning big enough to saturate all, or most, of the facets of their lives. "I became a very different person right away," Molly explains, attributing her rapid transformation to the power of God's love. In this way, they are like the goths, for whom subcultural affiliation is also a master frame.

Unity Christians formulate Christianity as a "personal relationship" with Jesus, but their identities are much more formally structured than the identities of either the goths or the Puerto Rican wannabes. Unlike goth and wannabehood, Unity Christian identities are embedded in a network of formal, international, hierarchical organizations with thriving cultural and political agendas. These organizations include older adults, whose responsibility it is to mold the identities of younger initiates. Thus, although these young people deploy the resources offered by their Unity identities for a variety of strategic purposes, these negotiations necessarily entail some interplay with the norms and concerns of the larger institution. In other words, while the Unity Christian identities here are still given specific shape by local norms, as the goth and wannabe identities are, they are more significantly shaped by a national movement via the institutional context than are the others. Although this context constrains their negotiations, it also offers (some) older adult validation for their identities that the goths and the wannabes do not have.

The Christians in this study organize their identities around participation in University Unity. Because churches cater to the concerns of families and older adults, church plays a much lesser role in their lives. Indeed, several report that they attend church only sporadically, that "going to church isn't necessary" to be a Christian.[2] The campus organizations structure their weekly schedules and their school breaks, and is the basis for their intra-Christian networks. University Unity claims about forty active members, has a weekly meeting, sponsors six different student-led Bible studies, and coordinates regular trips and events, including fall retreats and evangelizing spring break trips to popular spring break locales.

Race, class, and Christianity

Christianity has a complex relationship to race and class. It is not the case, as with the goths, that conservative Christianity is white and middle class at the national level. Blacks swell the ranks of conservative Protestantism (Wilcox 2004); Latino/as are faithful to Catholicism (Kelly and Morgan Kelly 2005);[3] and Asians convert to evangelicalism in increasing numbers (Alumkal 2004). Black churches, moreover, have historically embraced self restraint and respectability as strategies of upward mobility (Higginbotham 1993, Harvey 1997). And yet the history of conservative Christianity in the U.S. is a history of racial separation. After the Civil War, white and Black churches developed separately. This separation spawned not only religious segregation but also distinct political orientations. Harvey (1997, 13) writes in his history of Southern Baptists:

> Southern religion in the white sense has produced a profoundly conservative stance, while southern religion for blacks, while rarely assuming any revolutionary bent in the postwar south, has supported prophetic voices of change. The religious cultures of blacks and whites in the south provided the moral and spiritual voice both for the Civil Rights movement and for the dogged resistance to it.

In recent years, some white evangelicals have lamented the church's role in unequal race relations, calling for racial reconciliation between Blacks and whites (e.g., Tapia 1997). These projects have forged friendships across

2. Most do attend church, but they don't all attend the same church. Instead, University Unity clearly provides the important structure for their identities.

3. 56 percent of Latino/as are Catholic, while 23 percent are evangelical (Kelly and Morgan Kelly 2005).

racial lines, but their emphasis on personal relationships leaves structural inequalities intact (see Heath 2003). Moreover, Christian cross-racial
friendships depend on common adherence to moral values that are central
to contemporary racial politics.

Nevertheless, evangelicalism remains predominantly white (Alumkal
2004). Emerson and Smith (2000) argue that the organization of religion
in the U.S. unconsciously contributes to the process of racialization. People
look for congregations in which they feel comfortable, gravitating toward
those comprised of people from similar race (and class) backgrounds.
At the same time, they make in-group and out-group comparisons that favor their own groups. They thus see their own race and class homogenous
congregations as more desirable. Moreover, because social organizations
like congregations facilitate access to resources, the homogeneity of congregations perpetuates racial inequalities (and class as well, although that
is not the focus of Emerson and Smith's work).

Like most religious organizations, University Unity is not integrated.
University Unity is white and middle-class—although there are three or
four Asian, Latino/a, or Black participants, including Carolyn, whose story
I discuss later. As in other organizations, the presence of a few, highly visible nonwhite members creates the impression that campus Christianity
isn't segregated, even while separate campus organizations cater specifically to Black Christians and to foreign students. Moreover, all student
leaders and paid staff are white. For Unity participants, race and class are
invisible resources.

University Unity recruits from the general college population, but integration into the organization, I slowly learned, requires a kind of informal sponsorship. Unity members describe the organization as a warm,
inviting, comfortable space in which everyone feels welcome, but I did
not experience it as such. At the first meetings I attended, someone—
always a woman—introduced herself to me, but returned quickly to her
conversation with her friends. Even the people I knew, who I had spoken
with at length, acknowledged me only with a nod or quick smile. At first,
I couldn't tell if this lukewarm reception was personal or if it was typical, although Unity participants I spoke with eventually confirmed that
they felt initially uncomfortable at those meetings as well, sometimes for
as long as an academic year, and only began to feel welcome when they
chose a mentor from the established members or the leadership.

Because people typically make connections with socially similar others,
this sponsorship mechanism reproduces the composition of the community,

foreclosing the full integration of people who cannot achieve this comfort. Sponsorship becomes a mechanism for proving one's University Unity identity. Unity Christians themselves conceptualize it differently, however, portraying themselves as having made a conscious decision to get to know people in the community. Brian describes approaching the leadership of different campus Christian organizations until he finally found leaders he could talk with. Kevin explains that he regrets "last semester not getting involved in groups. I've kinda learned the benefit of being friends with more Christian people."

Unsurprisingly, Unity Christians attribute their successful integration into University Unity to their personal efforts and not to their social commonalities with other members of the group. This way of thinking about community membership masks the ways in which commonalities make University Unity more accessible to some people than to others. For example, Kevin explains, "Sometimes, you know, you'll go into a group of people and they'll judge you on how you look and stuff. The Christians aren't like that." But Kevin doesn't experience them as judgmental because his cultural practices are like theirs; it is probable that if he violated their practices, he would not feel as accepted.

Community membership matters. One's Christian identity is perceived differently if one isn't a member of University Unity. Unity members make in-group and out-group comparisons that favor themselves. Specifically, they differentiate between "Christians who act like Christians should (Unity members) and Christians who act like everyone else (non-Unity members)." Unity participants invoke this boundary to explain their dismay that some Christians conduct themselves in ways that don't meet the expectations of the University Unity community, effectively defining members of their own group as authentically Christian and thus morally distinct.

Although they use their identities to draw moral and cultural distinctions, Unity Christians are not virulent Christians shrieking about moral values, although they may become them.[4] Instead, they are happy, academically committed, rather ordinary young people, struggling to make sense of their lives. Their identity does not intentionally retrench race or class progress; indeed, as with the goths, race and class are invisible to them. And yet, by breathing new life into old values, they unwittingly resuscitate race and class hierarchies.

4. Irvine (2002) describes the ease with which the Christian Right transforms formerly nonactivist Christians into activists.

Race, class, and the performance of goodness

It is a Thursday night near the end of the semester. Students roam the campus center, meeting friends to go out. Most are dressed in "going out" clothes—Thursday is a big party night at the university. University Unity members wander the campus center too. Instead of the glittery, revealing clothes worn by their peers, they are dressed in casual college wear: jeans and university sweatshirts, t-shirts, button-down shirts, small "tasteful" crosses on thin chains around their necks. Clothes aren't too tight, makeup isn't noticeable, hair is neat but not styled. Neither unfashionable nor flashy, these students look "ordinary." Opting out of the drinking and "hooking up" that earned the university its reputation as a "zoo," they get together on Thursday nights in formal meetings organized and run by adults (typically in their late twenties and early thirties) who are trained and paid by an international Christian organization based outside of the northeast.

The evening follows a standard, familiar format: singing, announcements, a few student speakers, a talk by the organization's leader, and finally more singing. The songs are usually accompanied by one or more men strumming acoustic guitars. The lyrics are projected onto a screen, encouraging everyone to sing along. The audience stands for the songs. A few clap their hands, a few others sway to the music. Some people do both. The music seems to focus the participants, creating a break between their lives as college students and the fellowship of their community. The participants describe this time as joyful, but the mild music and swaying is more constrained than the enthusiastic, spontaneous free-for-all associated with charismatic churches. Afterwards, participants go to a local diner to hang out.

At other times, Unity Christians are dispersed across the university campus. They take classes, live in dorms, hang out in the campus center. In the college classroom, they are difficult to pick out. But they think of themselves as distinct, and they maintain these distinctions by avoiding the activities that they perceive as central to many of their peers—partying, goofing off, gossiping, complaining, sex.

Unity Christians embody a social type with which most of us are familiar. They are "goody-goodies," "whitebread," "vanilla." They always do the "right" thing, refraining from engaging in any behavior that even suggests rebellion. In keeping with this image, they dress in conservative attire, play board games and have ice cream socials, and commit themselves to studying, praying, and reading and discussing the Bible. They thus resist contemporary expectations of youthful rebellion and cultural experimentation, and instead embrace conservative adult values.

Goody-goodies are favored by some adults, but not by most other youth; in their seeming failure to challenge any expectations of young adulthood, goody-goodies are boring. Although being a goody-goody seems like an individual characteristic, it is a structural position linked to race, class, and gender. Bettie (2003) argues that the category prep, like the category teacher's pet, is a means of "displacing" race and class (see also Luttrell 1993). Young people understand that these categories are not random, but in fact require conformity to particular sorts of performances; the race, class, and gender dimensions of these performances, however, are often invisible to them. Despite the efforts of Unity Christians, goodness is associated with boringness. Thus, when I speak of Unity Christians as "boring," I am not talking about a personality trait or an interpersonal dynamic (in fact, many are engaging and likable), but about a collective quality attached to a social position. In this sense, boring is the opposite of cool: it is a quality of posing no challenge to the existing structure. There is much to be gained from being good, but there is also much to lose from being boring. Unity Christians, both women and men, attempt to manage this paradox by working hard to show that they are not only good Christians, but are also interesting and authentic people.

The Unity strategy is likely shaped, in part, by the particular class locations of these mostly white youth. The Unity Christians in this book hail, in general, from slightly lower class locations than do the goths. In the broader sense, both goths and Unity Christians are middle-class, but the goths tend to be more upper-middle-class, while the Unity Christians tend to have fewer economic and cultural resources. For example, Unity Christians are more likely to cite economic concerns as a limitation on their education. The Unity strategy makes sense for young people who have something to lose but fewer class resources to fall back on.

Opting out

It is Lucas's week to speak at the Thursday night University Unity meeting. A member of the University Unity leadership team and a competitive ballroom dancer, he is slight and blonde with an eager smile. He seems geeky and awkward. Still, he takes the stage, using the platform to tell his own story of Jesus's work in his life. By design, this story is at once intimate and formulaic. As Lucas outlines the ways in which Christianity changed his life, he weaves biographical details into a familiar storyline. Over coffee, he tells me his tale again, but in more detail. Lucas's story, like the stories told by other Christians, is as much about the negotiation of young adult social worlds as it is about a spiritual awakening.

Lucas was raised in a family in which Christianity was preeminent: his father was a Baptist pastor. Yet, until he was fifteen, Lucas "hated going to church." He credits his parents, whom he speaks of fondly, with giving him a choice about attending church, rather than forcing it on him. Lucas made this choice when he was in high school. He associates becoming a Christian with his "sweet sixteen," though he can't remember exactly which year it was. Lucas explains that his initial interest in church wasn't God so much as girls:

> In high school, I was like not very popular so I was trying to get a girlfriend. I wasn't very popular and they were all very mean to me so I decided to go where there would be nice and good-looking girls...church. So when I saw there was this group of seniors who were different. They just seemed to shine. It got me on this search for God and a few months later, I accepted Christ.

Lucas went to church looking for a practical way to solve his social problems—by getting a good-looking girlfriend. Things didn't work out quite that way, though: "I was always trying to fit in, to find my place, to find intimacy. I found my identity in God. It gave me so much joy. *Things didn't get better for me at school*" (emphasis mine).

Gretchen, a twenty-one-year-old white junior at the university, also fared poorly at high school status competitions. Describing high school benignly as "not too fun," she explains that she spent a lot of time trying to be cool by lying and talking about sex with boys. At first it worked, but by senior year, "all the girls became whores....one up on me," she says. So when she came to college, she was "looking for something different." Her first week at the university, she discovered University Unity through a table in the campus center. She went to the meeting because the "girl [at the table] was so nice." But although Gretchen was introduced to University Unity immediately upon coming to college, substantial life changes occurred more slowly. She was "still getting into bad relationships [and getting] wasted with some people from high school." She "thought that was kind of cool." But the day after, she recalls, "I wanted to kill myself."

The real change came after a Unity spring break trip to Mexico on which she found empathy for her pain and a group of people who wanted to help her change.[5] She says, "I liked my life a lot more. I thank God because God was showing me that my life had meaning. It wasn't just about other people. It was about His love for me." Now fully integrated into University Unity, Gretchen leads a Bible study of her own, did an internship in Washington, D.C., with the Christian Coalition of America, and hopes to do missionary work in Asia in a few years.

Like goths, most Unity Christians were high school geeks. A few tried to be cool, but weren't very successful. Others claim not to have cared about being cool, describing the cool people as immature. Molly, the exception, *was* cool, but she worried about the costs to her reputation. Unity Christianity, like goth, works out these problems, but the solution is different. Goths claim some status and power for themselves by remaking themselves as freaks. But Unity Christians withdraw from peer directed status systems altogether, creating a distinct identity. Instead of being hip, exciting, or notorious, Unity Christians are safe and restrained.

For both Lucas and Gretchen, Unity Christianity resolved their struggles with coolness by providing them with alternative identities and communities. In becoming Christians, each was able to reject the youth status hierarchies at which they had been unsuccessful, developing successful identities as Christians. For Lucas, church was the obvious place to go to opt out of the high school popularity quest. Even though he had found church boring, it was familiar. Because his father was the pastor, he did not even have to sort out churches. Gretchen's discovery of Christianity was less structured, yet it served a similar purpose for her, allowing her to replace unsatisfying behaviors and friends with supportive friends who engaged in behaviors that didn't make her feel bad about herself.

Lucas's and Gretchen's struggles with coolness are shaped by gender. Lucas was humiliated by his failure to demonstrate his heterosexual competence by attracting a girl; Gretchen felt ashamed of her overt expression of heterosexuality. Moreover, Gretchen's stories incorporate a sense of skirting danger. Part of this is rhetorical; the notion that one has abandoned a scandalous or dangerous past in favor of goodness is stock material for Christian conversion stories. But there is also real danger lurking

5. This trip was important. It provided a chance to solidify alliances with other Christians, and to prove one's central interest in evangelizing. Thus, the ability to participate in costly trips is an important means of marking one's commitment to the Christian identity.

in Gretchen's stories, including the physical and psychological consequences of undesired sexual exchanges, as well as costs to her reputation.
Gretchen feels ashamed, in large part, because the behaviors in which she
engages "to be cool" threaten her sense of being a respectable woman (issues
I take up again in the next chapter). For Gretchen, moreover, respectability isn't just threatened by her sexuality, but also by activities like drinking.

The gravity of Gretchen's story reminds us that the expectations of coolness pose different dangers to women than to men. Coolness is a raced,
classed, *and* gendered concept. When young women engage in the practices associated with cool, they jeopardize their claim to (respectable) femininity. For young men, as with Lucas, the problem is often reversed: his
failure to be cool created a crisis of masculinity that he initially sought to
mend through heterosexual success, and eventually circumvented by becoming a Christian.

Not partying and social boundaries

Instead of incorporating shocking accoutrements and practices, as both
the goths and the wannabes do, the Christian identity is conveyed through
its ordinariness. In many ways, Christians look and act mundane. There is
nothing about their style, for example, that makes them stand out on the
streets or in a college classroom. Yet because they do not participate in
many of the key rituals of the university student community, they are not
quite ordinary.

In particular, Unity Christians don't "party," a general term that refers
not only to the act of drinking (and sometimes taking drugs) but also to a
"wild" social scene in which drinking is central. Jillian explains:

> One thing in college I notice is definitely like the party atmosphere and getting
> drunk all the time....A lot of my friends who aren't Christians go out and
> get drunk every weekend, but that's not what Christians think they should be
> doing.

Being a University Unity Christian requires adherence to this norm, although maybe not total abstention—a few participants admit to the occasional beer *outside* of the college atmosphere or tell me they think moderate
drinking is okay for those of legal age. But for Unity evangelicals, *not*
drinking is an important mark of distinction from the general college pop-

ulation. They don't drink in front of their college peers in a purposeful effort to mark their difference.

For some this expectation brings relief because it provides a viable alternative to a party culture at which they were neither successful nor interested. Aaron recalls that in high school, he "made friends just to have them and not because I had anything in common with them. They were immature—got drunk and stuff. I never really saw the point of it. They'd bag on me for not joining in." As a Unity participant, Aaron is able to sidestep the pressure to drink and the harassment he received for choosing not to. Susan also explains that she was socially isolated in high school in part because she didn't party. She says another time, "One thing—like a lot of choices about my personal convictions. I wouldn't have had any reason to make them. Like not drinking at college or waiting to have sex until marriage." Similarly, Kevin explains:

> I think like before I came to school I knew I didn't want to get involved in drinking. I've had a few friends who have said that but as soon as they came here, got involved in it because it's hard not to. I knew I shouldn't do it and was able to be firm in that.

Aaron, Susan, and Kevin all claim that they didn't want to drink even before they became Christians. Unity Christianity, then, doesn't so much motivate them not to drink as provide a rationale and social support for their desire not to. In turn, they are able to use their abstention as a sign of control. In explaining their decisions not to drink, they portray themselves as more mature or more controlled, better able to live up to their "personal convictions" than are non-Christians.

For others, abstaining is more difficult. Molly, who partied her way through high school, had a hard time committing to the Unity expectations. "It's hard to find things that are fun but aren't like drinking," she confides:

> When I first became a Christian, I remember really struggling with it. I would justify it to myself. It's really hard because it's harder to let loose and all my friends from home, all they do is drink, and I love them all so much and they're like, "What are you doing? Just have a beer."

Carolyn describes similar problems, explaining that following the Unity expectations disrupted her friendships with non-Christians.

Because drinking is so pervasive in the undergraduate community, the expectation that Unity Christians will not drink makes it difficult to sustain social relationships with non-Christians. Even when hanging out with people who are drinking is not forbidden, Unity members may have a hard time managing their abstention. Maybe, like Molly, some want to drink, and find it more difficult to abstain when in the company of people who are drinking. But, because drinking is often a social ritual, not drinking also effects the people who *are* drinking. Kevin explains how mutual discomfort can make friendships with non-Christians difficult:

> I like that I can feel comfortable with them [other Christians]. We have the same beliefs. I don't have to worry about being judged for being Christian. Sometimes people don't want to be friends with me because it makes them uncomfortable if they're not really into [the Christian scene].

When the purpose of a get-together is to get drunk, then choosing not to drink pushes you to the sidelines, may make others uncomfortable, and likely makes you look uptight and judgmental. Moreover, as most of us have probably experienced, hanging out with drunk people can be annoying if you're not drunk yourself. Jon explains:

> I don't have a lot of friends out here these days. I kind of started going to parties but I stopped doing that. I don't even want to be at it because I don't want to condone it necessarily. Underage drinking is illegal but I also have a lot of problems with it. I don't like the smell and sometimes the way people acted [*sic*]. The people I hung out with usually kept it under control, but when they didn't ... [trails off].

Not drinking, then, provides an important point of distinction between Unity Christians and non-Christians—one that stands in for a range of assumed differences: maturity, resoluteness, strength of character. Not drinking also creates other kinds of social distance; managing non-drinking raises practical difficulties that pull Unity Christians away from social relationships with non-Christians. To avoid drinking, Unity members spend more and more of their free time with other participants. "On weekends and stuff," Jillian says, "there are socials you can go to. . . . I think a lot of times for people who aren't into the party scene, [they're] an alternative thing to do." Thus, the expectation that Unity Christians won't drink also has the effect of narrowing the participants' social worlds.

This creates tensions. Almost every Unity Christian I spoke with was adamant about her or his friendships with non-Christians, explaining how important it was to have non-Christian friends. Yet these relationships, they all also confessed, were often fragile and tenuous. It seemed important to them to see themselves and to be seen as socially available, rather than as cut off from non-Christians, yet the expectations of their identity, and its disengagement with the young adult rituals so central to the lives of their non-Christian peers, militated against the possibility of meaningful friendships across the Christian boundary. The Unity Christians who reported the most success at maintaining friendships with non-Christians were those who participated in a secular activity, either organized or informal, but even those relationships often suffered.

Becoming disciplined

Turning their backs on the university party scene, Unity Christians instead cultivate self-discipline, hard work, and long-term planning. Christianity is neither a requisite for nor a guarantee of academic discipline, but Unity Christians attribute their academic ethic to their religious identity. For example, Kevin says: "Christianity helped me with my study habits. I've always had a big problem with procrastination." And Lucas: "I wanted to focus on schoolwork and on my relationship with God." Catherine also credits Christianity with her ability to exchange partying for schoolwork. Although she drank when she first came to college, since joining University Unity she:

> realized I could have fun without it.... It makes me feel better to know I can have fun on my own terms, without doing any of that stuff.... I'd say last year I spent more time with college friends and this year a lot more time with my Christian friends. It helps me get down to studying more. With floor mates and all it can get ... [trails off]. I'm more focused when I'm out with them [Christian friends]. I don't get caught up. Last year I'd get bored and go hang out with floor people and do stupid things. Throw things out the window.

The Unity Christian community promotes academic discipline both because of its own internal academic culture and because it teaches techniques of self-discipline that translate well into diligent study habits. Authentic Christians, in their formulation, have personal relationships with

Jesus, relationships which require time and commitment. Jillian explains that, although she was raised in a Christian family, she didn't really grow as a Christian until Caragh, one of the Unity staff people, encouraged her "to set time apart everyday to spend time with God or to study the Bible." Developing an authentic Unity Christian identity requires routines—daily time spent praying, reading the Bible, and reflecting in journals. Hannah identifies the importance of this time for herself:

> God is a daily, constant presence. I try to take an hour each day to read the Bible and pray and write in a journal. If I don't take the time the day would get all frazzled when I interact with people.

In learning to be authentic Unity Christians, young people acquire habits and practices that prepare them not only for the expectations of coursework but also those of middle-class adult life. Importantly, the expectation of routines is daily, not just a Sunday thing, and saturates their lives, accustoming them to repetitive schedules and self-direction. As Hannah's comment suggests, successful self-discipline is central to the understanding of themselves as authentic Christians but also as competent people—without time to herself, Hannah feels too "frazzled" to deal with people. This link between habits and self-concept teaches Unity Christians to monitor themselves, *and* gives them tools with which they can think of themselves as disciplined, controlled people. Susan says:

> [God]'s given me the strength to make decisions that I'll wish I had made. . . . I see things in terms of long-term benefits now, I'm purposeful about when I do things, analyze things as I go.

Like other Unity Christians, Susan portrays her Christian self as wiser than her pre-Christian self. By attributing her changes to God, she is able to claim confidence without seeming self-serving. This is a useful strategy, but one that suggests that authentic self-knowledge is exclusive to Christians.

"Actually, sometimes Christians are boring"

To be "normal," as Kenny (2000) argues, is a critical feature of white middle-class identities. The cultural dominance of the white middle class depends on its being unseen and taken for granted. But Kenny also identifies a condition she describes as "false normal." Girls who fail to take part in any of the rituals of girl culture, the rituals that break up the monotony of their "soooo boring" lives, appear normal on the surface but are unable to integrate themselves socially and are unprepared for any deviation from their narrow social worlds. In some ways, Unity Christianity ameliorates some of the problems with false normality; it provides a social network and subcultural symbols that add social and cultural depth to daily lives. But because they withdraw from the status hierarchies and symbolic exchanges of their peers, Unity Christians also run the risk of teetering into abnormality. Indeed, outsiders often perceive Christians to be abnormal.

To varying degrees, each person I spoke with worked to convince me that she or he was a "normal" person—that is, that she or he had interests beyond Christianity. Jillian confessed that she watches movies like *Austin Powers;* others told me that they listen to popular music and attend concerts. They snowboard. Some go out dancing with their friends, albeit dressed more conservatively (they add). Some participate in secular, though not necessarily "cool," activities: Lucas is on the ballroom dancing team; Susan is a member of an a capella group. In these ways, Unity Christians present themselves as engaged in or knowledgeable about youth cultural practices as well as Christianity.

This is rocky terrain. The authentic Unity Christian identity depends on separating themselves from the attributes of coolness, but they don't want to be boring either. Jon explains the dilemma:

> I suppose sometimes I try to be a little more outgoing because I think sometimes people have the impression that Christians are boring and not interesting as people.... Actually sometimes Christians *are* boring.

The idea that Christianity is boring is a problem that has been taken up by evangelicalism at the national level as well, resulting in "contemporary" church services and youth events that integrate elements of popular culture into the Christian format. With some disdain, Hannah describes this phenomenon: "I went to this thing where the church is trying to be cool with pyrotechnics. I was fully aware that the church was trying to imitate the secular world." Hannah's disdain suggests her difficulty reconciling Christian attempts to "be cool" with an authentic Christian identity, yet less spectacular examples of this tension filtered into many of the Unity events I attended. Chuck, the Unity leader, for example, peppered his talks with boisterous sports metaphors and with references to Red Bull, an "energy drink" also popular among the goths. His talking style came across as a Christian version of masculine braggadocio. Chuck suggests that he is a "real" man who knows what's "going on," while only engaging with symbols of popular culture that don't jeopardize his central identity as "good." Pictures on the organization's Web site do similar identity work for the group. While women often have their arms around each other, men stand with their arms crossed in front of themselves, in postures that evoke a moderated kind of "cool pose" (Majors and Billson 1992).

Aaron is especially proud of his interest in secular pursuits. He explains that he is "not a cultural Christian," proving his point by referencing the band he's in with a good friend who is pagan. Aaron uses Lucas as a foil. Lucas, who only listens to Christian and ballroom music, is Aaron's example of a boring, culturally monochromatic Christian (Lucas, of course, sees himself as more complex). In becoming a Christian, Aaron (and others) suggest, he does not have to completely foreclose his participation in exciting and status-producing secular activities as long as they do not violate his Christian moral code.

In describing his musical interests and distancing himself from Lucas's "geeky" pursuits, Aaron refutes the "boring" stigma accompanying his Christian identity. Holding onto these interests also likely aids him in maintaining his Unity Christian identity by ameliorating its potential to become too restrictive. Moreover, it's easier to perceive yourself or be perceived as cool if your comparison group is particularly uncool. In becoming Christian, Aaron relinquishes his claim to externally defined coolness but sets himself up to be among the coolest of the Christians. Thus, by shifting his comparison group, Aaron can be more socially successful.

Aaron's strategy also has long-term benefits. In particular, it allows him to continue to develop and claim an eclectic array of interests, rather than a one-dimensional Christian persona. Omnivorous eclecticism, as Peterson and Kern (1996) argue, has replaced consumption of traditional highbrow tastes (like classical music) as a marker of class status. Aaron's integration of the secular and the sacred not only accomplishes similar ends, but also draws on similar assumptions about what makes a person cultured and interesting.

Carolyn: Asianness, class, and Christianity

Of the Christians I spoke with, Carolyn is the least successful at integrating all of the demands of the Unity Christian identity. Although she describes herself as a Christian, Carolyn explains that she isn't yet fully "good" like her friends Molly, Susan, and Jillian. She describes them as "level one" Christians, explaining that she's not there yet. For Carolyn, the balancing act between the expectations of University Unity and the expectations of her other college friends pose ongoing difficulties. A nineteen-year-old Korean woman adopted into a white, Irish Catholic family, she is the most loosely connected participant in my study, attending University Unity irregularly. While her loose integration likely prevents her from developing the "level one" Christian identity that would more resolutely foreclose the temptations of college, her ongoing interest in those temptations is probably also the reason she remains only loosely integrated. Carolyn's story is revealing, though, because in her partially developed Christian identity, Carolyn lays bare the ways in which the Christian identity negotiates the poles of coolness and (boring) industriousness, and the ways in which those negotiations are bound up in submerged race and class concerns.

Dressed in jeans, a sweatshirt, and Birkenstock-style sandals, Carolyn looks the part of a northeastern college student. Like the other Unity Christians I spoke with, she holds up finding evangelical Christianity through University Unity as a defining, saving moment in her life. University Unity, she explains, helped her focus and find herself. "It sounds so cliché when I say that," she laughs. "Last year," she tells me, again earnest, "I was dependent on them. I needed them every week. I used to be a pathological liar. I felt this need to make myself seem cooler."

Uncomfortable with her family's Catholicism, she came to the university with the intention of figuring out who she was. She recalls:

> Freshman year, I accepted Christ as my savior. I'm a sinner. I'm always going to sin. I spent the whole second semester trying to fit into the image in my head. It wasn't till the end that I came to realize I couldn't live up to it. I didn't drink, [went] to bed early, read the Bible and prayed every night, shunning my friends because lots of them were big partiers. It was exhausting.

As she talks, Carolyn formulates two competing selves. The self who was a "pathological liar [and] want[s] to be the popular, pretty girl" and the self who "aspires to be more like . . . the people [she] sees as really good Christians." In Carolyn's stories, she isn't successful at either, but this portrayal is misleading. By positioning herself as a "level two" Christian (by her assessment, she knows she needs Christ but doesn't always listen), Carolyn avoids the exhausting Unity Christian identity she attempted to achieve her first year, even while the promises of Christianity continue to redeem her when she strays. She explains: "There are days when I just shut the door on Christ. I live the ways other teenagers do.... I do things to make people like me better. But yeah, when I do things I don't like, I can repent. I can change and I can try to learn from my mistakes."

Carolyn is able to use the components of a known, collective identity to manage the competing pressures of coolness and long-term middle-class expectations. For Carolyn, Christianity softens her difficulties with popularity competitions (including, as I'll show in the next chapter, heterosexuality) not just by providing an alternative model of desirable behavior but, even more, by providing an explanation for her lack of success. At the same time, it limits the potential costs of coolness by providing a cloak of respectability. As Carolyn explains, although her parents think University Unity is like a cult, "My mom has seen that it's focused me. It's not like I really had a troubled teen but there were moments when she thought I was going to be the 'bad seed.'"

Carolyn's story is also about race. A number of scholars have tried to make sense of the explosion of evangelicalism among Asian American college students. These scholars have noted that the conventional interpretation of evangelicalism as an assimilation strategy for Asian immigrants is inadequate for explaining evangelicalism among a new, postimmigration generation of Asian Americans. For these young people, Alumkal (2004) argues, evangelicalism does not represent assimilation into the mainstream because, like other evangelicals, Asian Americans perceive evangelical Christianity to be outside the norm. Instead, evangelicalism provides "an alternative—and preferable—way of understanding their marginality" (208). Yet Asian Americans are more likely to join Asian evangelical organizations than white ones. This pattern reflects the contradictory needs of second generation Asian Americans. Unlike their parents, college-age Asian Americans are more likely to have grown up outside of ethnic enclaves; their experiences are thus distinct from both those of their parents and those of their white peers. Joining Asian American evangelical organizations allows them to find an ethnic community (Hall 2006). Moreover, although Asian Americans are typically welcome in predominantly white evangelical organizations, Kim (2004) finds they are excluded from leadership positions in them. In Asian American organizations, race is not a barrier to leadership.

In contrast to the overall pattern, Carolyn joined a white-dominated organization rather than an Asian American one. Carolyn, however, is not the child of immigrants, but instead is the adopted child of white parents. The only thing about Carolyn that is Korean is her phenotype, yet this phenotype elicits reminders that she isn't quite the same as her white peers. She never really thought about race, she explains, "until some kid called [her] a 'chubby chink.'" At the university, Carolyn is more relentlessly reminded of her ethnic ascription:

> Especially at [the university], there's so many Asian groups. They sit together in their classes. I feel like I'm a traitor to their cause because I say 'wicked.' In my mental picture—I'm not Asian. I don't know if that's healthy or not. I'm Daddy's girl—I feel Irish. Other Asians shun me. I checked out the Asian groups, thought I should know my background. I do. I'm American.

For Carolyn, Christianity shores up an unmarked racial identity at a moment when her racial identity had become uncomfortably marked as Asian. In her study of African-descent girls raised in white homes, France Winddance Twine (1997) similarly found that identity politics in the university challenged the race neutrality of the young women in her study, encouraging them to claim new identities as Black. These identities had costs, including more difficult relationships with their white mothers. Carolyn faces the same pressures as the young women in Winddance Twine's study, but chooses to maintain her racially neutral identity. Becoming a Unity Christian helps her do this.

Christianity provides Carolyn with authentic membership in a predominantly white group. It thus, as Alumkal (2004) suggests, replaces the marginality of Asianness with an alternative, ostensibly race-neutral identity. Hall (2006) contends that one of the reasons Asian immigrants don't object to their children's participation in evangelical organizations is because evangelicalism is consonant with their conservative values. Stereotyped as the "model minority," Asian Americans are expected to be diligent, above-average students. For many Asian Americans, these expectations are narrow and burdensome (Lee 1994). But for Carolyn, one can imagine, University Unity's emphasis on hard work and discipline provides a way to commit herself to school without it being attributed to ethnicity. Evangelical Christianity, then, provides a way of being "good" that isn't Asian.

Just good people: emotions and the authentic Christian self

"A lot of the Christians I know seem happier than a lot of the non-Christians I know," Kevin says. As Unity Christians tell it, Christianity brings relief, happiness, even joy—the good feelings that come with know-ing that "you are truly loved" and that your "burden has been lifted." Sim-ilarly, they draw clear lines between their non-Christian pasts and their cur-rent Christian selves. Before they were Christians, they tell me, they were bored, depressed, angry, or cold, but they are now happy, joyful, and at peace.

Unity Christians explain that they feel good because Jesus works in their hearts. This logic means that one is not *really* a Christian unless one has good feelings. Accordingly, Unity Christians use emotions to gauge their progress as Christians and, thus, to determine authenticity. Gretchen explains that when she first began to explore Christianity, she was still having a "lousy time. . . . I had a hard time staying in the Scripture. I hadn't made God a priority. I read the Scripture about once a week, if things were going wrong." After she made a more serious commitment to God (and thus to her Christian identity), she says, "I liked my life a lot more. I thank God because God was showing me that my life had meaning." Jon tells a similar story, recalling that before he became a "real" Christian, he hated reading the Bible. "I was a fidgety person," he says, "Then I found that I enjoyed the intimacy and fellowship that I found with God. When you're in the presence of God, it *feels* so good" (emphasis mine).

Although Unity Christians attribute their feelings to Jesus, they are learned. The University Unity community initiates new members into its feeling rules, teaching them not only how they should feel but also pro-viding them with methods for banishing the wrong feelings and sustaining the right ones. When Tom feels like he's "going to explode," he refocuses his energy on God through reading and prayer. This technique allow him "to come back and think, why am I here, why am I with God." Now, he sleeps with worship music on so that he can "wake up praising Him." Tom deliberately contains the emotions that might otherwise explode as a first step in his effort to create the joy he considers appropriate to his Christian identity. Hannah also describes how she works to change her emotional responses:

> Sometimes I get annoyed like everyone else in the world. And I'll start dissing people and He'll stop me in the middle of it and I'll be in the middle of a dia-tribe and I'll have to stop and apologize. It's hard because I'm steamed but I feel better because I didn't just spew poison. I don't want to dishonor people.

Hannah's comment at first seems to be describing a behavioral adjust-ment. She starts "dissing people," but then catches herself and apologizes to the recipient of her "diatribe." But Hannah's story is really about emotional readjustment. In "dissing people," she is "spew[ing] poison." Thus, her inner feelings, which she describes as toxic, are spilling out. To stop this spillover, she needs to transform her coldness into "love." Hannah's story, like those told by her peers, reveals the intensity of Unity Christian emotional self-discipline.

I cannot overstate the centrality of emotions to Unity Christians. For them, emotions are the most important boundary between themselves and non-Christians (and inauthentic Christians), perhaps because they are an almost irrefutable "proof" of the desirability of Christianity. But for Unity Christians, feelings also matter because, in their formulation, they are the key to being really, truly *good*. The right emotions prove not only the authenticity of one's Christianity but also the moral worth of one's self. Carolyn describes the Unity essence:

> [Unity Christians have a] warm aura. My friend [Molly] has such a respect for the world. The way I see them they have a lot of things going for them and they're not cocky about it. They're just good people. . . . They're not spiteful.

In Carolyn's description, Molly's moral self is defined by her emotions: her warmth and the absence of spite. Katz (1975, 1370) argues that "persons conceive of essences as personal qualities which exist independently of, and cannot be verified in, observed conduct. . . . [P]ersons give moral significance to the essences they impute." For Unity Christians, one's emotions communicate one's essential goodness in a way that behavior cannot.

It is not enough, then, to be nice to other people; one's conduct must be motivated by authentic emotions. Hochschild (1983) describes the process by which people align their inner emotional states with their outer emotional comportment as "deep acting." Mimi describes the importance of deep acting to her sense of herself as a good Christian:

> I feel like there are times when I've just known how to do things well. I know how to help but I don't know how to have the love. When I help sometimes it's like a task but I don't have the *feeling*.

Unity Christians use emotions to draw lines between good and not-good people. They use the same sets of emotions to draw lines between authentic Christians and both non-Christians and inauthentic Christians. Thus, to be an authentic Christian is to be *good,* and to be good is to be an authentic Christian.

Contemporary U.S. emotional norms favor "good cheer" (Kotchemidova 2005), or what the goths described as compulsory happiness. Twentieth-century American emotional culture is characterized by a "cooling" of emotions that discourages any emotional intensity and expects pleasantness as an everyday standard in social interactions (Stearns 1994). These contemporary emotional norms contribute to the creation of the smooth, tension-free social relations necessitated by the organization of late capitalism (ibid.; Kotchemidova 2005). Kotchemidova (2005) argues that expectations of cheerfulness have spread and intensified over the twentieth century, but historically cheerfulness has been a symbol of middle-class virtue. Today, both good cheer and emotional control contrast with stereotypes of Blacks and Latino/as as fiery, volatile, or "in your face" (see Wilkins 2004a). Unity Christians internalize dominant emotional expectations and learn to feel them more than anyone else.

Unity Christian emotions, however, run into the same problem as other University Unity strategies. There is something not quite *normal* about being happy all the time. We expect people to experience a broader range of emotional ups and downs. Unity happiness is a bit *too* controlled. Because of this, Unity Christians run the risk of seeming fake. Turner (1976) argues that we increasingly identify our "authentic" selves by the impulses that break out of institutional constraints. Authenticity is imagined as raw and rebellious, as throwing off the shackles of emotional control. This celebration of the "wild" self makes sense in a context in which middle-class jobs increasingly demand intense emotion management (Hochschild 1983). "Real" people, then, are not always emotionally controlled. Recall, as well, the goth's derision of too much happiness as emotionally inauthentic. In contrast, goths interpreted their own interest in darkness as a sign of their emotional authenticity.

Unlike goths, Unity Christians vanquish darkness, pursuing instead relentless happiness, love, and joy. But like the goths, they portray their emotions as authentic. Being a Christian, Aaron explains, is about "getting to know who I am, who I was, and about who God wants me to be." Mimi says "the biggest change [in becoming a Christian] is knowing who I truly am." For both the goths and the Unity Christians, the right emotions prove their authenticity; but for Unity Christians, authenticity is also an antidote to the perception of their relentless happiness as fake. To be seen as fake is a cultural problem (e.g., Goffman 1959, Lamont 1992), and

Christians are not unaware that their happiness might be interpreted that way. For Mimi, the perception of emotional authenticity was critical to her ability to take seriously the first Christians she met. She recalls her reaction: "There's so much love there, [and] they're not even faking it!"

Emotions were an important boundary to everyone I spoke with, as well as being a central feature of the organizational material. But it was women, more than men, who connected their emotions to caring for others. Niceness is a much more thorough expectation for women. In her study of flight attendants, Hochschild (1983) finds that more general emotional expectations of women spill over into the workplace. Expected to not only provide services but to also make people feel good, flight attendants "manage" their emotions by finding ways to suppress or eliminate feelings of anger or irritation.[6] Niceness is not just a gendered expectation, but also a raced and classed one. Loudness and combative emotional expression—"attitude"—are associated with lower status women (e.g., Wilkins 2004a). Niceness makes Unity Christian women good, but in particular raced and classed ways.

For some University Unity women, the emotional expectations of Unity Christianity serve as a means of tempering unfeminine emotional impulses and thus pull them back into line with the emotional expectations of white, middle-class womanhood. Hannah says:

> Before I was a Christian, I used to look at people how I could use them, a really cold way to be. I really didn't want to be that kind of person. I wanted to love them the way [Jesus] did. I've always related to guys more than girls. I was in a sorority house for two and a half years. A guy would break up with a girl and she'd be crying and friends would be hugging her and I would be cold on the inside. I didn't want to be like that.

In Hannah's story, becoming a Christian not only made her a better person but also transformed her undesirable (masculine) inner coldness into an emotional response appropriate to femininity.

Unlike the flight attendants in Hochschild's study, however, Unity women do not have "off" time. Instead, their Unity Christian identities require constant vigilance over their feelings, both in social relations and in solitary contemplation. The emotional requirements of Unity Christianity

---

6. Skeggs (1997) also describes the centrality of "developing and monitoring a caring self" to British white working-class women's respectability.

thus reinforce and make more explicit the emotional rules at play more generally for middle-class women. Moreover, they shut off emotional outlets that exist for other middle-class women, including and perhaps most importantly, the possibility of a separate interior life in which negative emotions can be entertained. As we will see in the next chapter, they also shut off other socially acceptable outlets for negative emotions, such as the break up sadness and self-absorption associated with the rhythms of the dating ritual. Finally, they ratchet up the penalties for violating the rules: noncompliance threatens not only the middle-class femininity of the Unity woman but also her claim to a Christian identity.

Conclusion

The Unity Christian community structures its participants' daily lives in such a way as to leave little time to be either lonely or idle. As Molly points out, the full slate of Unity activities means that there is seldom any time left for anything else. In addition to their commitment to their studies, Unity participants run a constant circuit of meetings and Bible studies and social events that diminish their opportunities to hang out with non-Christian students. Through these daily rhythms, they learn the community's behavioral expectations: they don't party, they commit themselves to their studies, and they develop personal habits of self-discipline and introspection. They use these practices to think of themselves as different kinds of people—more disciplined and focused, more mature, more confident. Together, these perceived differences allow them to see themselves as good and worthy people; "I've become a better person," was the common refrain.

Unity Christians learn to see themselves as "good people" through specific practices (not drinking, academic discipline, not having sex, and so forth) and through specific emotions (happiness, joy). Although they describe these qualities as coming from God, they pour their energies into learning how to behave and feel like "real" Christians. For some, the requirements of the Unity Christian identity are easier than for others, but they all describe relentless self-monitoring. In the case of emotions, this monitoring is more intense for women than it is for men.

The claim to "good" personhood is complex. Although references to "good people" are frequently used in a way that implies conceptual universality, the specific content is much harder to pin down: the banality of the concept masks its complexity. Claims to goodness rely on contestable cultural assumptions about what constitutes good behavior. Why, for example, is it "good" to spend time studying and not to spend time hanging out with friends? The particular behaviors defined as "good" align in important ways with the values that are assumed to propel upward mobility or defend against downward mobility, but the invocation of Christ as the author of goodness clouds the normative assumptions embedded in the definition of goodness, reinforcing the notion that "good people" are necessarily *good,* i.e., morally superior, and that the specific contours of goodness are more socially and morally desirable. Furthermore, goodness is more than just behavioral. The notion that someone is a "good person," rather than an ordinary person who does good things, implies an essential moral self that shapes outward behavior. For University Unity Christians, this moral self is conveyed through one's disposition—being happy and loving.

Being a "good person" has long-term pay offs, but it can be a drag, as Carolyn's story reminds us. Unity Christianity is a demanding identity to fulfill: its behavioral expectations are stringent and tedious. In a world of dizzying MTV-style images, instant gratification, and commodity fetishism, Unity Christianity can seem dull. In the more immediate context of college, when young adults are living away from their parents for the first time, and when partying and sexual exploration are expected, Unity Christianity may be especially dull.

Unsuccessful at coolness, Unity participants opt out. Instead, they invest in the "geeky," "boring" characteristics associated with goody-goodies, transforming them into sources of validation and distinction. This process is not a new one. Marginalized groups create "badges of distinction"— alternative criteria for worthiness at which they can be successful—as a means of feeling good about themselves in social spaces that don't value their cultural traits (Sennett and Cobb 1972, Fordham 1996, Schwalbe and Mason-Schrock 1996). But Unity Christians are located a bit differently from many of the groups in other works. Although they are marginalized in young adult hierarchies, the characteristics they bolster are associated in the dominant culture with long-term success and moral virtue. In solving their own problems, then, they unwittingly remake the cultural oppositions between "good" and "cool" that shaped their dilemmas in the first place. In turn, their strategies legitimate moral and cultural hierarchies used to justify the exclusion of people of color and the working class/poor.

Nonetheless, these Christians are marginal in their university community, in which "devoted" Christian identities and their attendant practices are uncommon. Their withdrawal from normative youth rituals like partying and gossip contributes to their marginalization, making them seem not only boring but also, sometimes, not quite normal. This marginality, however, means a different sort of thing than it does for youth of color or even for the goths. Their marginality is not only chosen, but also temporal and spatial. There are many communities in which evangelicalism is, if not normative, then at least common enough. As Unity Christians embark on their postcollege lives, they are able to choose to be embedded in strongly evangelical communities. Indeed, this is clearly the goal of many of them, who propose religion-based careers (missionary work, ministry, Christian political organizing, etc.). Thus, while they may be embattled in the short run, their identity opens up not only specified, reserved career paths, but also provides them with access to an established, supportive adult community. This identity path is safe, ameliorating many of the anxieties that accompany contemporary transitions into adulthood (e.g., finding a job and finding a meaningful community). Unity Christians shut out outside influences that could derail them and develop practices that will pave their transition into white (or race-neutral) middle-class adulthood. The University Unity project, however, is not a path to affluence; the careers at which participants are aimed are low-earning but stable. The University Unity strategy trades middle-class consumption for middle-class respectability.

The similarities between Unity Christianity and goth—seemingly antithetical subcultural projects—reveals the ways in which cultural practices that seem to be starkly different can be used to similar effect. Goths and Unity Christians both use their particular subcultural practices to formulate themselves as self-disciplined, emotionally controlled and authentic, and (as I will show in the next chapter) sexually respectable. Like goths, Unity Christians use their subcultural practices to understand themselves as distinct, worthy people, and attribute their distinctiveness to the particular characteristics of their subcultural identity. In other words, goths see themselves as distinct because they are *goths,* and Unity Christians see themselves as distinct because they are *Christians.* In both cases, they use similar rhetoric to validate their subcultural practices.

But Christians are also different from goths in important ways. Goths push against the behavioral boundaries of the white middle class, while Unity Christians narrow them. These differences become most clear when we turn the lens to Unity sexuality.

CHAPTER FIVE

Abstinence

"Not having sex before marriage is a big thing for Christians," Jillian tells me. I am not surprised, nor does she expect me to be. Unlike the sexual strategies of goths or even wannabes, the sexual politics of the Christian Right, whose reactionary platform has infiltrated federal policies, are hard to avoid. It is thus hardly astounding that sexual abstinence would be a "big thing" for Unity Christians. Because of this hypervisible association with the Right and because abstinence stakes a seemingly absolute behavioral boundary, abstinence appears to make clear identity claims. Abstinence sides young people with conservative (and many mainstream) adults, as well as with a well-oiled political machine. To others, however, abstinent Christians are prudes.

At the university Unity Christians attend, sexual exploration is an expected part of the rhythm and ritual of daily life. Like other components of the University Unity identity, abstinence distinguishes Unity Christians from their classmates. Nonabstinent students often scoff at abstinence, describing abstinent peers as repressed, oppressed, deluded, or disingenuous. They are eager to find contradictions in the claims of abstinent students; for example, someone once sent me an Internet link to pictures of an "abstinent" (but not Unity Christian) student in less-than-virtuous poses. I, too, began this project with preconceived notions about abstinence, primarily because of my feminist concerns that abstinence restricts women's sexual agency.

In turn, non-Unity Christians have not been shy about telling me what they think of my own sexual decisions, and one abstinent student (also not a Unity member) told me, with some embarrassment, that I was "living in sin." Unity Christians treated me with more respect; perhaps because, as a struggling single mother, they saw me as a victim, perhaps because of the age difference, perhaps because I represented institutional authority, or perhaps because they really are tolerant, as they claim.

These distinct stances reveal the starkness of the moral and cultural boundaries between abstinence and nonabstinence, but they also point to inconsistencies in contemporary young adult sexual culture. Today's young adults are pulled by competing currents. On one hand, the sexual revolution opened up sexual options. Although the sexual double standard persists, young women have been especially impacted by the sexual revolution; increasingly, they are able to exercise the kinds of sexual choices made by the goth women. Pro-sex feminists laud sexual independence as central to women's well-being, but even what Carpenter (2005) calls the "moderate majority" do not expect that young people—men or women—will wait until marriage to initiate their sexual lives (see also Montemurro 2006).

On the other hand, beginning in the 1980s, HIV/AIDS and the resurgence of conservative Christianity brought back sexual fear. As the country grows increasingly secular, the sexual platform of the Christian Right shapes sex education curricula in an ever expanding number of public schools (Carpenter 2005). And abstinence, it seems, is everywhere. In gossip magazines. On President Bush's tongue. On interstate billboards. On PBS. And, of course, in University Unity materials. High school youth take virginity pledges, making public promises to remain virgins until they get married. Ones who have already had sex proclaim themselves "born-again virgins," expressing regret for their shameful pasts and committing to a new life of sexual virtue. Although teens do seem to have retreated from sexual intercourse in the '90s (e.g., Risman and Schwartz 2007), among young adults mixed cultural messages about sex are more likely to result in sexual contradictions than in abstinence.[1] As Risman and Schwartz (2007, 316) report, "Nine out of ten Americans are sexually active by the time they are twenty." For young people seeking to negotiate the treacherous terrain of nonmarital hetero-relations, however, University Unity's broad injunctions against sexuality provides clear rules, pointing a bright light through the fogginess of contemporary heterosexual negotiations.

University Unity not only proscribes sexual intercourse but also prohibits homosexuality, discourages casual hetero-relationships, and encour-

---

1. Montemurro (2006) argues that the new phenomenon of bachelorette parties symbolizes women's ambivalence about their new sexual roles.

ages participants to choose Christian partners. The wide net of Unity Christian sexual culture forecloses almost all young adult dating and sexual rituals and experiments. Indeed, most Unity participants have sworn off not only physical intimacy, but also dating, engaging in a practice I call "romantic abstinence."

Unity Christians understand sexual maturation as a transition, appropriate only in marriage, rather than a process. In this model, marriage signals social adulthood, as it did for previous generations. The timing of marriage, however, has changed for many young people; increasingly, college-educated young people postpone marriage until they have established careers (or later). These changes mean that abstinent people could have many adult years in which sexuality continues to be off limits to them. Thus, the imperative to "wait until marriage" requires longer durations of sexual control for many youth than it did in previous generations.

Flouting these expectations means sacrificing one's Unity Christian identity. Consequently, participants like Lucas acknowledge that "it's not something people would talk about." This paradox suggests that perhaps there is more to Unity sexual practices than Christians are willing to admit—an idea endorsed by some of my nonabstinent students and further animated by recent films. The movie *Saved!* (2004), which depicts a Christian high school in which students, faculty, and parents say one thing about sex and do another, suggest that Christian sexual rules are hypocritical. Similarly, the documentary "The Education of Shelby Knox," which aired on PBS in 2005, contends that Christian youth are not as abstinent as they might seem. "Shelby Knox" follows the political transformation of an evangelical high school girl from Lubbock, Texas. The movie opens with Shelby's own virginity pledge ceremony. But, after learning that Lubbock teens have among the highest rates of STIs and pregnancies in the nation, Shelby takes on the school board's abstinence-only policy. Shelby Knox is not alone in her conclusion that abstinence-only education and virginity pledges increase STI transmission and unintended pregnancies. Abstinence-only policies, decriers argue, deny young people accurate information on STI and pregnancy prevention, and encourage them to misrepresent their sexual behavior in the name of maintaining their abstinent, Christian identities. Central to these representations is the idea that, for many Christians, abstinence is a sham.

Some academic work backs this up. Bearman and Bruckner (2001) found that "abstinence pledges" do not reduce STI rates, because pledgers are less likely to use condoms or to be tested for STIs. In this way, then, the

goth community norms about safe sex are possibly more helpful in reducing STIs and pregnancies that is abstinence. Pledging works best, the
authors find, when there are neither too few nor too many fellow pledgers. When there are too few, social control and/or support is inadequate.
When there are too many, the pledge becomes *expected* and thus loses the
distinctiveness that gives it personal meaning. I have no way of ascertaining whether or not Unity Christians are abstinent in practice. However,
they are most similar to the middle group in the Bearman and Bruckner
study: they have adequate social support for their commitment, but they
are unusual enough that their commitment makes them distinct. Because
Unity participants acquire their identities in a context where evangelicalism is not normative, it is likely that sexual abstinence is important or desirable to them for multiple reasons, as I will argue, not just because it
makes them good Christians.

For my purposes, though, sexual abstinence is a rhetorical strategy, used
by Unity Christians to make claims about who they are and who they are
not. Abstinence, in this sense, is not so much a behavior as a style. Abstinence is useful as a symbolic boundary in so much as it is internalized as an
aspect of self and proclaimed as an identity marker. Thus, it is the rhetoric
of abstinence (its explanation and rationale, the difficulties it poses—or
not—in daily life, its connection to emotional well-being, etc.) as much
as the "not doing" itself, that communicates who Unity Christians are.
Like other aspects of Unity Christianity, abstinence is uncool, as it shuts
out the status-producing possibilities of sexual competence and adventure. At the same time, it enhances claims to innocence, moral worth, and
self-discipline.

The meanings of Unity abstinence cannot be extricated from the Right's
national agenda, which imbues abstinence with much of its meaning, provides Unity Christians with the language they use to make sense of their
strategies, and, in many ways, sets the terms of Unity sexual culture. Yet
in the hands of these college-age Christians, sexual abstinence is a more
intricate personal strategy than it initially seems. For many Unity Christians,
abstinence is as much an opportunity as it is an imposition. Like the goths
and wannabes, Unity Christians use sexuality to solve a range of problems,
many of which are bound up in gender expectations. Like goth freakiness, abstinence has both surprising and contradictory effects. In particular, abstinence has a more complex relationship to feminist goals than
my presuppositions had led me to believe. In the end, however, the Unity
strategy of abstinence binds them to conservative gender relationships.

Abstinence in national politics

The Right's abstinence-only campaign is effective because it mobilizes a cultural model of childhood innocence. By framing its agenda as an effort to protect children from sexual knowledge, the Right limits the terms of the debate. In this rhetorical context, proponents of more expansive curricula risk being seen as tarnishing children's "natural" innocence (Irvine 2002). As a consequence, discourse about youth sexuality is limited: even voices that seem discordant share the assumption that young people, especially girls, are having too much sex, too early, with too many people. We (adults), the discourse continues, have a responsibility to persuade them to stop having sex by teaching them the paramount importance of premarital abstinence. The disagreement is over whether we should also offer young people the tools to prevent STIs and pregnancies should they "fail" to live up to the expectation of abstinence. Those who object to the abstinence-only agenda argue that failing to provide adequate information about sexual health endangers young people, but, with few exceptions, do not argue that young people have the *right* to have sex.[2] Even moderates such as Hillary Rodham Clinton and Donna Shalala have jumped on the abstinence bandwagon. In the words of *Salon*, "Lunacy about teen sexuality is not the exclusive property of the lunatic fringe."[3] The contours of these debates rely on what Fields (2004, 12) calls the "adultist" assumption that "young people have little legitimate claim to pleasurable, agentic sexuality."

The rhetoric of youthful sexual innocence is powerful, in part, because it seems universal. After all, everyone begins life as a child. But assumptions of childhood innocence are not universally applied. Instead, innocence is apportioned along racial lines. While institutional authorities read white children's mistakes as outcomes of youthful innocence, they read Black children's mistakes as signs of inherent deviance: they are "adultified" (Ferguson 2000), or, in Roberts's (1997) words, "born guilty." Gender matters. While Black boys are often treated as criminals in the making, Black girls are seen as "always and already sexually opportunistic, excessive, and a drain on public resources" (Fields 2005, 560).

The abstinence-only agenda assumes that white youth are different from youth of color, and reinscribes these differences in its curricula.

2. See Fields 2005 and Irvine 2002 for excellent discussions of these debates.

3. See http.//dir.salon.com/story/sex/feature/2002/02/20/powell/index.html. (Accessed on January 8, 2007.)

Abstinence-only programs are aimed especially at protecting the innocence of white youth, particularly girls, while programs for inner-city youth (presumed to be of color and poor) assume not sexual innocence but sexual risk (Patton 1996).[4] Again, gender is central to these definitions, as girls and women are responsible for upholding the purity of racial and ethnic groups (Das Gupta 1997, Espiritu 2001, Nagel 2000, Wilkins 2004a). Historically, white women have claimed purity in juxtaposition to the presumed hypersexuality of women of color (Hill Collins 1991, 2004, Ferber 1998, Jewell 1998, Wilkins 2004a). Since the sexual revolution, however, the sexual behavior of unmarried white middle-class girls and women has grown more liberal, sullying white claims to sexual purity.[5] In this context, abstinence-only education is consistent with historical efforts to maintain racial purity by "protecting" the bodies of white girls and women (Hill Collins 1991, Solinger 1992, Odem 1995, Ferber 1998). In debates about sexual innocence, however, racial assumptions are typically submerged (Fields 2005). Irvine (2002, 77) argues: "the Right found that public arguments about sexuality could perform significant rhetorical work. For one, they could serve as a code for race; a way to implicitly tap racial fears." Thus, sexuality both marks gendered racial differences *and* mobilizes racial fears.

A 2006 push to target unmarried adults for abstinence-only programming (Jayson 2006) makes clear that the Right's agenda is not just about childhood innocence. Abstinence is also about families. The Heritage Foundation's Robert Rector makes this connection explicit. He writes on his blog: "Abstinence programs can provide the foundation for personal responsibility and enduring marital commitment. Therefore, they are vitally important to efforts aimed at reducing out-of-wedlock childbearing among young women."[6] These aims of abstinence education are paired with small, often unnoticed assaults on girls' and women's reproductive freedom. Together, these agendas retie "proper" sexuality to morally conservative definitions of family (see also D'Emilio and Freedman 1988, Coontz 1992).

As Rector's blog suggests, Christian Right attacks on sexual freedom coincide with moral panics about nonmarital childbearing. Luker (1996)

4. But see Fields 2005.

5. Risman and Schwartz (2007, 315) note that it is "boys' sexual behavior [that is] becoming more like girls' behavior," not the other way around.

6. Entry dated April 8, 2002. See http://www.heritage.org/Research/Abstinence/BG1533.cfm. (Accessed on January 9, 2007.)

argues that concerns about the "epidemic" of teen pregnancy are less about the age of the pregnant women, and more about their unwillingness to legitimate the pregnancy by getting married. "First Comes Junior in a Baby Carriage: Four in ten kids are now born to unmarried moms," screams the headline of a December 4, 2006, *Newsweek* article (Rosenberg and Wingert 2006, 56). Sociologists have documented the similarities between unmarried mothers and married mothers, noting especially that both sets of women value marriage, relational quality, and commitment (Edin and Kefalas 2005, Hertz 2006), while conservatives portray unmarried mothers as both a moral and an economic problem.[7] Poor women and women of color are significantly more likely to have children outside of marriage (Edin and Kefalas 2005), but white middle-class women are increasingly choosing single motherhood as well (Hertz 2006). Because these changes signal the increasing independence of women across race and class lines, they portend a muddying in the use of sexual and family patterns to mark race and class distinctions. In this context, the abstinence of white unmarried girls and women takes on additional symbolic weight, but this context also matters for the sexual performances of boys and men.

Unity Christians are not the people about whom moral alarms about family formation have been sounded. Instead, morally conservative rhetoric provides Unity Christians with tools they can use to further their own, not always conservative, ends. Nonetheless, the University Unity strategy works because it draws on hierarchies of sexual and family meanings that disadvantage people and groups who cannot or will not live up to them. Moreover, because Unity Christians use those meanings to make sense of their choices, they not only fail to challenge, but also extend, these moral hierarchies.

The stories Unity women and men tell about abstinence share similar themes, but like goth sexual freakiness, abstinence has different implications for women than for men. Although abstinence is no longer normative among young women, it corresponds with traditional notions of femininity. Definitions of feminine sexuality as passive and chaste persist, despite some revision, in contemporary culture. Abstinence is one means for women to enact traditional gender roles (Carpenter 2005). In contrast,

---

7. Robert Rector, of the Heritage Foundation, "calls unwed births the primary cause of child poverty and welfare dependency" (Rosenberg and Wingert 2006, 57). The Bush administration's "Healthy Marriage Initiative," which aims at getting poor people to marry by fostering relationship skills, presumes that culture is the problem.

abstinence defies normative definitions of "real" men, which equate masculinity with heterosexual prowess. Thus, it would seem that abstinence would be a more stigmatized, and perhaps more radical,[8] choice for men than for women. Nonetheless, within University Unity, as with goth polyamory, men accrue more status from abstinence than do women.

Abstinence and masculinity

Unity Christian men claim abstinence in a context in which young men are assumed to be sexually voracious. Images of young men's relentless sexual desire are everywhere—even in the materials used by Christian organizations aimed at young adults. For young men, then, sexual abstinence is indeed a distinctive identity. Because men are seen as sexually voracious and women are not, abstinence distinguishes Unity men from non-Christian men in a more profound way than it does for Unity women (for whom sexual abstinence is not perceived to be so difficult).

Abstinence creates particular identity tasks for Unity Christian men. First, they must explain their abstinence in a way that is culturally credible. They do this by emphasizing that abstinence is a *choice.* The rhetoric of choice, I argue, allows them to retain a sense of authority and autonomy while also masking other potentially more troublesome deviations from dominant masculine expectations. Second, University Unity men must prove their manhood in the absence of conventional forms of heterosexual success. They do this through collective performances of temptation and by linking their resistance to alternative masculine qualities of self-control and commitment. Thus, although Unity men engage in heterosexual performances at odds with those of most men their age, they do not, in the end, propose an alternative definition of manhood. Rather, they piece together conservative rhetoric about men in ways that best suit their needs. This strategy, in turn, maintains gendered assumptions about what men (and by extension, women) "are really like" (Wilkins forthcoming).

Almost all University Unity men report a lack of heterosexual success before becoming Christians. Most, like Jon and Lucas, recount a history of rejection at the hands of girls. Others, like Kevin and Jesse, suggest

---

8. Carpenter (2005, 100) suggests that, for contemporary young men, violating the mandate to be sexually voracious is a means of "rejecting a traditional style of masculinity for a more relational, less aggressive alternative." But see Wilkins (forthcoming).

that they aren't interested in heterosexuality. Aaron describes the vulnerability he feels in intimate relationships. For young men, rejection, heterosexual disinterest, and expressions of vulnerability are all social problems.
Abstinence is a clever, if surprising, solution to these problems. In claiming abstinence, Unity Christian men transform unmasculine heterosexual
experiences into a *choice*. In doing so, they regain control over their sexual identities. The experiences of Jon, Lucas, and Kevin illustrate how this
works.

Jon laments, "I wasn't that popular with girls in high school. It's kind
of embarrassing." Lucas's story, told in the previous chapter, reveals the
same problem. He says:

> In high school, I was like not very popular so I was trying to get a girlfriend. I
> wasn't very popular and they were all very mean to me so I decided to go where
> there would be nice and good-looking girls...church.

Not being able to attract girls incurs social costs that may have little to do
with frustrated sexual desire or a lack of intimacy. Jon describes embarrassment, rather than frustrated desire or loneliness. Lucas sought out a
"good-looking girl" in an attempt to become more popular, or at least to
challenge the social basis of the bullying. For Lucas, getting a girl—especially a good-looking one—was a means of proving sufficient masculinity.

University Unity provided Jon and Lucas with tools to manage their
rejection. Each, somewhat differently, uses Unity Christian rhetoric and
rationales to mold the terms of heterosexual success in ways that better
fit their experiences. Jon explains, "I think I have changed my image...I
used to value physical features a lot but now I really value someone I
can talk to and be on the same playing field. I still have some attraction
too." Jon doesn't fully relinquish the importance of heterosexual success
(note that his admission of embarrassment is in the present tense rather
than past), but he rewrites it, emphasizing the value of communication
and common ground rather than physical attraction. Jon's shift in heterosexual expectations reduces the range of possible suitors, and thus the
potential for rejection.

University Unity provides an explanatory structure for Jon's emphasis
on relational, rather than physical, qualities—a shift that, in turn, provides a comprehensible explanation for why he doesn't have a girlfriend.
"I haven't found someone I can talk to" returns agency over his heterosexual experiences to Jon (who is being choosy rather than being rejected

or disinterested), *and* allows him to perform heterosexuality. Christians, of course, are not the only men who decide communication is more important than physical attraction. Jon's shift in interest could be credited to a maturation process, but Jon attributes it to his development of *Christian* values. This is an important piece of his strategy, as it not only provides a comprehensible explanation for his changed perspective but also tools for thinking of it as the right thing to do (see discussion below).

Lucas, like many of his Unity peers, rejects dating altogether. He explains:

> I still haven't had a girlfriend. I made a conscious decision. I just saw people who had girlfriends. They always broke up, and as soon as they broke up, they wanted another girlfriend. It's like obsessive.

Lucas uses Christianity to turn abstinence from a sign of masculine failure into "a conscious decision." Moreover, by labeling dating "obsessive," Lucas draws on pop cultural language to demonstrate his own comparative self-control.

Kevin didn't date in high school either, but he never describes himself as unpopular. Instead, he explains that he was so busy "having a good time" in high school that he didn't get much work done. He describes a whirlwind of activities. As an afterthought, he adds:

> [In high school], both of my best friends had long-term girlfriends. I never really, I don't know, I never really worried about it. I couldn't get involved in after-school things because I had to babysit my baby sister when my mom went back to school.

On the surface, this explanation makes sense. Kevin seems unaware of the ways in which it contradicts his animated recounting of a busy high school social life. It wasn't that he didn't want to date or that girls didn't want to date him, he suggests, it's just that he didn't have time and he couldn't participate in activities where he would meet people. His family responsibilities provide him with a credible, status-protecting explanation for not participating in the dating rituals that are so central to adolescent life, even while he was able to maintain relationships with his two best friends.

In college, where he no longer has the shield of family responsibilities, University Unity provides new reasons for not dating. Offhandedly, he says:

I do plan to [date]. I just let things happen. I think if I ever want to have a serious relationship, I can imagine the problems of being with a non-Christian. I'd want them to come to church with me, and it's so important to me, I'd want to be able to talk to them about it.

As with his earlier shift in energy, Kevin's comment suggests that, for him, dating is an abstract idea, not particularly interesting, something he "plans to do" if it happens. His desire to date a Christian, as with other Unity participants, restricts his pool of potential partners, reducing the chances that it will "just happen"—especially given the commitment to postponing dating among the University Unity women with whom he interacts (as well as the general prohibition against homosexual relationships).

For young men like Kevin, Unity Christianity is a useful means of navigating a nominal interest in heterosexuality. University Unity's norm of romantic abstinence provides structural support for being single. Not only is it normative to be single in the Unity community, but social activities are structured around single people rather than couples. Thus, for Kevin, there are always activities in which he can participate that neither depend on nor highlight his singleness. As Kevin says, he "has a lot more fun" hanging out with Unity members because they "organize stuff to do as a group"; he is thus freed from dependence on the heterosexual social culture of the dorms.

For men whose heterosexual histories deviate from masculine social expectations, transforming abstinence from a sign of failure into an active choice is a useful trick. Configured as a choice, abstinence allows Unity men to sidestep pressure to demonstrate heterosexuality. Their heterosexuality is assumed to be on hold, rather than absent. They are thus able to avoid, at least among like-minded friends, the speculation about sexual preferences that might elsewhere attend a man's lack of interest in dating. Among non-Christians as well, Christianity serves as a plausible, if derided, explanation for avoiding competitive heterosexual posturing.

Because Unity men don't participate in expected heterosexual practices, they must prove their masculinity some other way. For these men, masculinity is achieved, in part, through the rhetoric of temptation. Temptation talk does two things for Unity Christian men. First, it allows them to perform a kind of heterosexuality, demonstrating to themselves and to others that they are *really* heterosexual. Second, it turns abstinence into an act of self-control, intervening in problems of masculinity by validating an alternative definition of masculinity. This alternative recalls a Victorian model of manhood in which masculinity was premised on self-restraint achieved, in part, through sexual continence (Carpenter 2005, 24).

Unity Christian men perform temptation collectively. At the last University Unity meeting of the academic year, the participants prepared for the long summer ahead—a time that often tested their faith. A few of them would spend the summer in the company of other Christians, either in the churches they grew up in or at the summer programs organized by University Unity. But others would go home to their non-Christian (or, more precisely, nominally Christian) families, to work summer jobs among non-Christian peers. The differently structured time and the lack of daily support from Unity peers challenged their sense of daily, intimate connection with God, they said. What they didn't say, but seemed to understand, was that it also reduced community regulations on their behavior, minimizing the social risks of sexual choices other than abstinence.

In preparation for the time apart, Chuck, the staff leader, distributed summer survival packets called "More than a Summer, Survivor 2002."[9] "Let's face it," page one announces in bold, "Summers can pose a major challenge to our faith and obedience to Christ." Identifying three "essentials" for survival as a Christian—self-discipline, fellowship, and time with God,—the packet encourages Unity Christians to structure their time, set goals and priorities, find a local Christian community, communicate via e-mail and "prayer requests" with the campus community, and spend time reading the Bible and praying daily. It also includes detailed instructions on keeping a journal, memorizing Scripture, studying the Bible, and helping others find Christ (evangelizing). The pamphlet, then, reiterates the practices by which the Unity Christian identity is consolidated. University Unity anxiety that their identities might fray outside of their community underscores the importance of community to social identities. But it also suggests the fragility of an identity that stands in such opposition to the other cultural practices of young adulthood.

A third of the "survival guide" is about sex. The space that sexuality warrants makes clear its centrality to the Unity Christian identity. Chuck reinforced this point in his talk. Both the packet and Chuck's talk encour-

---

9. Although the pamphlet was produced and distributed locally, it was "adapted" from materials used by a staff leader on another major university campus in a different part of the country. Thus, although the Christian identities I discuss in this chapter are local, they draw on nonlocal Christian discourses.

age young Christians *not* to have sex. The explicit message is that sex is a universal, ongoing temptation that must be constantly managed. For example, question three in the "Personal Purity Bible Study," which was exclusively about sex, asks: "Why does everyone struggle with the temptation of immorality?" Question eight repeats this point, beginning: "You are not alone in your struggle of immorality."

Although University Unity materials sometimes portray temptation in gender-neutral terms, Unity Christians see sexual temptation as a problem for men, while they see the desire for romantic intimacy as a problem for women. For example, Susan told me a story about a University Unity–sponsored summer retreat at which she "learned," in a conversation with the young men, about their struggle with temptation: "I really had no idea like for guys, struggling to be sexually pure, they were brutally honest, it's a minute-by-minute thing for us, even a spaghetti strap can be hard. I think girls struggle with different things." Conversations like these do two things: first, they reinforce the notion that men and women are different (it's interesting that Susan and her women friends had to "learn" this); second, they provide another collective performance of temptation, "proving" the collective heterosexuality of Unity men. Instead of talking about scoring, Unity Christian men talk about how hard it is to manage temptation. The virtual absence of temptation talk in Unity men's individual stories clarifies the role of these public rituals as community performances of "properly" heterosexual masculinity.

On the surface, it seems ironic that a group whose identities are built on *not* having sex would be so preoccupied with discussing it. Mullaney (2001) argues that abstinent identities require both temptation and public performance. First, not doing identities "are less about absence and more about *resistance*. For this reason, *temptation* plays a central role ... " (6). Second, "identities based on 'not doings'" need to be demonstrated in some way to be socially meaningful. For Unity Christians, the organizational performance of sexual temptation fulfills both requirements. Unity temptation talk transforms heterosexual nonparticipation into *abstinence*—a moral identity achieved through self-discipline and commitment (see also Wilkins forthcoming).

Sexual abstinence is a more powerful moral boundary when nonmarital sexuality is understood as pervasive, if not in practice, then at least in desire. Because university students both postpone marriage *and* encourage sexual experimentation, Unity Christians believe that sexuality needs to be closely managed in college. In turn, this need for management increases the intensity of sexual abstinence as a moral boundary. In short, sexual abstinence is the ultimate form of self-discipline, but it is only such if it is the ultimate temptation in the first place.

The links between abstinence, resistance, and self-discipline are strengthened by the age of the Unity participants. Unity Christians are no longer children whose innocence needs protected. Instead, they occupy a liminal social position between youth and full adulthood. Because the average age at first marriage is increasing, this liminal position may stretch out for a number of years. Attitudes about nonmarital sexuality among adults are more divided than those about adolescents. Most young adults, married or not, have had sexual intercourse (Carpenter 2005). The Christian Right push to direct sexual-abstinence education at unmarried adults, mentioned earlier, is more fiercely ridiculed than are programs aimed at teens. Today, most people agree that adults have the right to make their own sexual decisions (within gendered, raced, and classed bounds). Thus, age alters the meanings of sexual abstinence in important ways. The putative innocence of younger youth suggests purity rather than resistance to temptation, and thus does not allow for claims to self-control (see Mullaney 2001).

Temptation performances are not the only way in which Unity Christian men prove their manhood. Unity men negotiate masculinity in a climate in which notions of sexually voracious men coexist with concerns about men's irresponsibility. Although men's heterosexuality is not subject to the same scrutiny and alarm as women's, the reproductive behavior of poor men and men of color has come under political and moral attack. Subordinated men are demonized, in part, for their inabilities to fulfill breadwinning responsibilities and for their presumed lack of commitment to either their biological children or their children's mothers. In response to widespread concern about a decrease in men's familial commitment, some Christian organizations have promoted an alternative style of manhood that encourages men's emotional and financial commitment to their families. While desirable to many women looking for a stable and involved partner, this Christian alternative reinstitutes the patriarchal family as a source of masculine authority and esteem (Donovan 1998, Heath 2003).

Unlike married Christian men, University Unity men have no *actual* family responsibilities. Instead, "family values" rhetoric supplies Unity men with resources they can use to claim masculinity through the language of family commitment, rather than heterosexual performance.

Family values talk is doubly useful to them. First, it further justifies their abstinence. Second, it allows them to claim that they are not only *real* men but, in fact, *better* men (Wilkins forthcoming). Listen, for example, to Jon:

> I think [premarital sex] is wrong. The Bible says it's wrong. Also the divorce rate is higher. There's so much temptation on this campus. Mentally I trip a lot. I don't know if I could work through a lot of it. Not just the divorce thing, but also STDs and getting a girl pregnant. I'm not ready for a family yet. The things I've worried about is that if I get too deeply involved with someone...two or three years...I don't know if I'm prepared to spend the rest of my life with that person.

Jon's comment fuses abstinence, temptation, and family values rhetoric. At once, he suggests that although he is tempted (a "real" man), he resists this temptation because of his commitment to traditional norms of family formation. His opening gesture to God ("the Bible says it's wrong") anchors his self-discipline and sense of family responsibility in his Christian identity. At the same time, his comments hint at his own trepidation about intimate relationships and draw attention away from other reasons for heterosexual nonparticipation. (Remember Jon's embarrassment that he couldn't get a girlfriend.)

Kevin achieves similar ends by talking about commitment:

> I think [people should wait until marriage to have sex]. I mean, that's something that I want to do. I mean, I don't look down on people who don't [wait until marriage] but that's what I want to do. Because I think it should be something important, not with someone you might be with a week or something. It should come with a commitment. I think you can have a commitment without marriage. I think marriage more represents the commitment, kind of declaring it. I do think you can have a commitment outside of it. I just think if you marry, when you're married to someone, it's a lot more incentive to work things out with them. You can't just break up.

The language Unity men use to explain sexual abstinence allows them to see themselves as different kinds of men: principled, committed, disciplined, authentic, and concerned about the future. Their gender strategy props up a model of manhood that doesn't rest on heterosexual prowess. For the Christian men in this study, this strategy makes sense, as it emphasizes elements of masculinity at which they are more likely to be successful. At the same time, its assumptions are entwined with race- and class-hued distinctions among men. Moreover, because the rhetoric of temptation maintains the notion that Unity men are *really* heterosexual, it doesn't undo the link between masculinity and heterosexuality that shapes the dilemmas of University Unity men in the first place. Finally, the emphasis on commitment, as with the goths, is not incompatible with hierarchical gender relations within heterosexual couples (Wilkins forthcoming).

Abstinence and femininity

Women are often enthusiastic members of conservative religions. Because women seem to have less to gain from participating in subcultures that institutionalize their subordination, their enthusiasm begs explanation. Some studies find that women seek religious communities because of, rather than despite, their traditional models of gender; women use the religion's conservative gender norms to solve personal problems (Davidman 1991, Read and Bartkowski 2000) or to claim resources (Mihelich and Storrs 2003). Other researchers argue that traditional religious gender hierarchies may be less rigid in practice than in ideology. Conservative Protestant couples, for example, may combine norms of male-headship with the reality of women's economic participation (Ammerman 1987, Stacey 1990, Gallagher and Smith 1999). These studies remind us that it is important to pay attention to the meanings and strategies of participants themselves. Chong (2006, 702) cautions, however, that "despite these liberating and empowering functions of women's faith, women's very efforts to cope with their personal dilemmas through religious beliefs also result in consequences that are highly oppressive for women."

Unity women's relationship to abstinence reflects many of these tensions. For Unity women, sexual abstinence is nonnegotiable, reviving inflexible assumptions about feminine purity. Yet Unity Christian women also use University Unity sexual norms for their own ends. Like their non-Christian peers, Unity women don't want to be rejected or to feel unattractive. They are concerned about their reputations. They worry that guys are only interested in sex. And they fear that romance will distract them from other pursuits. These concerns are entangled in cultural notions of appropriate sexual behavior, but they are also about the gendered inequalities and insecurities of the heterosexual marketplace. As with the young men, abstinence provides a way out of gendered heterosexual challenges, but the problems Unity women contend with are in many ways more complex, more painful, or more dangerous than the problems faced by the young men. Abstinence is not experienced in identical ways by all Unity Christian women, even while their stories contain similar elements. Below, Molly's and Gretchen's stories profile the complexity of Unity women's sexual strategies.

Molly: "I've always been... boy crazy"

"I've always been like boy crazy," Molly explains breathlessly. "But it's something that I'm trying to get under God's control 'cause I don't want to be that way." To achieve this, she explains, she has established rules. She isn't dating anyone for six months, but that's over June first, and so she's also going to try to make it through the summer without a date. And she's not going to "casual date" anymore: no dating "unless there's marriage potential." This means she can only date Christians, because "the Bible talks about being yoked.... It's so central to my life. If I couldn't share that with my boyfriend, it would bring me down."

Molly's rules regulate her sexuality. Her rule about casual dating means that most potential suitors are off-limits. Her "Christians only" rule narrows the pool of potential future suitors to (presumably) sexually like-minded Christian men. Together, these strategies allow her to better patrol her own desires by keeping tempting situations at bay. Molly understands that maintaining sexual boundaries within relationships, even when both partners are Christians, requires self-vigilance and cooperation. She explains:

> Like I used to have sex but that's changed. It's so weird because my boyfriend who introduced me to Christ, he and I were having sex. I knew as soon as I became a Christian I wanted to stop but he didn't want to so it took about six months or so to stop. It says in the Bible, the idea that my body is a temple and it's the closest you can get to someone.

In this story, Molly's sexual desires, and the expectations of a relationship in which sexuality had already been initiated, vie with her new ideas about appropriate sexual behavior. It's possible that Molly's story also reflects women's unequal bargaining power in heterosexual relationships, although I heard a similar story from a man whose girlfriend didn't want to stop having sex. My sense is that Molly's story, like his did, reflects the conflict between her desires and the expectations of her Unity Christian identity.

Molly uses Christian abstinence to remake herself as a good girl. She explains: "I used to have the idea that if you've got it, flaunt it. When I look back at what I wore in high school, no wonder people thought what they thought." Molly's new chaste style and behavior protect her from the potential fallout of her formerly "wild" ways. She is self-consciously changing her reputation. The fresh start provided by the transition to the university helps her with this, but her University Unity identity makes it stick.

Molly's strategy only works because she has been redeemed from her prior sexual activity. In part, this redemption rests on her reevaluation of her past as shameful: "I feel bad that I didn't save it for my husband," she tells me. In becoming a Unity Christian, Molly learned to evaluate herself from Unity's moral perspective. "No wonder people thought what they thought," she says, newly owning the old idea that all performances of sexuality are inappropriate for unmarried women. Molly's redemption talk positions her current choice of abstinence as morally superior rather than just a choice among many. At the same time, it forces her to denigrate her prior choices and limits her ability to remake herself again in the future.

Yet, even while resistance narrows Molly's sexual and social options and requires her to reinterpret her past as shameful, it clears space for other pursuits, including her studies and her friendships with other University Unity women. Unity rhetoric provides her with a personally compelling reason to resist the pull of heterosexuality, a temptation that is fun and exciting, but one that can also delimit women's options. As I discuss more below, in resisting heterosexuality, Molly lays claim to a definition of self that does not rest on her ability to get a man.

Gretchen: "I was still getting into bad relationships"

In contrast to Molly's exuberance, Gretchen is grim. The stories she tells about her pre–University Unity dating experiences are painful. Like the stories told by many Unity Christians, her stories suggest that she is not competitive at the heterosexual game. Gretchen explains that, in high school (before she was a Christian), she used sexual knowledge to jockey for "coolness" and for attention, but was ultimately out-knowledged: "I knew a lot of sexual stuff and talked about it with the guys. They were like, how do you know all this stuff? Then all the girls became whores senior year—one up on me." Gretchen's description points to two familiar problems. First, her efforts to use sexuality to be cool were unsuccessful because she was less skilled than some of her peers. Second, this strategy was potentially costly, as it is for all women, sliding too easily into a reputation as a "whore." Like Molly, Gretchen accepts, without ambivalence, the sexual hierarchy that creates this cost.

But Gretchen's story suggests other problems as well:

> I went to two high schools. At Catholic school, everyone was evil. I transferred to public school. My boyfriend was there. I didn't tell my family that. They didn't like him, thought he was forcing me to do stuff...sexual stuff. He kind of was I guess.

In college, Gretchen reports more unsatisfying and exploitative heterosexual relationships. "I was still getting into bad relationships. I had a boyfriend who was kind of a jerk. God really helped me see that.... Guys who were only interested in sex," instead of what she wanted—"someone who was interested in me and who I am."

Like other Unity Christians, Gretchen draws on broader cultural scripts[10] to make sense of her bad relationships. But it is in University Unity that she finds the language to justify her choice. Gretchen attributes her change to God, but her involvement with the University Unity community, and the timing of a Unity spring break trip right after she broke up with the "jerk," gave her tools to reassess her needs and the support to end the relationship. Now, she's not dating. "I'm staying away from guys. I mean I have a few crushes but I don't think they're the right person. I haven't heard God say so. I think I'd just know."

Like Molly, Gretchen expresses shame for her sexual past, but her shame takes on a tinge of self-disgust that Molly's doesn't. For Molly, abstaining from hetero-relations is an ongoing struggle, but Gretchen says that she never desired sexual intimacy. She explains: "I don't want to have sex before I get married. I didn't actually have sex before. I just did other things. I don't want to do those things either. I didn't feel right about it before so it's not a huge change." The differences in their stories likely

10. "Guys who were only interested in sex" is a version of what Phillips (2000) identifies as "the male sexual drive discourse."

arise from the distinct ways in which they experienced heterosexuality before becoming Christians. Gretchen seems to have experienced little pleasure. Not only does she describe her relationships as exploitative, but she
was disadvantaged on the heterosexual marketplace in a way that Molly
was not. Given these differences, Gretchen's self-disgust makes sense.

Shame legitimates women's unequal sexual position, but it may also promote solidarity among Unity women. Because "shame is a social emotion,"
the act of sharing it "can bring about particular closeness with other persons" (Lynd 1958, 66; in Scheff 2000, 97). Shame, then, creates common
ground between otherwise different women like Gretchen and Molly. For
Gretchen, moreover, the disclosure of shame and the redemption offered
by Christianity were important tools in her efforts to stake out her own
sexual terms.

Waiting for "God to say so" allows Gretchen to put off further relationships with men, but it also pushes back other sexual dilemmas:

> [Homosexuality] is kind of an iffy thing to talk about. I think it's a wrong thing.
> I wouldn't totally condemn it. I struggled with it when I was like twelve or
> thirteen. I thought I might be gay. I don't know. I liked my friend but it didn't
> work out. I don't know. I kind of think you could be born with it. Some people
> argue that. Or it could be a choice. I feel like it's a really personal thing, whether
> you do it or not. Or whether you agree with it or not.

Gretchen is not the only Unity Christian to claim uncertainty about the
conservative Christian prohibition on homosexuality, but she *is* the only
one to admit that she had ever grappled with the possibility of her own
homosexual desires. Moreover, unlike her discussion of her heterosexual
past, she doesn't present those desires as coercive or inauthentic, but instead attributes their latency to circumstances—"it didn't work out." She
also leaves open the spiritual door for a return to those desires: "I believe like if you're doing it and you don't want to be doing it or if you're
doing it and you really love God, then you can be forgiven." In taking
on a Christian identity that advocates postponing romance and sexuality in favor of developing a relationship with God, Gretchen seems to be
able to push back the immediate need to confront issues of her own desires. Gretchen uses the notion of God's forgiveness to leave a wedge in
the door—despite the lack of room in mainstream evangelicalism for homosexual desire (see Wolkomir 2006). Although most University Unity
members I spoke with were reluctant to out-and-out condemn homosexuality, they also explained that the lack of organizational support means

that "people wouldn't say if they were." Active exploration of homosexuality would thus burst Gretchen's Unity Christian identity, but because heterosexual exploration is equally off limits, Gretchen can delay (or hide) sexual ambivalence.

Redemption, shame, and femininity

Because women are seen as less sexual than men, they are less able to achieve self-control through sexual resistance. Instead, for women, abstinence is linked to sexual purity. Mullaney (2001) argues that sexual purity hinges on "neverness"—having never engaged in sexual behavior. Among Unity women, however, neverness is not universal. For sexually experienced women, the claim to sexual purity requires redemption. Redemption happens, in part, through shame.

Shame, in these cases, is flexible enough to redeem a range of sexual pasts. As we saw with Molly, a woman doesn't have to dislike sex to be redeemed by shame; she need only feel ashamed that she had it too early, endorsing outsiders' views of her as impure. Molly's expressions of shame rehabilitate her white middle-class femininity, returning her to a state of sexual purity.[11] But despite its flexibility, shame is not available to all women as a strategy. Its potential to rehabilitate depends on a race-based presumption of potential purity: "white girls can be pulled back into the fold, while their nonwhite counterparts can't" (Kenny 2000, 157).[12] Thus, University Unity women's strategies are unwittingly grounded in racialized (and classed) hierarchies among women (see Wilkins 2004a), as well as a perhaps more visible hierarchy between men and women.

Notably, Aaron, the only Unity man to admit to any prior sexual experiences, expresses regret but not shame for his sexual past. For Aaron, nonmarital sex was wrong because it led to vulnerability. He explains:

> I just remember when Laura and I had sex and then when we broke up, it was the biggest mess. Even then I wished I could take it back. Because I think having sex—I'll say for everyone—a nice blanket statement—is by nature a very intimate, very personal act, a gesture of acceptance and love and depth,

---

11. Her strategy is akin to the now popular notion of the "born-again virgin," advocated in abstinence-only curricula like True Love Waits, although Molly didn't describe herself in these terms to me.

12. See also Solinger 1992, Roberts 1997, Reich 2005, and chapter 6.

and after doing that and being dumped, it's like baring yourself to someone
and saying, ooohh, I don't like what I see.

Aaron is what Carpenter (2005) calls "a gifter"; he envisions his virginity as a gift requiring reciprocity in the form of commitment. Although
his understanding of sex is associated with a feminine approach to sexuality (Carpenter 2005), redemption through shame is not part of Aaron's
story. For Unity Christians, shame is not just about having sex outside of
marriage but about tarnishing one's feminine purity.

Shame teaches individual women to scan their inner selves to make
sure they line up with social expectations. Unity women accrue the benefits of sexual purity only if they both act and *feel* the right way. In this
way, shame is consistent with other emotional expectations for University Unity women. Although shame is in these ways individually experienced, it has collective implications. Irvine argues that "[c]onservative
opponents [of sex education] depend on a normative emotional climate
of sexual shame" (2002, 146). In the same way, Unity Christian sexual
narratives rely on "traditional affective conventions of sexuality" (ibid.).
Unity women experience shame because shame is a feature of broader
cultural expectations for women's sexuality. At the same time, by embracing shame as not only normative but appropriate, they legitimate the
link between a woman's moral personhood and sexual purity. In these
ways, shame is a powerful and unsurprising mechanism of social control.
Nonetheless, inasmuch as sexual abstinence clears the way for romantic
abstinence, it has surprising benefits for Unity Christian women.

Romantic abstinence

University Unity women don't just avoid sex, they avoid all forms of heterosexual intimacy. Unity women, on the whole, don't date. Some evangelical romance manuals contend that Christians should avoid dating until
they are ready to marry. Although not all evangelicals adhere to this perspective, its influence is seen in a range of evangelical texts, which propose
"modified" versions of dating that purportedly better reflect evangelical
values about love and sexuality (Schweingruber and Meyer 2007). Unity
Christians, in contrast, never make an explicit argument against dating,
nor do they explicitly link not dating to Christianity. Nevertheless, for the
most part, they avoid dating.

To outsiders, even to some other conservative Christians, Unity women's "romantic abstinence" is inexplicable in a way that women's sexual abstinence is not. Holland and Eisenhart (1990) argue that college women are indoctrinated into a "culture of romance," in which the ability to get (and keep) a man is the most important thing about a woman, superseding academics or other social roles. The pervasiveness of this culture means that women are always held accountable for the decision to forego participation. As Catherine laughs, "People are like, what do you mean you don't want a relationship?" Through romantic abstinence, Unity women sidestep the culture of romance altogether.

For Molly, this is not easy. She struggles with her desire for guys. She is constantly meeting someone who turns her head. "It's easy to say [I'm not going to date]," she sighs, "but then I'll meet this great guy. And I already did meet this great guy." And, I suspect, she is constantly turning heads. She works hard to control these temptations, though, because "it's really easy to mess up in other ways" when you're "being controlled by something other than God." As with Unity men, Molly ties together temptation, self-discipline, and one's moral self.

For Molly, temptation is not sexual but romantic. She struggles to resist relationships, not sex. The Summer Survival packet, discussed earlier, reiterates the idea that, for women, temptation is primarily emotional. An article called "Why You Shouldn't Marry or Date an Unbeliever" cautions Christian women to avoid casual dating. "Every marriage starts with a first date," the author counsels, reasoning that if you date a non-Christian, you may fall in love with him; your love may blind you to the problem of his nonbelief (or let you think he'll come around), you may marry him, and then you will be locked into a marriage that cannot be satisfying because a non-Christian cannot meet your spiritual needs. The article is written by and directed at women, for whom the dangers of emotional blindness are presumably more intense. Just as men have to manage their sexual desires, the material suggests, women need to manage their desire for love. Thus, for women, romantic abstinence (or abstaining from dating at all) is a way to manage emotional impulses. Failure to control one's romantic desires can sabotage one's Christian identity, as the article makes clear. The author's final warning says:

> If you can find peace and contentment in a relationship with someone who doesn't love God, then you must ask yourself how much you really love Him. After all, if you find you have more in common with those who walk in

darkness...It may be because you are both walking down the same path!
(1 John 1:6–7. John 3:21).

This essentialist thinking not only leaves the responsibility for romance
firmly within women's court, but maintains the notion that women need
relationships more than men do.

Yet not all Unity women struggle with romantic abstinence. Instead,
most formulate romantic abstinence as a benefit of sexual abstinence. The
commitment to postponing sexuality makes postponing romantic involvement logical: the desire to avoid the temptation of nonmarital sexuality
provides them with a coherent explanation for withdrawing from the dating rituals omnipresent in the college scene. For many, as with the men,
University Unity assumptions about dating provide them with a way to
make sense of their deviations from feminine expectations. Like other
Unity women, Catherine uses the rhetoric of God's will ("if I'm meant
to") to justify her disinterest in dating. She explains: "it just isn't important to me. As long as I have friends and family, I'm happy. If I'm meant
to have someone, I'll find him."

Carolyn, the Korean American woman introduced in the previous
chapter, would like to be "pretty and popular," but she sees herself as unattractive. Her lack of success at dating makes her feel bad about herself.
University Unity peers provide sympathetic ears. But more than that,
Unity relationship rhetoric allows Carolyn to put a less stigmatizing spin
on her experience of heterosexual exclusion. Carolyn invokes Unity Christianity especially in moments of heterosexual failure. For example, she
says, "University Unity means the world to me right now. This weekend I
took a huge step backward. I thought I could do an adult relationship...."
Carolyn's talk both salves her pain and deflects attention from the failed
"adult relationship" itself. As with the men, Unity norms create a rationale for postponing dating, transforming heterosexual inactivity from failure to choice. Note that Carolyn's explanation, like that of the men, is not
really about God. Instead, Carolyn uses broader cultural concepts to au-
thorize her feelings. University Unity naturalizes particular understandings about sexuality (it is for adults, it should be accompanied by particular emotions, it should involve commitment and so forth) by linking them
to the Unity Christian identity. Carolyn continues:

A part of me doesn't trust myself enough [to date]. I'm selfish, still growing up.
I don't trust myself not to hurt someone in a long-term relationship. That and

I still have the "fat girl" syndrome. All my friends are in long-term relationships....I'm romantic to the core. Prince Charming will come along—I don't
want to kiss a lot of frogs.

Carolyn's explanation transforms feelings of heterosexual failure into a
rational response to emotional unreadiness. To be sure, this is not a perfect strategy. Carolyn still admits to feeling fat (and therefore unattractive). Nevertheless, the restricted terms of Unity Christian sexuality help
her manage her feelings of unattractiveness and regain agency over her
sexual and romantic experiences.

Abstinence allows Unity women to resist compulsory romance, albeit
temporarily. Moreover, in opting out of romance, Unity women also opt
out of other aspects of "girl culture," including talk about boys, sex, and
the consumption practices involved in heterosexuality that forge connections among girls and women (McRobbie 1991, Bettie 2003).

Thus, the Unity Christian identity bends the rules of femininity in unexpected ways. Unity Christianity expects women to focus their emotional
energies on their spirituality, and to supplant a heterosexual relationship
with a relationship with God. In these ways, Unity Christianity provides
them with a way to step off of the otherwise compulsory "sexual auction
block" (Holland and Eisenhart 1990). Unable to accomplish sexual and
romantic intimacy on their own terms, Unity women choose to postpone
participating altogether, rather than attempting to alter the terms of participation, as the goth women do. In turn, by postponing romance, Unity
women defer the diversion of energy and attention often entailed by romantic coupling, making room for personal development and for friendships with other women.

Molly laments, "I didn't really make any friends my first year because
I was always going to see my boyfriend." Dating, she explains, is "dis-
tracting. That's all I think about when I meet a guy." Molly's experience
probably seems familiar: because women are typically responsible for the
emotional labor in heterosexual relationships, the relationships can take
over everything else. In withdrawing from the heterosexual market, Unity
women carve out room for themselves to develop identities independent
of alliances with individual men. Thus, abstinent women are less centered
on men, at least temporarily, than are either the more radical seeming
goths or wannabes. By prioritizing God, they are able to focus on inward-
directed pursuits. Hackstaff (1999) argues that the development of individualism means different things for women than for men. "For men, putting

the self first remains a way to sustain male dominance in marriage. For women, putting the self first is a way to counter male dominance in marriage" (3). For these Christian women, withdrawing from the other-directedness of hetero-romance provides a window of time in which they can focus on their selves.

The idea that God is responsible for the timing of their heterosexual relationships enables Unity women to prioritize their own needs over the needs of heterosexual relationships. The space cleared by romantic abstinence is important to Unity women. The emphasis on introspection, as I detailed in the last chapter, encourages women to focus on their inner lives (even while it also prescribes a narrow set of acceptable emotions). In addition, when time and emotional resources are not siphoned off into heterosexual relationships, women are better able to develop supportive relationships with other women. Women-only, student-run Bible studies, as well as personal mentoring relationships with other Unity Christians, provide structured opportunities to develop these relationships.

Unity women all discussed the importance of their friendships with other Unity women. Gretchen, as I discussed earlier, described the support of Unity friends as central to her ability to dump her boyfriend the "jerk." Catherine describes her friendships with Christians as more authentic, "I feel like at church they care about a person more than friends. Non-Christian friends will do anything to keep my friendship but don't care anything about me as a friend." With the "support" of other Christians, she explains, her "confidence has grown."

The friendships formed among University Unity women are premised on emotional disclosure and spiritually guided advice. This pattern may create enduring and supportive bonds between women, but it has costs. First, as discussed in the previous chapter, it impedes friendships with non-Christians. It is not just that Unity women are not likely to have things in common with non-Christian women, it is also that the structure of emotional closeness that University Unity creates is hard to replicate in their other friendships. In Susan's words, "the more I get to know God, get excited, it naturally has the effect of . . . the more I can't talk about that with other friends. I don't know, it's frustrating." Second, the structure of University Unity facilitates emotional and behavioral monitoring. Bible studies and mentoring relationships premised on disclosure create an "incitement to talk" (Harris 2004) that exposes inner lives. This exposure, in turn, allows for greater community control and amplifies internal monitoring. Susan points to the contradictions in Unity norms when she says, "If friends have problems, I'll see really, really clearly [what to do]." At once, Susan bespeaks a self-assurance that is unusual among the college-aged women I know, and claims her right to intervene in her friends' problems, denying them the same self-assurance.

As we saw in the last chapter, the Unity Christian identity fosters self-discipline, hard work, and long-term planning. Sexual and romantic abstinence makes room for these concerns. Without the distraction of hetero-romance, Unity women are able to better concentrate on developing academic and leadership skills. Thus, sexual and romantic abstinence both protects feminine reputations and facilitates educational acquisition in ways that have historically been reserved for men. For Unity women, the emphases on academic discipline, leadership, confidence, independence, and personal development contradict stereotypes of selfless and submissive Christian femininity, resonating instead with many of the aims of liberal feminism. "I say what I think," Gretchen says, "I used to sit back and let people walk all over me. I got more assertive." Unity women's use of Unity Christianity as a tool for resisting expectations that they be other-directed and romance-oriented, however, is undercut by their reinvention of romance.

Reinventing romance

The decentering of heterosexual intimacy in college is transitory. Unity Christian culture, like most conservative Christian cultures, emphasizes the importance of eventual marriage. Unity women and men alike explain that temporary heterosexual withdrawal reaps greater heterosexual romance and emotional satisfaction down the road. This perspective keeps them safely heterosexual while also limiting their options to a singular relationship structure, a singular sexual trajectory, and a singular type of partner.

Like goths, Unity Christians argue that their sexual practices are more desirable than others because they improve the quality of heterosexual intimacy. In the Christian formulation, "saving" sexuality for marriage will intensify marital intimacy. In addition to invoking the Bible, Unity Christians explain their abstinence by using the language and concepts of pop psychology, which, in turn, rest on modern notions of companionate marriages.

Jillian says:

I feel like that's a good thing [the Christian emphasis on no sex before marriage], not just because it's what the Bible says. I just think it would be a good thing to do. I just think it would be a more fulfilling thing to do. Just like, emotional attachment. Like there's more if you do that [have sex] and more hurt and I feel like I would just want to wait.

In addition to promising to increase the emotional intimacy of the hypothetical marital relationship, sexual postponement allows Unity Christians to lessen (or avoid) the pain of uncoupling, as Aaron's comments indicate: "Sex isn't wrong but God designed it for something. It's so intimate that to do it without that strong commitment that marriage brings could just be hurtful for both people." Like other Unity Christians, Aaron views sex as inherently (intensely) emotional, and the marital relationship as the natural location for emotional intimacy. This understanding allows Unity members to frame waiting in positive terms; they anticipate being able to give a gift to their (hypothetical, future) spouse (especially husbands). In this sense, Unity Christians portray themselves as saying yes to greater marital intimacy, rather than as saying no to present desire.

The ideas Unity Christians express are consistent with the growing exploration of marital sexuality within evangelicalism. Emerging tentatively in the seventies, these ideas back away from universally restrictive sexuality, endorsing sexual satisfaction for both men and women but within the singular context of marriage (Irvine 2002). This shift within evangelicalism replaces the need for a lifetime of sexual control with the promise of intense sexual satisfaction upon marriage. Thus, Unity Christians and other contemporary unmarried evangelicals are not required to internalize a permanent rejection of sexual desire, but are invited to imagine greater future sexual and emotional fulfillment.

In this regard, Lucas's dream is perhaps the most extreme. A bit shyly, he says, "My dream is to tell my wife she's the only one I've ever liked or loved. I want to lie down on the beach and know she's the only one." Lucas tells me that he never tells anyone this—perhaps because it sounds a bit odd even within the University Unity community or perhaps because sharing it would tarnish his dream. Either way, Lucas uses the community's insistence that physical intimacy equals emotional commitment to elaborate a hyperromantic dream in which he avoids intimacy (or, one can imagine, heartache or disappointment) of any kind until he meets his wife. It is hard to imagine how this will work out, since Lucas's dream forecloses almost all contemporary options for ascertaining which woman he wants to marry. Perhaps this is the point—the dream allows him to endlessly avoid hetero-intimacy. It seems more likely that the dream is temporarily useful to Lucas, but will become more unmanageable as he reaches a life stage in which he wants to get married.

As with the goths, however, the promise of emotional intimacy is not egalitarian, but is premised on essentialism. As we have already seen, Unity Christians believe that relational emotions matter more to women than to men. After telling me his romantic dream, Lucas, for example, said, "Women and men are different. Women are more emotional than men. Women focus more on love and loving. Men focus more on significance, acceptance, and making themselves known."

For Unity Christians, the clock is turned back: their strategy recreates an environment in which the marital bargain is privileged. In exchange for their sexual postponement, Unity women are promised a committed and devoted husband. The problem, of course, is that the possible outcome— while perhaps desirable to some women—is narrow, prescribing a singular relationship model. The discourse surrounding sexual abstinence valorizes that model, positing the marital dyad as the site of intense emotional satisfaction. Thus, this ideal integrates a marital model of unwavering lifelong commitment with a marital model of satisfying emotional and sexual companionship, but without acknowledging that these models emerged out of different socioeconomic concerns and are consequently often antithetical (see Coontz 2005).

Unity women are thus set up with high expectations for marriage but without the resources to address potential marital pitfalls. First, their strategy denies them "trial run" relationships that would help them accumulate relationship skills, including tools for anticipating and resolving conflict as well as a more realistic understanding of relationships. Second, their strategy doesn't address issues of heterosexual inequity in relationships, and thus provides them with only a temporary reprieve from gendered relationship concerns. And third, because it doesn't address women's economic disadvantage in marriages, theirs is a risky economic strategy, since Christian distaste for divorce doesn't guarantee protection from actual divorce, abandonment, or their spouse's death.

I conclude with a story from Hannah that illustrates the temporariness of Unity women's gains. Of all the women I spoke with, Hannah is the most firmly guided by career aspirations (perhaps because she was a bit older, twenty-three, at the time of the interview). Hannah takes herself seriously. Academically disciplined and ambitious, she carefully considers every life decision. She went to graduate school right after completing her undergraduate degree (at the same university), she tells me, because of a talk she heard at the end of high school, in which a professor encouraged her audience not to postpone graduate school "if you have the opportunity…because it will be hard later." Hannah's life, neatly organized around her career aspirations and her Unity Christian identity, has recently been unsettled by the possibility of hetero-romance:

> Right now I'm dealing with being with this guy who's very passionate about missions, very transient, at odds with a life of being in the computer lab and teaching students. I journal a lot. I was thinking about why I'm attracted to this guy cause lots of guys have wandered through but I've been able to disqualify them. He's the first guy I ever thought was a possibility. I just did well at a conference. I feel like I have a future in academia. [I asked] God, "does this allow me to disqualify him?" [God said,] "trust me."

Like other Unity women, she has used God's word to "disqualify" previous potential suitors. She is now using God's word again to take seriously the possibility of embarking on a heterosexual relationship. Despite her invocation of God, Hannah's confusion raises common dilemmas about balancing individual aspirations with the uncertainty of heterosexual intimacy in a society with an increasingly mobile workforce. Hannah justifies her indecision in terms of her own vocational, and not romantic, desires and retains a recognition of the instability of intimacy. In the end, however, it is God's voice saying "trust me" that leads her to consider retreating from her academic dreams; the career switch she considers would move her off a more competitive and prestigious academic path and onto the faith-bounded path shared by other Unity Christians I spoke with.[13]

Conclusion

The preeminence of sexuality in national discourse and on college campuses makes sexuality particularly fertile ground for moral distinctions.

---

13. Glass and Jacobs (2005) find that childhood religious conservatism accentuates class differences in adult earnings attainment, depressing the earnings of lower-class women (Black and white), and slightly raising the earnings of middle-class women. The women in this study, however, were not all raised in conservative religions; instead, many sought out conservative religion as older adolescents. My findings suggest that Christianity is protective to women in the short run, but will likely depress adult earnings in the long run because of University Unity's emphasis both on marriage and on women's carework.

But sexual abstinence is a different sort of moral boundary if it takes work to achieve. In other words, if sex is a temptation that needs to be constantly battled, then successfully battling it proves (at least) two things. First, that the person is *truly* a Christian, i.e., God must really be working in the person if they are able to abstain from the temptation of sex. Second, and related, a Christian proves his self-discipline, her moral fiber, by being willing to allow his or her "love for the Lord" to supersede his or her natural, embodied desires. This does not work as well for women, however, as they are seen as less desiring in the first place. Instead, women prove themselves by redeeming past transgressions through shame and by refraining from emotional temptations. Even though both men and women engage in abstinence, then, the explanations they use and identities they construct rely on gender difference.

Abstinence would seem to be a more difficult strategy for men, as it works against the equation of masculinity with heterosexual prowess, but men benefit most from it, just as goth men benefit most from both polyamory and bisexuality. University Unity men's benefits, however, accrue according to a slightly different logic than do goth men's. Like goth men, Unity Christian men gain status from their performance of an alternative masculinity. Unlike goth men, though, Unity men are "nice guys"—an identity that, by popular lore, is less heterosexually desirable than the "bad boy." This is a strategy, then, with a long-term payoff but possible short-term costs. For University Unity men, however, Unity Christian abstinence is less costly in the short-term than heterosexual failure, as it provides them with tools to salvage their masculinity in other ways.[14]

Unity women also use abstinence to their advantage. Abstinence provides them with language and logic that they can use to opt out of a heterosexual marketplace that is unequal and often dangerous for women. They use the space cleared by their withdrawal from heterosexuality to invest in themselves, acquiring many of the characteristics that feminists have hoped for young women: confidence, direction, strong friendships with other women. These outcomes, however, should be celebrated cautiously. On one hand, independence and confidence are important gains. On the other hand, these traits are tied to their performance of a good Christian identity, one that requires both shame and goodness, and that therefore binds women's confidence and independence to their ability to live up to gender conservative expectations. As we saw in the last chapter,

14. See Wilkins (forthcoming) for a more developed discussion of this point.

the expectations of Unity Christian femininity train them to relentlessly survey and adjust their own behavior and inner lives, and to be constantly industrious. In this way, they are a Christian version of the "can-do girl" (Harris 2004): the postmodern symbol of feminine confidence, ingenuity, and productivity.

The can-do girl, moreover, depends on her symbolic opposite: the economically and socially marginal "at-risk girl" (Harris 2004; see also Bettie 2003). In as much as Unity women's industriousness and confidence is linked to abstinence and a narrow version of "goodness," it updates racialized and classed sexual hierarchies. Whereas previous generations of young women were urged to remain pure to be marriageable, University Unity women claim purity both as a marital strategy and an empowerment strategy. Sexual purity, while it may bring gains, is a limiting strategy. Sexual purity, does not, Fields (2005, 567) writes, "allow for the possibility of having full, complicated, active sexual lives that might include desires, pleasure, violence, missteps, *and* respect and care from adults in their communities."

As with the goths, race and class are submerged in the Unity Christians' talk about sexuality, but race and class assumptions are nonetheless embedded in the rhetoric of commitment, discipline, responsibility, and marriage. By resuscitating the value of purity, Unity Christians partake in a historical pattern in which the white middle class claims status and morality in contrast to the presumed sexual and relational licentiousness of the poor and communities of color. Unity Christian sexual strategies thus take on meaning in a context in which culture is used to explain not only economic outcomes but also moral personhood. Unity Christians justify their strategies by drawing on reactionary rhetoric about gender, sexuality, and family. This language, while never explicitly racialized, turns back the cultural clock, linking moral worthiness to sexual patterns that are now rare among young adults. Unity Christians naturalize these patterns by attributing them to God's will.

In the course of solving their everyday problems, then, University Unity participants license moral boundaries that have economic and social consequences for people who do, or are presumed to, violate them. These consequences are seen most devastatingly in the increasingly punitive social policies of the last two decades. In these ways, sexual abstinence is unsurprisingly conservative.[15] Unity Christians, I think, are not

15. White middle-class Christians are not the only ones who engage these strategies. Higginbotham (1993) documents the ways in which the Black Baptist Women's Movement, at

(at least fully) conscious of the links between their strategies and race and class.

Like other aspects of the Unity identity, abstinence provides a clear path through murky expectations, and allows Unity Christians to navigate dominant expectations that they find difficult or burdensome. At the same time, it maintains the central pieces of the dominant logic that created their discomfort in the first place. In particular, Unity abstinence reduces the burden of expectations that they use heterosexuality to perform masculinity and femininity, but does not undo the link between gender and heterosexuality. University Unity strategies are temporary, meant to be abandoned with the advent of eventual marriage. In the end, abstinence tightens the gendered rules attached to heterosexuality, especially for women, as it is premised on the importance of sexual purity and on notions of essential differences between women and men that reproduce unequal heterosexual relationships in the long run. Unity Christians use abstinence in clever ways to craft a heterosexual reprieve, but their strategies prevent them from envisioning or achieving any other ways of remaking unequal heterosexual expectations.

---

the turn of the twentieth century, engaged in a strategy of respectability, which included sexual continence. Today, the Nation of Islam, as well as conservative Black churches, promote self-restraint and conservative gender norms as the means to gain respectability. As Harvey (1997) notes, historically, Black southern churches have packaged personal restraint with progressive political change. This combination would seem to have different implications for Black Christian youth and young adults. We need a thicker investigation of the identities Black Christian youth weave, to better address this question.

Puerto Rican Wannabes

"Well, then there's this other group of girls," Carrie told me, as I sat cross-legged on her bedroom floor. She was describing the social geography of her high school, and was almost embarrassed to bring them up. The "other girls" are "Puerto Rican wannabes," she explained. White girls who "don't know who they are." They're loud, annoying, always fighting, too proud of having sex. They wear the wrong clothes. They smoke the wrong cigarettes. They talk wrong, have the wrong attitudes, and have the wrong priorities. And they have the wrong boyfriends. In sum, Puerto Rican wannabes are white girls who date Puerto Rican (and sometimes Black) guys and adopt a particular, class-associated hybridized version of Puerto Rican and Black hip-hop femininity.

When I talked to Carrie, I didn't know to ask about Puerto Rican wannabes. Bringing them up, it seemed, wasn't particularly polite. When I brought them up in subsequent conversations, young people rolled their eyes, communicating that everyone "knows" about wannabes and everyone thinks they're ridiculous. Licensed to talk about them, they filled out the image Carrie sketched, often in a barrage of invective. Wannabes, they told me, wear baggy athletic clothes or tight, trendy clothes, dark makeup, and slick, time-consuming hairstyles. They smoke Newports. They often mimic a Spanish accent and sometimes speak in Spanish, but always speak in loud voices and use nonstandard grammar. They act tough, openly fighting with each other and threatening outsiders. They have sex with their boyfriends and with each other's boyfriends—and they let people know. They are too loud, too flamboyant, too publicly sexual.

The caricature of the Puerto Rican wannabe that these young people describe is the local manifestation of a broader phenomenon. The label "Puerto Rican wannabe" is local and contemporary, applied to a particular kind of white girl in a particular geographical context and in a particular historical moment. But the wannabe is seen across the United States in adolescent and now young adult cultural lore, popping up frequently as a "Black wannabe" or a "Wigger." Black wannabes, like Puerto Rican wannabes, embrace hip-hop culture to a degree that is considered racially inauthentic by both white youth and youth of color.

The caricature of the wannabe that the young people articulated with such certainty is just that—a caricature. In the first chapter of this section, I analyze the ways other youth talk about the wannabe in order to manage their own race, class, and gender anxieties. Young people talk about her as a means of communicating important information about themselves and their own relationships to race, class, and gender. But they also talk about her to police each other: the wannabe is an important means of articulating the parameters of acceptable race, class, and gender behavior. In the second chapter, I tell the stories of the wannabes themselves—stories that deviate in important ways from the caricature, but that are nonetheless penned in by its assumptions.

As I was finishing work on this book, a friend still living in the area in which this study takes place called to tell me about the T-shirts he saw a group of three white girls wearing in the mall. Two of the girls had on T-shirts that said "I love Puerto Rican guys"; the other said "I love Dominican guys." I couldn't imagine anyone in Missouri, where I was living at the time, wearing such a shirt, but back in my hometown mall, "loving" Puerto Rican guys has become a popular enough identity to merit a T-shirt, sold, according to Shawn, in a shop in the mall. Wannabehood has become a market niche. He and I laughed over the outrageousness of the T-shirts, but, humorous or not, the shirts condense many of the issues raised in the next two chapters. By suggesting that desire for a particular ethnicity of men is akin to a preference for a brand of shoe, the T-shirts support the notion that wannabehood is merely a fashion statement. Printed on a baby-doll style designed for young women and not young men, the T-shirts presume heterosexuality. And by reducing identities to "love" for a particular kind of man, the T-shirts reduce young women's identities to spectatorship, emerging out of their relationships with men, and not out of their own interests, desires, or concerns. The T-shirt's simple declaration flattens out the complex race, class, and gender meanings that the spectacle of the wannabe puts into play. It is these meanings that are at the heart of the next chapter.

CHAPTER SIX

Why Don't They Act Like Who They Really Are?

The spectacle of racial boundary crossing embodied in one instance by the Puerto Rican wannabe fascinates journalists, academics, and the public.[1] A number of mainstream media productions testify to this fascination, including Hollywood blockbusters like *8 Mile* (2002) and *Save the Last Dance* (2001), which turn on the integration of individual whites into Black-dominated cultural and social worlds. A 2003 episode of *Girlfriends,* a sitcom based on the lives of four thirty-something Black women, explored the adoption of Black style (clothes, hair, food, and music) by a white woman with an adopted Black sister. In this episode, the Black wannabe was palatable until, singing along to a popular Jay-Z song, she used the word "nigga." This moment exposed the boundaries of acceptable racial identification: it's okay to appreciate Black culture, as long as you don't think you know what it's like to be oppressed.

Racial crossover isn't new. Instead, the U.S. has a long history of "non-white" people claiming whiteness through "passing," legal challenges to the definition of whiteness, and group adoption of white behavioral standards (Loewen 1971, Roediger 1991). But what is fascinating in the media spectacles and in the Puerto Rican wannabe is the white claim to Blackness and Puerto Ricanness. It might seem understandable to want to claim the material and status benefits of whiteness, but, to many, the desire to claim a lower-status racial identity is incomprehensible.

From the start, I also found the Puerto Rican wannabe fascinating, but for reasons that were a bit different. I was fascinated by her audacity,

---

1. See Roediger 2002 for a detailed discussion of media accounts of racial crossover.

her flamboyant clothes, and her "don't fuck with me" attitude. To me, the wannabe was exciting and intimidating. She seemed to have thrown out the rulebook of white middle-class girlhood. I wanted to be able to throw it away too. Although not unique, my reaction is uncommon: when I tell young people about my research, they chuckle knowingly, sharing a laugh over the wannabes' preposterous behavior. When I tell older adults about it, they look perplexed until I explain. Most people, I've learned, think wannabes are weird or ridiculous, and have no problem telling me why.

This chapter is about those explanations. To other youth, the wannabe is a spectacle. They deride and condemn her for violating everyday assumptions about the performance of race, class, and gender: "she doesn't act like who she really is," proclaim Black, Puerto Rican, and white youth— as if this statement explains everything. In response to these violations, youth defend their social order by castigating the wannabe; at the same time, their reactions make clear their expectations for race, class, and gender comportment. In telling stories about what *not to do,* youth tell stories about what *to* do. Stories about the wannabes reveal their own race, class, and gender assumptions, anxieties, and desires.

Interpretations of sexual behavior are critical to these stories, playing a central role in marking classed gender and racial boundaries. Seemingly contradictorily, the Puerto Rican wannabe defines *and* effaces racial boundaries through her sexual transgressions—her "preference" for interracial dating and her "inappropriate" sexual self-presentations. In turn, non-wannabes, both girls and boys, use the wannabe's sexual transgressions as a foil against which they make claims about their own class, race, and gender locations.

Performing race

The performance of racial identities is an ongoing, everyday process (West and Fenstermaker 1995). In addition to this everyday, often unthinking enactment of our racial identities, race is performed symbolically through ritual participation in ethnic celebrations or through the display of specific commodities (Gans 1979, Waters 1990). But unlike more mundane performances, the Puerto Rican wannabe's racial performance is treated as a spectacle and contested. The explanation for this, on the surface, is simple: the Puerto Rican wannabe's racial claim is challenged because she is not, in fact, Puerto Rican; she is a wannabe, and so she should act like "who she really is." This explanation assumes that race is fixed and knowable, and that it translates neatly into sets of behavior. It also glosses over the complexity of the racial criteria that the spectacle of the wannabe puts into play. In practice, racial boundaries are not static, but are malleable and mobile; youth throw them up strategically to block the wannabes' access to community membership. The criteria for authenticity are slippery, molded to accommodate the ends of the person employing the criteria. These criteria begin to expose what is at stake—for middle and working-class white, Black, and Puerto Rican youth—in this particular struggle over "real" Puerto Ricanness.

The mantra-like claim that wannabes are a problem because they aren't acting *white* crystallizes race as *the* problem with the wannabe. But, as my initial celebration of her reveals, the wannabe is a spectacle of failed middle-class girlhood as well as of racial transgression: she is so symbolically loaded because she violates understandings about appropriate gender and (middle-) classed behavior for white young *women*. The wannabe is tough, confrontational, and loud. She opts out of status competitions based on educational attainment and career goals. Most audaciously, she violates notions of "proper" white, middle-class feminine sexual conduct, claiming the "wrong" young men as her sexual partners but also displaying her sexuality flamboyantly.

The local icon of the Puerto Rican wannabe is a girl, but white boys can be wannabes too. Indeed, in the popular media, white boys as wannabes are the visible spectacles, while girls are invisible. And yet, for the youth in this area, the boy wannabe is not the problem. He may evoke chuckles, but he doesn't elicit anger, concern, or even much discussion. His sexuality never comes up. This polarity in youth reactions indicates the centrality of gender to the wannabes' violations. The "dangerous" or "illicit" behavior engaged in by wannabes is consistent with expectations for boys' comportment, even if it is draped in a cultural style associated with a different race.[2]

Youth alternatively imagine wannabes as fallen middle-class white girls or as poor white girls. As the next chapter will reveal, wannabes come from a range of class backgrounds. But imagined class in these stories

2. Carter (2005) also finds that young people associate "acting white" with femininity. She is concerned with the implications of this association for boys' school success. Here, I highlight the ways in which it makes the white girls in my study more vulnerable to charges of racial transgression.

matters as much as "real" class. Class is used to validate or invalidate the wannabes' claims to racial crossing and, in turn, to bolster each person's own claims to moral, intellectual, or cultural superiority. The white youth in this chapter inflexibly conflate class and race; to them, white youth are always middle-class. The youth of color, on the other hand, are more open to the possibility that wannabes come from various class locations, but assume that whiteness confers a set of invariable economic and educational privileges.

Youth culture and racial crossover

Youth and young adult spaces, while still segregated, more frequently provide opportunity for real cross-racial contact than older adult spaces. Even when such contact is limited, youth culture's emphasis on consumption and leisure allows for cross-group influence and experimentation (Hebdige 1979, Thornton 1996, Maira 2002, Roediger 2002). These spaces may be celebrated as sites in which meaningful cross-racial interactions can occur, fracturing hard boundaries between white and Black. Perry, for example, argues that cultural cross-pollination allows youth to create identities that are "multiple, ambiguous, and contradictory" (2002, 21).

The Puerto Rican wannabe, who mixes white heritage with hip-hop style, seems to be an ideal example of the flexibility and multiplicity of youth racial identities, but young people don't celebrate the wannabe as a symbol of racial hybridity; they denigrate her as a race traitor. That the wannabe is condemned by both white youth and youth of color suggests a universal interest in maintaining the integrity of bounded racial categories, but the wannabe activates different kinds of unease for white youth than she does for Black and Puerto Rican youth.

Moreover, although the name "Puerto Rican wannabe" suggests that she is crossing the white–Puerto Rican border, she embraces a hip-hop style that is coded locally as both Black and Puerto Rican. Thus, the Puerto Rican wannabe raises anxieties about both the white-Black border *and* the Puerto Rican–Black border. The white-Black border is especially contentious.[3] Pride about Black culture contributes to an environment in which Black youth may censure each other for "acting white"

---

3. Youth interest in Asian martial arts or Asian-influenced clothing, for example, does not elicit moral panic.

(Fordham 1996), while white people fear the infiltration of Blackness into white spaces. The popularity of hip-hop allows Blackness access to white suburban homes that had previously been insulated from nonwhiteness. For white youth whose parents associate Blackness with gang behavior, hip-hop provides a ready-made form of rebellion. As Kelley (1997, 39) points out, hip-hop music provides a way for whites to consume Black cool, to believe that they are part of the "adventure, unbridled violence, erotic fantasy, and/or . . . imaginary alternative to suburban boredom" of the ghetto, *and* simultaneously reduces Black people and ghetto life to violence and sex. Thus, whites are concerned that the breakdown of the white-Black border undermines their unqualified claim to race and class privileges, while Blacks are worried that white interest in Blackness is not only another example of cultural appropriation without structural costs, but one that feeds racial stereotypes.

The Black–Puerto Rican border is also contentious. Because mainland Puerto Ricans are concentrated in areas (like East Harlem) that have been associated with Blacks, and because they are structurally disadvantaged in ways that are similar to the disadvantages faced by American-born Blacks, they are the Latino/a group most likely to identify with Blackness, and to be stereotyped in similar ways (see Bourgois 1995, Moore and Pinderhughes 1993). Puerto Ricans have staked out some territory, albeit often marginalized, for themselves in hip-hop culture (Rivera 2001). Allegiance with Blackness is not embraced by all Puerto Ricans, however. Middle-class Puerto Ricans are more likely to resist this identification, exalting Spanish components of Puerto Rican culture as "authentic" and excluding aspects of Puerto Ricanness that are African or Indian (including hip-hop). Carter (2005, 121) found that Puerto Rican identities also vary by gender. The working-class Latinas in her study "created more social distance between African American urban youth culture and Latino cultures." The derisive label "Nu Yorican" condenses these tensions. The Nu Yorican label suggests inauthenticity, based on both poverty and a "too Black" performance of Puerto Ricanness (Bourgois 1995, Negrón-Muntaner 2004). Thus, debates over the Black–Puerto Rican border reflect issues of race, class, and gender.

Locally, the connections between Puerto Ricanness and Blackness are similarly complex. The Puerto Rican wannabes in this area are also sometimes called Black wannabes, indicating a connection to Black culture rather than to Puerto Rican culture. These cultures often (but not always) overlap, sharing different versions of hip-hop culture. Thus, the Puerto

Rican culture that the Puerto Rican wannabes adopt is more of a mainland urban, Nu Yorican, culture than an Island culture. That either racial
label may be assigned to the same wannabe, depending on who is doing
the labeling, illustrates the fluidity and ambiguity of the racial categories
local youth engage.[4]

The more commonly used Puerto Rican wannabe label imperfectly
maps class onto race. The increasing invisibility of economic hardship in
these gentrified college towns pushes low-income youth to look to the
broader community for both a model of low-income membership and validation of their relative poverty. In the larger area, Puerto Rican median
household income is well below that of both whites and Blacks. As such,
Puerto Ricans are the local symbol of poverty. Hence, interpretations of
Puerto Rican culture and low-income culture intertwine: to be Puerto Rican is to be poor, and to be poor is to be Puerto Rican.

Sexuality is central to the marking of individual and group racial
boundaries (Roediger 1991, Nagel 2003). In her study of the racial identities of girls with mixed-race parentage, Winddance Twine (1997) found
that, while consumption and residential patterns had initially allowed
these girls to successfully acquire white identities, the advent of adolescent dating negotiations challenged their white identities. Social and political allegiance is marked not just by the choice of sexual and romantic
partner but also by (perceived) adherence to standards of sexual comportment (Higginbotham 1993, Das Gupta 1997, Espiritu 2001, Nagel 2003).

The Puerto Rican wannabe challenges dominant performances of
whiteness. She is a spectacular symbol of the ways in which racial boundaries are being challenged in contemporary youth culture. And yet other
youth don't applaud, but deride the challenge she poses, exemplifying the
limits of a politics of racial crossover. These limitations outline the gender
and class contours in contemporary formulations of race, and demonstrate,
again, the ways in which sexuality is used to mark and remake gendered
and classed racial categories.

4. Carter (2005) finds that Latino youth are clear about the differences between "black
and Spanish cultural styles" (128). Carter's research takes place in a larger metropolitan area,
and so likely finds different patterns in the local racial order. But in this area as well, some
distinctions are made between Puerto Rican (also called Spanish by local youth of color)
and Black culture. The distinctions often emerge in larger communities. But even in these,
working-class and poor Blacks and Puerto Ricans tend to presume that they occupy a common place in the racial order. This presumption of political common ground is also true in
Carter's study. From the perspective of whites, there are often few distinctions.

The wannabe doesn't just challenge the sanctity of biological racial categories. She questions the assumed desirability of being white. In doing so, she brings whiteness into the spotlight, challenging both the norm of color blindness and the invisibility of whiteness. In addition, she makes visible anxieties about white consumption of Blackness and Puerto Ricanness, about the connection between race and class privilege, and about the roles of feminine sexual restraint and intraracial sexuality in defining racial superiority (for whites, Puerto Ricans, and Blacks). In the face of the wannabe's racial defection, young people reconsolidate—rather than expand—racial, class, and gender categories.

The people in this chapter

I began my study with an unfocused interview with Carrie, a white middle-class girl. It was in this interview that the concept of the wannabe emerged. I was fascinated both by Carrie's palpable and uncharacteristic contempt, and by the distinction she made between the behavior of the wannabes and my own relationship with a Puerto Rican man. My conversation with Carrie motivated me to explore the wannabes from a variety of perspectives. I hoped to interview young people occupying a range of race and class positions. However, the constant policing of race, class, and gender borders made the interviews difficult to arrange. My original contacts—the white middle-class youth whose social locations were most like mine—were eager to talk to me about Puerto Rican wannabes, but youth of color were reluctant to talk to me at all. To them, I learned, I was "that (white) lady." I was able to secure interviews when the initial contact was made through a Puerto Rican: my boyfriend or one of my friends. Once they established my legitimacy, I successfully attained trust and rapport with my informants; indeed, they were frequently delighted to educate me on their terminology (e.g., "kicking it") and their dating norms. Each interview generated at least one more contact.

At the time of the study, my informants ranged in age from fourteen-year-old ninth graders to twenty-two-year-olds. I conducted thirty formal interviews, but had dozens of informal conversations with these and other young people. Although I draw primarily on the formal interviews here, my understanding of the people and issues in this chapter is much more broadly based. Interviewees determined their own race/ethnic categorization. I determined class by parental occupation and residential location.

I designated class as "ambiguous" when class markers conflicted. For example, Mani's mother is low-income but his father and stepmother (with whom he lived for a number of years) are middle-class professionals (although not highly paid ones). It is ironic, of course, to designate race and class when I am arguing that these identities are unfixed, but I do so because the designation of these categories matters for how people understand themselves as well as how others understand them.

In this chapter, young people tell stories about the wannabes. The storytellers are students at two local high schools whose social scenes overlap. Occasionally, I also bring in the perspectives of recent graduates of these high schools. Although wannabes are a phenomenon of the high school, wannabes spill over into young adulthood as well. Indeed, one of the recurring concerns about wannabehood is that the birth of a "mixed" baby will make it permanent.

The wannabe was not interesting or important to every young person I talked with, but she was the subject of extreme and uncharacteristic scorn for most. This scorn varied in its content and emphasis. Youth with different race, class, and gender locations have different things at stake in the spectacle of the wannabe. The stories they tell reveal as much about the narrators as they do about the wannabes; as I will show in the next chapter, these stories often have little to do with the wannabes' actual lives.

I divide the stories thematically into five sections, beginning with the stories about the wannabe that I heard first—the ones told by middle-class white girls. These girls demonize the wannabes for their failure to live up to the expectations of white middle-class girlhood. But they also express concern for them, lamenting the putative "insecurity" that leads the wannabes to be victimized by Puerto Rican boys. These two storylines allow white middle-class girls to distinguish the wannabes' failed girlhood from their own successes. In the next section, I introduce the perspectives of white middle-class boys. Rather than differentiating themselves from the wannabes, these boys hope to "save them from themselves," reviving the notion that white men are the protectors of white womanhood.

I organize the youths of color's stories differently. I first combine the stories told by Puerto Rican and Black youth, both girls and boys, from mixed class backgrounds. These youth come from families with a range of economic and educational backgrounds, but their circumstances and futures are all much less certain than those of the white youth in the first two sections. These youth share a set of race and class concerns that come across most clearly if they are heard collectively. In the second half of the section, I discuss their distinctly gendered concerns.

The final two empirical sections of this chapter tell the stories of youth for whom the wannabe label is an ongoing threat. First, I tell the story of a Puerto Rican couple, Mariella and Jose, whose experiences illustrate the difficulties of negotiating a middle-class Puerto Rican identity, and the role of sexuality in policing racial authenticity. Mariella's middle-class performance deems her inauthentically Puerto Rican, and she is labeled a wannabe because of the mismatch between her class and race performances.

I end this chapter with a section on white working-class girls. Perhaps it seems logical to group these girls with the other white youth, but their experiences are shaped so distinctly by class that they have little in common with either the white middle-class girls or the white middle-class boys. Instead, the experiences of these girls foreshadow the stories told in the next chapter by young women identified as Puerto Rican wannabes. The line between these white working-class girls and the wannabes is blurry. Their experiences reverse Mariella's. Their stories expose the problems girls face in negotiating a white working-class identity in a context in which whiteness is presumed to be middle-class. Together, these accounts show the ways the wannabe label is used to police a range of girls for behaving in ways that don't line up with local expectations for race and class performances.

Sexuality is central in these accounts. Youth castigate the wannabe for claiming the wrong boys, for being too easy, too flamboyant, and too open about her sexuality. Her desire for Puerto Rican and Black young men disrupts assumptions of intraracial sexuality. Studies of racial attitudes indicate that while it is no longer as acceptable to voice blanket disapproval of interracial relationships, most white Americans continue to disapprove, particularly of relationships that cross the white-Black color line. This disapproval is cloaked, for example, through "concern for the children" (see Bonilla-Silva 2003). Wannabes not only cross the color line, but they flout it flamboyantly. But the sexual threat posed by the wannabe extends beyond her desire for Puerto Rican and Black boys and men. The perception of improper feminine sexual behavior also locates her in a race/class system that degrades women of color and poor/working-class women through images of hypersexuality or exoticism (Davis 1981, Hill Collins 1991).

White middle-class girls: "and then there's that other group of girls"

I sat cross-legged on Carrie's bedroom floor as she mapped out the social groups in her high school. Confident, poised, goal-oriented, and pretty in

an understated way, Carrie is everything a white middle-class girl is supposed to be. I liked her immediately. It was clear that the high school was
her turf; her descriptions were breezy, evincing a tolerance for the many
groups of people sharing her halls and classrooms. Until she introduced
the wannabes. "Well, and then there's that other group of girls," she said,
almost as an aside, as if they weren't important enough in the school's
social geography to warrant mentioning, and yet Carrie's voice dripped
with contempt as she indicted the wannabes for a variety of sins.

Carrie is typical of the girls in this section. White and upper-middle-class,
they live in large homes, do well in school, and plan to go to expensive,
prestigious colleges. They are what Harris (2004) calls "can-do girls." Coming of age at a time when they can take for granted many of the gains of
second wave feminism, they have been molded to be confident, competent,
independent, and ambitious. By performing class-coded Puerto Ricanness,
wannabes fail on all these fronts. They flagrantly reject the expectations
of white middle-class girlhood.

The white middle-class girls I talked with respond to the wannabes' un-
apologetic transgressions with a combination of anger and concern. Their
anger suggests that wannabes deliberately reject the behaviors of white
middle-class femininity. Their concern, in contrast, strips the wannabes
of agency, presenting them as insecure dupes exploited by their Puerto
Rican boyfriends. Often overtly antagonistic in their expressions, these
responses inscribe a boundary between these middle-class white girls
and the wannabes, reinforcing the normalcy and "goodness" of the non-
wannabe white girls and justifying their own choices.

White middle-class girls tell a tale of fallen white girls: Puerto Rican
wannabes, they explain, used to be like us (proper white middle-class girls)
and then they changed. Carrie says, "They become involved with a crowd
of Puerto Rican guys in high school and they take on attributes of that
culture." Now they're "loud and obnoxious"; they "yell obscene things."
"They act tough, yell a lot, and talk about getting in fights," says Courtney.
And Laura remarks, they're "too proud of their sexuality." Wannabes,
then, reject norms which expect that white middle-class girls won't make
scenes, get in fights, be vulgar or flashy, or make their sexuality visible.
Although these transgressions are also about gender and class (note that
each of these complaints could be read as annoying but acceptable behavior from boys), these girls attribute them to Puerto Ricanness.

Courtney says, "I've never seen a white girl date a Puerto Rican boy
and not be a Puerto Rican wannabe. But it depends on the boy. How

many Puerto Rican friends does he have? How Puerto Rican is he?" Court-ney's model allows for a range of Puerto Rican performances among boys of Puerto Rican heritage, but it seems to restrict girls' performances. Instead, she suggests, like the "I love Puerto Rican boys" T-shirt, that boys give girls their identities. But her comments, like Carrie's, also name race (Puerto Ricanness) as the wannabes' principal defection ("I've never seen a white girl date a Puerto Rican boy and not be a Puerto Rican wannabe"). Because so many of the wannabes' transgressions are about class, the centering of Puerto Ricanness both reveals and perpetuates the assumption of a cultural lockstep between race and class.

The intersection of race and class is again illustrated in Laura's de-tailed, biting portrait of the wannabes:

> Wannabes are so fucking annoying, loud, obnoxious, bitchy, always fighting—"oh, I'll kick your ass." They wear lots of hairspray, smoke Newports (a brand of cigarettes locally associated with people of color), big baggy clothes. They're always talking the Puerto Rican version of Ebonics with their friends. They hate school. They come across as academically ignorant because of the way they speak—not educated.

Laura sees wannabes as inexplicably rejecting the values of education and individual self-betterment she embraces. Her concerns are about class transgression, but Laura draws on racially coded symbols (Newports, Puerto Rican Ebonics) to exemplify her points.

"They make a point of acting like they hate their family or have no family," Laura adds, describing this "fuck-the-world attitude" as a front. She explains:

> Wannabes lov[e] the image . . . It seems like they want to forget what they really are. Maybe they do come from really good middle-American homes and don't like that because that's not dramatic enough or something.

In her accounts, the wannabes diverged from an otherwise uncluttered path to college and successful white womanhood. Because dissatisfaction with education and family are equally inconceivable to her, she uses them both as markers of the wannabes' inauthenticity ("it seems like they want to forget what they really are"). In her description, to be white is to be mid-dle-class, and to be middle-class is to be "good," stable, and achievement-oriented.

White middle-class girls criticize wannabes for a broad range of behaviors, but their most vehement critiques involve sex. Wannabes, they say, are too open about, and too interested in, sex. "Sex is a big part of their life, going to dances and openly grinding (explicitly sexualized dancing) on the floor with their friends," Laura says. They have sex with the wrong kind of guys: "older guys who appear to be drug dealers," Carrie notes. And they have sex for the wrong reasons. The wannabes' relationships are "sex relationships. It doesn't seem like they're friends," Courtney tells me, adding:

> Wannabes are seen as more sexual than other *white* girls. They're more open, they talk about it. They're proud, not necessarily more sexual. They seem like typical *boys*—sex is an accomplishment (emphases mine).

By describing the wannabes in terms of both race and gender transgression, Courtney makes explicit the intersecting race and gender contours of the wannabes' sexual deviance. Moreover, her comment suggests that the wannabes' sexual violations are as much about the perception of their sexuality and their (inappropriately "proud") attitude than it is about actual sexual behavior.

Laura adds another layer to the white middle-class girls' indictment, revealing again the class dimensions of the wannabe's sexuality:

> [Wannabes] seem so angry and pissed at the world, and "I'm cool because I have the ability to dress up like it's Halloween everyday with blue eyeliner and shit, and have unprotected sex with my boyfriend and risk pregnancy because I don't give a shit."

The problem is not just that wannabes proudly display their sexuality, and not just that their desires are directed at the wrong guys, but that the wannabes' sexuality could permanently sabotage class position via early pregnancy. As with her discussion of education and family, Laura attributes wannabes' (presumed) risky sexual behavior to their bad attitudes, to "not giving a shit." She assumes that wannabes have deliberately foreclosed their options, and that any choices other than the focused pursuit of academic success are wrong.

Biting comments like Laura's imply that wannabes deserve contempt because they deliberately violate the rules of white middle-class girlhood. But Laura, Carrie, and Courtney also portray the wannabes as victims.

Wannabes, they explain, are "insecure" and "lost," and "need something to fit into." Carrie says that wannabes aren't "grown up in any sense. It's just a way to get attention." Courtney comments, "It doesn't seem like they really know what they're doing." And Laura says, "wannabes get all their value from their relationships and boyfriends and big baggy clothes...not anything that matters....My friends and I have talked about it before," she adds, "and agree that it's sad." These comments appropriate popular feminist concerns that identify loss of self-esteem as a central problem of contemporary girlhood (e.g., Pipher 1994). Wannabes, this storyline goes, don't choose to defect, but instead are victims of sexually predatory and emotionally abusive Puerto Rican guys who take advantage of their insecurities. This rhetoric adds exploitation to the list of sexual distinctions: the wannabes' allegedly unequal relationships are further evidence of their failure to live up to the expectations of white middle-class girlhood.

Courtney describes the relationships like this:

> They get really involved.... Puerto Rican boys take them very seriously. They may cheat on them, but they're very possessive. They want the relationships to last. After a girl broke up with a boy, he came to her class. He didn't let her have any space. There's a lot of fighting and jealousy, getting mad at the girls for talking to other guys. The girls are possessions. It makes them feel wanted and loved. Girls get really wrapped up in it because the boys make them feel good about themselves. They're [Puerto Rican boys] expressive—more than white guys. They write letters. But they're not necessarily more truthful.

Courtney pins pop feminist rhetoric about adolescent girls to race, class, and gender stereotypes: Puerto Rican boys are the quintessential sexual predators, "choosing [wannabes] to become...like them." "The [Puerto Rican] boys are constructing these girls to be what they want them to be and to do the things they want them to do." "They want to have them under control." They isolate them: wannabes "stop hanging out with [their] friends." They exploit them: their boyfriends keep "side girls they talk to, cheat with." In turn, wannabes "have sex with them just to make them happy." "Puerto Rican boys don't want to have safe sex ever," Courtney adds, "two girls got pregnant and had abortions." The Puerto Rican boys further derail wannabes, who are "not the smart, goal-oriented girls" to begin with, from a proper middle-class future by engaging them in "really weird, unrealistic, naive plans" (marriage and kids, but not college).

Courtney's long, detailed narrative seems sympathetic to the wannabes, but it relies on a string of racialized assumptions about Puerto Rican boys while assuming that wannabes have no agency or desires of their own. As a result, Courtney suggests that not only are the wannabes inauthentic, but so are the heterosexual relationships in which they engage. By delegitimizing the relationships established between Puerto Rican boys and white girls, these assumptions further normalize intraracial relationships.

This narrative strategy is useful. First, it comes across as concern rather than contempt, and is thus less morally threatening to white middle-class femininity. Moreover, the proliferation of media dealing with these issues has authorized this storyline as an acceptable axis of intrusion into girls' lives. This storyline, moreover, speaks to white middle-class girls so powerfully because they have been raised on its assumptions—girls should be all they can be, should focus on school instead of boys and clothes, and so forth. Second, although these girls' concerns are clearly about race (Puerto Rican boys are the threat, after all), their stories *seem* to be about other issues: interracial relationships would be okay *if* they weren't overly intense and exploitative.[5] Third, this strategy reestablishes white boys as the proper romantic and sexual partners of mature, secure white girls.

Finally, and perhaps most importantly, the braid these girls weave displaces the threat of sexual victimization onto the wannabes. By alternatively seeing the wannabes as sexual deviants and as victims of a particular (race, class, and age coded) kind of man, these girls draw a net of safety around themselves: it won't happen to us because we know better. As Carrie smugly remarks, "The girls I know wouldn't take crap from their boyfriends. They voice their own opinions."[6] They combine liberal feminist precepts of adolescent girls' self-actualization with traditional understandings of white middle-class girls' sexual restraint to position themselves as morally and politically superior and as sexually safer.

These girls depend on racist tropes of Puerto Rican femininity and masculinity to make sense of the wannabes' behavior and to give emotional weight to their concerns. But they want to see themselves as colorblind (as Laura says, they "hate how ['good' white girls like them] get

5. Bonilla-Silva (2003) argues that a central feature of "color-blind" discourse is rhetorical displacements like the one these girls use. He found, for example, that white people often expressed approval for interracial relationships, but followed them up with a list of concerns that belied their approval.

6. Note how similar this language is to the language of sexual self-actualization used by goth women.

sucked into stereotyping") and as nice girls. They resolve the dilemma posed by their intolerance by pushing responsibility back onto the wannabes.

"Wannabes," Laura complains,

> are taking the stereotype of Puerto Ricans and making it something they want to be. They're trying to be something they're not.... They seem so ignorant about what it means to be Puerto Rican, what the group really is.... People like that make it hard because they glorify these stereotypes by dressing up like that, and that makes me even more mad.

By constructing themselves in opposition to the wannabes, these girls situate themselves as "together," authentic white girls making individual "choices." Indeed, in a historical period characterized by widespread unemployment, increasing poverty, rising numbers of single-parent families, and the persistence of gender discrimination, it is perhaps important for these girls to see themselves as psychologically advantaged, as emerging strong and intact from the minefield of female adolescence, as making the right choices, as having the self-esteem and integrity required for career and financial success. At the same time, this construction veils both the race and class advantages that allow them to see themselves as authentic individuals and the future limitations to individual success they are likely to experience as women. Moreover, it perpetuates a narrow vision of proper sexual conduct for girls.

As "can-do girls," the girls in this section have faith in the promise of individual self-betterment. They believe that they can and should be all that they can be, and direct their energies at taking advantage of the institutionally sanctioned opportunities that previous generations of girls have been denied. But while their senses of competence and entitlement (Orr 1997) can be lauded as feminist victories, they can also be used as a means of further invalidating the paths of young women with fewer opportunities. As Bettie (2003) argues, "When prep girls are considered not in the context of boys of their own class and racial/ethnic location, but in the context of both boys and girls outside it, their demeanor becomes difficult to celebrate" (111).

White middle-class boys: "saving them from themselves"

The white middle-class boys I spoke with eschew the term Puerto Rican wannabe. They tell me it's "stupid" and "juvenile." At first, this dismissal seems to reflect a lack of investment in the construction of white middle-class femininity violated by Puerto Rican wannabes. But because traditional white femininity supports white men's exclusive access to white women, these boys do have a stake in its maintenance.

White middle-class girls indicted the wannabes for their failure to live up to the expectations of feminine competence, confidence, independence, and sexual restraint. But white middle-class boys weave together much more contradictory narratives. They portray wannabehood as a means by which white girls can exercise control and power in their own lives, and yet contend that wannabes are "insecure" and "confused about who they are." They suggest that wannabes "play" their Puerto Rican boyfriends, "using them for what they can get," yet they also blame those same boyfriends for leading wannabes into the "gangster lifestyle"—for introducing them to fast cars, drugs, and fighting. They are perplexed that anyone would "choose a lower status," expressing concern about the wannabes' class trajectories, and yet scoff at the wannabes and at Puerto Rican youth for claiming economic hardship that white middle-class boys say doesn't exist.

The boys in this section are attractive, college-bound, and reasonably socially successful. They come across as warm, friendly, and engaging. They are the kind of boys white middle-class girls are "supposed" to date, the kind that (most) parents like instantly. To me, they speak highly of their female friends and their girlfriends. They are the kinds of boys who have been raised to not only be color-blind but also to provide (at least verbal) support of girls and their accomplishments. Like the white middle-class girls, they use a discourse of concern to talk about the wannabes, but they sound much more tolerant and much less angry. Because these boys sidestep intolerance, it is easy to read their words and see these boys as the concerned heroes they paint themselves to be. Yet, like the white middle-class girls, they draw on widespread anxieties about race, class, and gender. Moreover, their narratives about the wannabes not only seek control over the white-girls-gone-astray, but also redefine proper white girlhood as passive and subordinate.

Although the white middle-class girls saw no reasons why a girl would want to be a wannabe, the white middle-class boys provide a litany of explanations. Both Eric and Bryan contend that the rejection of white middle-class femininity via the wannabe persona allows white middle-class girls to engage in a range of fun and interesting behaviors and to act on desires that were previously off limits to them. They also suggest that wannabehood provides girls with a source of power they didn't have as non-wannabe white girls; Eric explains that the transformation to wannabehood is about "wanting to be in control." After becoming wannabes, he says, girls "get more confidence" and "can tell people to fuck off."

Bryan suggests other gains as well. "It's pretty tedious being in high school right now," Bryan explains. In comparison to the "boring," "repetitive" routine of high school (which he codes "white"), the Puerto Rican "lifestyle" is glittery and hip: Puerto Ricans have "different connections, a different lifestyle...loud systems in their cars, lots of gold. It's attractive, you know, and if *I weren't secure* I'd probably find the coolest people...and be with them" (emphasis mine). In addition, becoming a wannabe alters people's expectations:

> In a sense you want to be a minority because they're treated so much different than whites. They're expected to do poorly in school, be obnoxious, problematic. White kids want that image that they could do poorly in school and if they happened to not do poorly they'd be looked at higher, like they'd achieved more.

Bryan equates Puerto Ricanness with poor academic performance and misbehavior, suggesting that claiming a nonwhite identity gives white youth license to sidestep expectations of high achievement and institutional obedience. Finally, Bryan sees Puerto Rican wannabehood as sexually liberating for white girls:

> If you're a guy and you get with many girls, you're the man. If you're a girl and get with anyone but your boyfriend, you're a slut. If you're a wannabe, you're not a slut. It's almost like you're a man. You can be with anyone. If I was a girl, I'd be jealous of wannabes...getting to sleep with lots of guys and not be called a slut. (He later contradicts himself, however, by noting that wannabes *are* called sluts.)...If I were a girl, I'd be a quote "slut" too and I wouldn't give a shit either.

In these stories, wannabehood not only provides girls with more sexual options but also gives them access to different sorts of relationships. Eric suggests that wannabes find their relationships with Puerto Rican boys more emotionally satisfying than relationships with white boys, even if the relationships also involve "fooling around" with other people. In his version, both members of the couple "cheat," and so neither the girl nor the boy is clearly victim or victimizer. "The relationships," he says, "are heavily emotional. There's a lot more riding on it. He treats you really well, drowns you in affection." Bryan also interprets wannabes as gaining from their relationships with Puerto Rican boys: "I've noticed that a lot of Puerto Rican wannabes play the guys, get what they want from them."

Although these boys draw on some of the same relationship dynamics cited by the white middle-class girls, their interpretations are different. White middle-class boys don't portray the wannabes as victims of Puerto Rican boys, but rather as sexual agents, seeking out satisfying and empowering relationships. This interpretation buffers the threat wannabes could pose to white boys' masculinity by suggesting that, although some white girls have chosen Puerto Rican boys over white boys, the Puerto Rican boys are not in a position of power in their relationships with wannabes. This interpretation paints the wannabes' cross-racial project as a means by which white girls can gain interpersonal control.

And yet white middle-class boys interweave these powerful portrayals with concern that wannabes need to be "saved from themselves." The boys' redemption tales are both general and specific, sometimes detailing their own interventions in the lives of particular wannabes. The same boys who suggest that wannabehood can be a way of gaining "confidence" justify their interventions through the narrative of "insecurity" used by the white middle-class girls. When a girl becomes a wannabe, Eric says, it's a "cry for help" that indicates her confusion over her identity. By changing the "way [she] speaks, thinks, and acts," he adds, wannabes "disrespect themselves." Similarly, Bryan explains the attraction of wannabehood to girls by saying, "In my school girls are not as secure as the guys. They're always looking for a different fad, a different group." People who are "secure," like he is, resist the appeal of the Puerto Rican "lifestyle." And Mark says, "I think they like to come off as being a bitch. They seem like they're just putting on this act. They all seem like pretty nice girls who just got caught up in the wrong crowd." On the one hand, then, these boys ascribe toughness, control, and confidence to wannabes and, on the other hand, dismiss these qualities as either inauthentic ("an act") or a "cry for help."

In response, these boys attempt to save them. Bryan unsuccessfully tried to save Kim, who he describes as "the biggest Puerto Rican wannabe in [the high] school." Kim "was the whitest white girl...rich as hell, nice cashmere clothes, almost a dork." According to his story, she's now living with her Puerto Rican boyfriend, seven months pregnant, dealing cocaine and marijuana, and "has about one thousand dollars worth of gold on her body." Kim's style shift crystallizes the symbolism of clothes. While both cashmere clothes and gold jewelry demonstrate consumption, cashmere clothes are associated with "taste" and restraint (both sexual, because cashmere is unrevealing, and financial, because cashmere is a "quality" investment) while the gold jewelry is linked to the stereotypically flashy, unwise spending of the poor. Giving up cashmere in favor of gold symbolizes Kim's rejection of her parent's money, the rejection of their cultural capital, and the rejection of white male approval.

But Bryan is attracted to Kim, despite (or because of) her flagrant racial violations. He first cheated on his ex-girlfriend with her and then went on a personal crusade "to get her back" while she was hospitalized after an illegal abortion. "I thought we had something," he tells me, "but she didn't want to come back."

Although Bryan's crusade was unsuccessful, Mark successfully redeemed his girlfriend Julie from wannabehood. Mark gives Julie credit for her own transformation, but his presence as her (white) boyfriend is clearly the crowning symbol of that change: "Her parents are happy that she's dating me. She's always had weird boyfriends." (Remember that those "weird" boyfriends were not white.) Mark has had a chance to get to know some of Julie's old friends, and he "totally thinks of them differently now," not as Puerto Rican wannabes like he used to. Nevertheless, he still sees Julie's old wannabe lifestyle as trouble:

> She (Julie) was considered as bad—you know, she snuck out of her house to go to [a roller skating rink]. . . . She knew she was headed in the wrong direction and hanging out in the wrong crowd. She was still getting A's so it wasn't totally ruining her life.

These boys tell their stories of attempted and successful redemption with earnest and compassion. It is easy, for example, to hear Bryan's story and be alarmed for Kim. But we need to constantly remind ourselves that these stories, while they likely contain some truths, are constructions. For example, when I asked Mark about Kim, he described her as "quiet and smart." He said, "She actually seems like she knows what's going on (meaning she 'has her head on straight'), but since she's pregnant maybe she doesn't." His comment doesn't necessarily negate Bryan's concern, but it does suggest that Kim's persona and life are more complex than in Bryan's portrayal.

Moreover, Eric's comments suggest that, at least for some white middle-class boys, the desire to "save" the wannabes is motivated by more than the desire to protect them. Eric begins with the now familiar refrain of adolescent distress:

> Girls who used to be run-of-the-mill, clean, become wannabes. People know there's something wrong. She wants things. Normally people don't put themselves in a worse-off position and that's what they're doing.

He expresses particular alarm that the wannabes are "warping their style" and "who they are" to "attract a certain kind of guy," a kind of guy he sees as an unsuitable partner for these girls because of his presumed involvement in the "gangster lifestyle" of drug dealing, stealing, and fighting. In this story, the girls pick up the "gangster" toughness from the boys. In these ways, his comments resonate with Bryan's story about Kim. But he goes on:

> Some guys think they can be revolutionary; they're out to break the girl, break some secret code or some such shit. Guys see an attraction in that (knowing there's something wrong). Guys have a puzzle to unwrap, he can analyze that girl, can be her savior.

He admits to desiring "tough girls" himself when they show "they have a weakness in them." By weaving together two seemingly incompatible ideas—"saving" wannabes and "breaking" them—Eric suggests a less altruistic motivation for the boys' interest. His story pulls together two sets of transgression: the wannabes' desire for the wrong kind of guy, and her nonpassive comportment. "Saving" them solves both a race and a gender problem: it brings wannabes back into the fold of whiteness by realigning them with white boys *and* refeminizes them by "breaking" them of their "tough," "bitch[y]" desire for "control." "Saving" wannabes is both a race and a gender project.

These stories are also about class. Indeed, these boys conflate class and race. Both Eric and Bryan are perplexed by what they see as the choice of a lesser status. "If you're Puerto Rican," Bryan says, "you're already on a lower [level], not only to teachers but to peers." Bryan was perplexed about my relationship with Carlos (most of the youth saw my relationship as distinct from those of the wannabes). He wanted to know why I would consciously lower my status by dating a Puerto Rican man, and his question fit with his other concerns. For Bryan and for Eric, it's not simply that white girls are dating Puerto Ricans or acting like Puerto Ricans, it's that *middle-class* white girls, "kids who grew up in good households," are giving up that privilege to "become like gangsters." The label "gangster," used by both Eric and Mark, highlights both the collapse of class into race, and the ways in which identities take on meanings in specific contexts. The original gangsters, Eric tells me, were Italian: the defining characteristic is thus not a specific ethnicity, but rather participation in a criminalesque lifestyle associated with a (lower-) classed ethnic group.

Rather than seeing the Puerto Ricans and the Puerto Rican wannabes as authentic "gangsters," Mark sees them all as wanting to be lower-class when they're not. He doesn't call them "Lower Class wannabes," but that's his point: "Kids in our school want to create these gangs, show they're a lot worse off than they are—growing up in the ghetto but there's no ghetto around here." Because [the town] is not New York or even a smaller nearby city, Mark suggests, *real* poverty and deprivation don't exist. Without a perceived legitimate class basis for "gangster" behavior, Mark sees both Puerto Ricans and Puerto Rican wannabes as inauthentic. The "gangsters" are easily dismissed as just the "wrong crowd," and their academic alienation dismissed as a result of their faulty choices. The real difficulties youth growing up in low-income housing face become mere friendship and behavior choices.

These boys' comments assume that white youth, regardless of economic circumstance or gender, have equal access to the privilege of whiteness. At the same time, they claim that the wannabes' behavior leads to the loss of class status. In particular, their savior stance suggests that girls' white middle-class privilege is contingent on the protection of a white boy, and that the boys' own privilege includes a proprietary interest in the sexuality of white girls. By passing up white boys in favor of Puerto Rican boys, Puerto Rican wannabes upset a conventional hierarchy that provides white boys and men, as a group, with unlimited access to white girls and women. The denial of this right crumbles part of the foundation of white masculinity. Thus, their position both allows and encourages them to "save [the wannabes] from themselves." By providing protection, they reassert their authority over the white-girls-gone-astray.

Like the white girls, these white boys justify their unsolicited protection through the language of pop psychology, interweaving it with a romantic hero discourse that signals the persistence of racial and gender hierarchies. They both desire the exotic and dangerous wannabes and they want to tame them. The wannabes offer the boys a chance to reassert their gender and racial dominance as protectors. More, the wannabes provide a way to reassert control over the behavior of "normal" white middle-class girls, to mark behavior that is too assertive or too sexually in control as nonnormative, and thus to maintain the importance of feminine passivity for all girls.

Youth of color: "Don't think just because you know Spanish you're already Puerto Rican"

> You always see like Puerto Ricans and Blacks chillin', you know what I'm saying? I'm not trying to be racial so don't take it seriously, okay? But you always see like white girls on one side of the thing, you know what I'm saying. Like most Black and Puerto Rican people don't like white people, you know? But we like most of them, you know what I'm saying? And so they try to act like Black or Puerto Rican people. They just trying to fit in, you know what I'm saying?—*Claudia, low-income, Puerto Rican ninth-grader*

This is what Claudia and her friend Imani, a low-income Black ninth-grader, say is going on: Puerto Rican and Black people are cool. White people are not. White girls hope that by hanging out with Puerto Rican and Black people, they'll be a little bit cool too. They speak Spanish, mimic clothing and hairstyles, try to act tough—all to try to fit in. But it doesn't work. They try too hard and it backfires on them. Imani explains:

> They're trying to be down and it's just like they try to be around you so much that it irritates you. Cause, it's just not them. For them to be Puerto Rican, you know what I'm saying? You can be friends but for them to try so hard, it's just not working for them because they're taking it too far.

Claudia complains most vehemently about Candy, who has nicknamed herself "Miss Puertorriqueña," and Tina, who insists on speaking Spanish even when Claudia initiates a conversation in English:

> She was like getting on my nerves all the time ... I'm all the time talking to her in English and she would just bust out talking to me in Spanish and things like that and she just started getting too much into my business and I was just like, yo, I need to push this to the side, so she got kicked to the side.

Similarly, Nia, a low-income self-identified "brown" tenth-grader, is disgusted with white girls who tout symbols of Puerto Rican or Black pride (e.g., wearing a Puerto Rican flag): "Why are you trying to be down with a culture that's not yours?"

Puerto Rican and Black boys sound like the girls of color. According to Rafi, a Puerto Rican, wannabes are "people with no identity who want to adapt something they think is cool." Wannabes may think they're "down," but listening to hip-hop, smoking "blunts" (marijuana rolled in cigar wrappers), and drinking "forties" (forty-ounce cans of malt liquor marketed to and associated with poor Blacks) doesn't make them any less white. So, Rafi rhetorically asks, "Why don't you act like who you really are?"

The youth in this section are less easy to characterize than the white youth in the previous sections. Some are Puerto Rican, others are Black. Nia's mother is white. They occupy a range of class locations, although are more likely to be poor than affluent. Some live in public housing; some are headed to college. Nevertheless, as racial minorities in a predominantly white and affluent area, they share identities as "people of color," aligning their political interests with each other. Many have white friends or white mentors—all must interact daily with white people as peers and institutional authorities. They each invoke Puerto Ricanness and/or Blackness as important to who they are and experience race as contested cultural and political terrain.

The emotional power of their stories comes from their shared assumption that race is inborn. Their message is clear: you cannot become Puerto Rican just by trying. Race is deeper than exterior cultural signs. "Don't just think because you know Spanish you're already Puerto Rican," Claudia warns. Yet they dismiss wannabes on both biological and cultural grounds—both for not acting white and for performing Puerto Ricanness inadequately.

Claudia and Imani tell me that wannabes don't have friends because they're "fake" and "because they don't act right." "If you was born, I'm just saying, if she wants to fit in, she can just be herself, you don't have to try to be somebody that you ain't," says Claudia. It's not the behavior itself that makes them unlikable, but rather the inconsistency between their perceived biological race (white) and their enacted culture (Puerto Rican). Wannabes, Rafi explains, are so invested in their "hard-ass" image that they always have "something to prove." "If you're Puerto Rican then pretty much people expect that you're going to act like that," but if you are white and you "act like that," you are "fake." He goes on:

> [Wannabes think that by] acting Puerto Rican ... they can pretty much just look
> down on people.... More of an attitude you know they never had and they

somehow fucking changed and they think they're bad and they want to fight. *Because she's white and she acts like that, people look down on her. That's the only reason* (emphasis mine).

But while Rafi trivializes the wannabes' toughness because he sees it as racially inauthentic, other youth of color scoff at the wannabes' passivity. Claudia laughs:

> [Tina] got beat up by a Puerto Rican and she let the girl beat her up and Puerto Ricans don't let nobody just beat them up.... And then everybody was like, if you're so Puerto Rican, how come you didn't show your Puerto Rican when you needed to beat somebody up?

She similarly mocks Candy's unwillingness to verbally spar with her:

> Like, okay, she says she's Puerto Rican, okay? But us Puerto Ricans, we don't shut up by nobody, you know what I'm saying? You dis us, we'll dis you right back and things like that. With [Candy], she'll stay quiet.

Nia, too, contends that the wannabes aren't "as hard [tough] as they think they are." And Shamar, who's Black, explains that when he gets in fights, "minority girls jump in and help; white girls pull you out." In these accounts, wannabes are invalidated as fake both because they're tough when white girls shouldn't be and because they're not really as tough as Puerto Rican girls. Wannabes are both insufficiently white and insufficiently Puerto Rican.

The wannabes' behavior is more than inauthentic: it is also embarrassing. "They're like a disgrace to [Puerto Rican] culture or something," Nia comments. And Hadley (Black) complains, "They're acting all ghetto. They're not acting like us and participating in the mainstream lifestyle. And it gives the connotation that being Puerto Rican is being ghetto." Rafi adds, "It's fucked up because it gives us a bad image." By flaunting behaviors associated with the urban poor and calling them Puerto Rican, the wannabes perpetuate images of people of color from which these youth would like to be distanced.

Nia's indictment of Christine, a wannabe, illustrates this problem:

> She's always been a little Betty Boop or something.... Then she started sleeping around with all these guys. She thought she was pregnant this year. Her voice is so annoying. [I] don't look at her when she's talking—speaking Ebon-

ics and stuff. All ghetto. . . . I hate her walk—it's nasty. She sticks her chest out, holds her hands out, and she has an attitude on her face, like she's all tough or something. And she's from [our town]. That's the part that makes me mad.

Christine's rejection of both the physical presentation and restrained sexuality associated with middle-class white femininity is coded as Puerto Rican or Black because of her appropriation of Ebonics, her "attitude," and the way she holds her body. Nia differentiates her own brownness from Christine's "ghetto" attitude and flamboyant sexuality. Her disgust and anger stem, in part, from her recognition that the racial marking of Christine's performance limits her own ability to create a respectable identity as a low-income brown girl.

Nia is also irritated by Christine's appropriation of what she sees as a false class-consciousness. She extends this critique to local Puerto Rican and Black youth as well. "They think we're in New York—straight out of the ghetto. They don't face reality, [and] try to pick fights with people." But while her comment may recall Mark's, her distinct social location imbues them with different meaning. Nia herself has grown up with a single mother in subsidized housing: by distinguishing local poverty from New York poverty, she again distances herself from the stigma of the ghetto poor. She is consequently ambivalent about the toughness that Claudia sees as essential to Puerto Ricanness. Recall that despite her assertion that her town is not New York, and that youth of color should "face reality" rather than fight, she scoffs at the wannabes for "not being as hard" (tough) as they think they are. Nia preserves her claim to coolness, but at the same time seeks to resuscitate brownness from its association with "low-class, ghetto" behavior.

Underlying these accounts is anxiety about the meaning of both Puerto Ricanness and Blackness. The symbol of Black and Puerto Rican pride they most frequently invoke is "coolness." The more relaxed attitude associated with "chillin'" and the mass popularity of Black and Puerto Rican cultural forms allow these youth to think of themselves as more interesting, as more desirable, or as having more fun than white youth. In the absence of traditional routes to socioeconomic success, coolness provides both an alternative definition of success and a point of racial pride around which solidarity can be built. Coolness is thus both a psychological and a political resource.

Like most resources, coolness is only valuable if it is scarce. These youth thus defend its borders, defining coolness as exclusively, even inherently, Puerto Rican and Black. To maintain the boundaries of coolness, girls and boys of color struggle with the meaning of race, concurrently invoking biological and cultural definitions. This struggle is most visible in the tension between race and class, as they sometimes contest the association of Puerto Ricans and Blacks with "ghetto" behavior, while they also frequently use "ghetto" behavior as a symbol of Puerto Rican and Black ethnicity. These complicated formulations reflect a more widespread anxiety about personal and collective strategies for success. Variously recognizing the constraints on their opportunities, these youth develop multiple alliances, pushing for solidarity while sometimes seeking status through individual and collective differentiation. They thus employ "strategic... essentialism" (Danius and Jonsson 1993) to claim the distinctiveness and exclusivity of their cultural space while they also make room for their own exceptionality (and thus, chances of individual upward mobility) by challenging the biological bases of race.

The association of coolness with race, and the behaviors associated with coolness, situate it as a resource at odds with the opportunities that come with the privilege of white skin and middle-class aspirations (hence, Nia's difficulty negotiating her position on toughness). Wannabes are seen as sacrificing white privilege in favor of Puerto Rican coolness. This trade is degrading because it implies that Puerto Ricans and Blacks devalue ambition and traditional socioeconomic success, disparaging the efforts of those Puerto Ricans and Blacks who seek upward mobility through these channels. "Basically what they're doing is limiting themselves because as whites they have opportunities; by being cool, they're limiting them," Hadley explains. On the other hand, Aiysha, a Black woman who just graduated from the local high school, suggests that for white youth, the loss of privilege is only temporary: "Like it was cool while we were in high school, but once we started filling out college applications... [they] knew they could rely on mommy and daddy's money."

Wannabes bring issues of coolness and mobility center stage, uniting Puerto Ricans and Blacks, girls and boys, in their concerns about the effects of white participation in their cultural spaces. But wannabes do more than just consume Puerto Rican and Black culture, they also claim Puerto Rican and Black boys. They thus threaten the racial unity between girls and boys of color. Unsurprisingly, girls and boys of color respond to her sexuality differently.

For the girls of color, stories about the wannabes' improper sexual behavior are the chief medium through which they express both derision and embarrassment. Nia, in particular, castigates the wannabes as sluts: "You hear all the rumors and you know they're true because you see all the hickeys and stuff.... Guys talk about all the things she's done with them— willingly.... They wear all these hoochie mama (slutty) things.... They're just walking down with their five kids and their attitude—makes them look low class, like trash.... I see someone and I know they're just struggling to be anything but white. Like they have a kid with a Black guy or something. It's just gross."[7]

Like Nia, Claudia and Imani use sexual behavior to draw a boundary between themselves and the wannabes. Together, they describe Tina's transgressions:

i: She talks to a lot of guys.

c: But she's not really going out with them. It's like kicking it with a guy but he hasn't asked you out yet.... If she's too easy, then the girl's a fool. Tina—she's a fool.

i: She talks to boys. She kicks it with them. She'll be talking to one boy and just messing with him and stuff, and then the next week she'll be talking to someone else.

c: That's what makes people talk junk about her, cause they'll just be like, "Oh, look at her, she has a different man every day of the week" or something, so they'll just call her a fool or whatever. All the boys want her for is just for that, you know.

Even though Tina "kicks it" with Puerto Rican or Black boys, Claudia and Imani reduce her heterosexual threat by invalidating her as a "fool" who's just being used by Puerto Rican and Black boys. In this case, Tina's sexuality is dismissed as an ill-informed and unsuccessful attempt to behave *Puerto Rican* (thus, reinforcing her whiteness).

Sometimes they claim wannabes have too much power. Claudia explains condescendingly:

Like [Candy] has this boyfriend, he's Spanish, Puerto Rican whatever. He's like twenty. She's like thirteen. And like she's getting married to him or whatever. She has an engagement ring, and she just tries to be down. She tries to be a player like most Puerto Ricans are players, I know I ain't, but most of them are or whatever, and she's just like trying to be playing them or whatever. Like she played him. She's engaged to him and she went off with somebody else.

---

7. Adding to the complexity of these boundaries is the irony that Nia's own mother is a white woman who had a child with a Black man.

Claudia can't dismiss Candy's relationship on the same grounds as she does Tina's, because her boyfriend has given her an engagement ring. Indeed, according to Claudia, Candy is the one using him "to be down." In this story, Candy's race situates her as a predatory victimizer, rather than as a victim, as is likely in other interpretations of the seven-year age gap between her and her fiancé, and was common in the stories told by the white middle-class girls.[8] Her efforts "to be down" fail because of her disingenuousness in her relationship—she "played him." In this story, Candy's Puerto Rican behavior (acting like "a player") undermines the possibility that her relationship will provide her with membership. What is never said here, but is implied, is that Candy failed because, in "playing" her boyfriend, she acted like a Puerto Rican boy and not like a Puerto Rican girl.[9]

In these stories, Imani, Claudia, and Nia all draw lines between themselves and wannabes. This line maintains the salience of race (constructed both biologically and culturally) to identity and thus the hegemony of Puerto Ricans and Blacks in their own circumscribed (but popular and appropriated) cultural space. At the same time, this line allows the girls to construct themselves as both "good" and "smart" in opposition to the gender transgressions of wannabes. Tina's a "fool," who gets "used" because she's too easy. Candy "tries to be a player" but Claudia "ain't."

Unlike wannabes, Imani and Claudia play the game right; they both capitalize on whatever their ("authentic") race can provide them with ("coolness," racial pride) and maintain whatever gendered power they can within their social network (by not "kicking it" without a commitment so they don't get "used," for example). Nia also claims authenticity by distinguishing herself from the false pride ("attitude") and "hoochie" behavior of wannabes and (more ambivalently) from the fake "ghetto" preoccupations of other youth of color. These girls of color, then, both concretely and symbolically reject the wannabes' attempts at solidarity.

The boys share the girls' contempt over the wannabes' perceived unrestrained sexuality. However, unlike the girls, who are often in sexual competition with the wannabes, many of the boys establish sexual and/or romantic relationships with them. Rather than establishing alliances with

8. This interpretation is similar to the white boys' versions.

9. Note that Claudia describes "most Puerto Ricans" as players, but differentiates herself. Her language suggests that normative Puerto Ricanness is defined in terms of Puerto Rican boys.

wannabes, the boys say that they have sex with them because they're "easy." Possibly, this strategy compensates for their (presumed) betrayal of Puerto Rican and Black girls. They thus preserve their solidarity with girls of color and their sexual access to wannabes.

These boys portray wannabes as a sexual opportunity to be exploited but not taken seriously. "People say they're easy," Rafi tells me,

> And they [Puerto Rican and Black boys] can get away with a lot more stuff, like fucking around. [White girls] are more naive than other girls. They usually put up with a lot more stuff. People call them suckers half the time.

By claiming that wannabes offer easy sexual access without commitment, boys of color can gain status in their own social networks. Teddy, a Black boy, laughingly told me that he and his (Black) friends can tell a "white girl who digs Black guys just by looking at her." At first, he refused to specify any particular characteristics that might lead to this interpretation. Finally, he described the caricature of the wannabe. For Teddy, his ability to "read" white girls' desires for Black guys was a victory, a means of keeping score. Status accrued from his perception of her desire for Black guys in general, not from his own physical sexual conquests. Mani, Puerto Rican, explained that sex with Puerto Rican girls was a bigger deal for Puerto Rican boys because it compromised the girls' purity and ensnared them in obligatory relationships. In contrast, sex with wannabes (or just their sexual desire, as Teddy's comment suggests) provides the boys with a chance to prove their masculinity (interpreted as virility and promiscuity) without tarnishing Puerto Rican or Black girls.

The appeal of this possibility rests on, perpetuates, and reconstructs a double double-standard. First, the equation of masculinity with sexual prowess and femininity with sexual restraint makes the boys' sexual conquests status-producing in the first place. It also provides the impetus to preserve the sexual "virtue" of Puerto Rican and Black girls. These behaviors then reinvigorate the sexual line that divides "proper" boys from "proper" girls. The second double standard (bad girls "do" and good girls "don't") bolsters and is bolstered by the drive to keep girls of color pure. But, by having sex with wannabes instead, the boys of color also invert the racial hierarchy that is inscribed on the Madonna/whore dichotomy. Historically, white men have sexually abused women of color. This practice additionally served as a bodily reminder of racial subordination, and simultaneously justified that subordination by constructing women of color as sexually other and white women as sexually pure. By using wannabes as disposable, exploitable sexual objects, boys of color turn white girls into whores, inverting this historical pattern. This inversion, however, is not equivalent, because wannabes have agency in their sexual liaisons in a way that slave women, for example, did not. Blackness and Puerto Ricanness triumph over whiteness, but at the cost of maintaining a gender hierarchy that positions men over women and good women over bad women. To participate in this racial triumph, then, girls of color must buy into the value of their own sexual restraint.

Dismissing the wannabes as fake and untrustworthy justifies their exploitation. For example, Rafi tells me, "I would never trust a girl like that at all. They're so fake; you never know what's going to come in that bag of chips." It also maintains the symbolic transposition of the hierarchy between (white) wannabes and girls of color, whose (perhaps similar) behavior is read as racially consistent and thus not fake, leaving solidarity between boys and girls of color at least partially intact. It is important to remember that this chapter deals with the construction of meaning, not with actual behavior. Thus, I am not arguing here that boys of color actually treat girls of color in a nonexploitative fashion or treat wannabes in an exploitative fashion, only that they portray them as being both sexually and racially different from the wannabes.

At the same time, this formulation leaves little room for a boy of color to take a wannabe seriously if he wants to. Hadley's jokes about Rafi's wannabe ex-girlfriends make salient this limitation.[10] The policing of this norm both limits the wannabes' ability to claim Puerto Ricanness through interracial dating and illustrates the strength of their threat.

Finally, although the story of the wannabe as "sucker" was a dominant theme in the stories told by boys of color, it was interspersed by references to a color-blind ideal in which, in Rafi's words, "It shouldn't matter who you date anyway." Boys of color offered this ideal as an antidote to stories in which relationships with white girls were sanctioned by Black and Puerto Rican girls. For example, Rafi says, "I get a hard time from Black girls [who say] 'you shouldn't date white girls.'" And Shamar tells me a story about being insulted by Black girls in the mall when he was there with a white girl. These stories suggest that portraying wannabes as "easy" and as "suckers" can also be a script that these boys use to au-

---

10. Since I conducted this research, Rafi began dating and ultimately married a white (non-wannabe) woman. They are currently expecting their first child.

thorize their relationships with white girls. The appeal to color blindness, though, only buries the significant issues of gendered racial solidarity that drive the Black (and Puerto Rican) girls' concerns.

Mariella and Jose: "I can speak Spanish ten times better than them"

The stories told by Mariella and Jose, a tenth-grade Puerto Rican couple, further reveal the ways in which racial allegiance can be challenged by behavior associated with the middle class or with the desire for upward class mobility (e.g., Fordham 1996). The experiences of Mariella and Jose further demonstrate two key points. First, the Puerto Rican identity that wannabes put into play is *as much* about class as it is about race. And second, this race-class identity is centrally maintained through sexual allegiance.

When Jose started dating Mariella in the second semester of ninth grade, Ricardo, one of Jose's friends in the "popular clique," was angry. Ricardo told Jose that Mariella (whose mother is Puerto Rican and father is Spanish) was lying about being Puerto Rican: "[Mariella] doesn't represent herself as Puerto Rican because she doesn't look like one, talk like one, act like one, or hang out with Puerto Ricans." Because Ricardo thought Mariella was inauthentically Puerto Rican, and because Mariella was dating Jose, Ricardo accused her of being a Puerto Rican wannabe. He called her a bitch. He made her cry. Girls in the "popular clique" hid Mariella's shoes in gym class. Jose's friends ostracized him.

Mariella's self-presentation and behavior do not match local youth assumptions about Puerto Rican identity. "Being Puerto Rican at [her high school]," she complains, "is a superficial thing based on how you dress, wear your hair, the people you talk to, how you talk. It's not cultural." Mariella is not accepted as Puerto Rican, she says, because she doesn't dress right or have dark enough skin or hang out with the cool Puerto Rican kids or "have a little attitude about [being Puerto Rican]."

Perhaps most importantly, Mariella comes from an academic family and is herself academically successful. Taking academically advanced classes separates Mariella spatially from other Puerto Rican students. "Divisions [in the high school] are based on intelligence," she explains, "this sort of ties into race" (see Fordham 1996, Bettie 2003). These divisions aren't just made by students; they're also made by teachers and

administrators, and Mariella finds the stereotypes insulting. "Just because
you're a minority doesn't mean you get bad grades…I think it has a lot
to do with people's economic status. If you go to Puerto Rico, there's a
lot of good, educated people." Mariella recognizes that behavior that is
identified as racial can be rooted in class differences:

> I think [the label] "Puerto Rican wannabe" is really sad and ridiculous. I think
> a lot of times they're [Puerto Rican wannabes] tough because they have to be.
> They grow up in tough neighborhoods and learn to deal with things that way.

To Mariella, the behavior described as Puerto Rican is really lower-class
behavior, and thus also natural for white people. In her formulation,
wannabehood is a phenomenon of class; she differentiates herself from
wannabes not by using the category of authentic Puerto Ricanness but by
using class categories: wannabes grow up in "tough (i.e., poor) neighborhoods."

Mariella endeavors both to assert Puerto Rican ethnicity and to distance herself from aspects of the Puerto Rican cliques that threaten her
current middle-class trajectory. Real Puerto Ricanness, she says, is about
culture. She boasts, "I can speak Spanish ten times better than them."
Language is "real" culture; style is not. Whether she is aware of it or not,
Mariella's distinction reflects a larger ideological debate over what constitutes "real" Puerto Rican culture: state-sanctioned Hispanic culture, or
an African-Indian-Hispanic hybrid. This debate cuts across class lines (so
that Hispanic culture reflects the interests of the middle class against the
interests of the poor/working class) on the Island and between (authentic) Island Puerto Ricans and (inauthentic) Nu Yorican (see Lao 1997;
Negrón-Muntaner 1997; Rivera 2001). Thus, the "cool" Puerto Rican kids
are performing an inauthentic Puerto Ricanness in the absence of a real
connection to the culture of the Island. Middle-class Puerto Ricans—
"good, educated people"—are the authentic carriers of Puerto Rican culture. Mariella thus establishes racial solidarity with Puerto Ricans that she
doesn't have with other local Puerto Rican youth.

Like Mariella, Jose is academically successful, but his success came despite serious economic and family obstacles. He does not share Mariella's
solidly middle-class position. Nevertheless, Jose also seeks to embody
middle-class behavior, behavior he understands to be a necessary step toward eventually claiming middle-class status. Labeled "the good Puerto
Rican" by adults in the school, he is considered an exceptional Puerto

Rican by others and by himself. "I'm not like other Puerto Ricans," he tells me, "I don't do drugs."

Jose's distancing behavior, however, is complicated by his clear sense of allegiance—not just to middle-class Puerto Ricans, but to low-income Puerto Ricans as well. He is articulate about the ways in which individual and collective experiences of racism (on the streets, in schools, in athletic leagues) reinforce his commitment to other people of color. "People complain how we [white students and students of color] don't hang out together, but it's kinda obvious why. If you were in our situation, you'd do the same thing." Although he invokes racial stereotypes himself, he is outraged over the "good Puerto Rican" label, which he understands assumes that "Puerto Ricans are . . . troublemakers and unsuccessful in everything we do."

Jose is stuck. To access the upward mobility he so badly wants, he has to distance himself from the community with which he shares experiences of racial oppression. Winddance Twine's (1997) research similarly ties middle-class membership to "racial neutrality" underpinned by an individual, rather than collective, orientation. "It's a choice to take advanced classes," Jose tells me, reflecting this individualistic perspective, "I disagree with the NAACP decision" (that school tracking is discriminatory). As he experiences academic success, an investment in meritocracy vies with his experience of collective racial oppression. Mariella's lack of understanding for (and trivialization of) her friend's "little attitude about being Puerto Rican" also suggests that middle-class membership should be accompanied by a restrained racial pride, rather than an "attitude."

Both Jose and Mariella forge their own racial identities against a classed construction of Puerto Ricanness. Seen as racially neutral, as white, and thus as not Puerto Rican, Mariella asserts a middle-class Puerto Rican identity. Because Mariella's (white) phenotype discourages inquiries into her racial background, though, her exercise of (middle-class) Puerto Ricanness is akin to the symbolic ethnicity practiced by European-descent Americans in Water's (1990) study. Mariella's claim to Puerto Ricanness may work to redefine what it means to be Puerto Rican, but it may also melt into racial invisibility. Jose, on the other hand, is exceptionalized by both himself and others as he fights to negotiate his relationship to a low-income Puerto Rican culture that he fears will derail him from his quest for upward mobility.

Mariella's and Jose's struggles are exacerbated and brought into bold relief by their dating relationship. Mariella's middle-class behavior did not provoke harassment until she started dating Jose. Her romantic involvement with a Puerto Rican boy signaled her claim to a Puerto Rican identity that wasn't previously apparent. Dating Jose upset her prior social location as a racially neutral, middle-class girl—marking her racial behavior as transgressive. Ricardo highlights this destabilization by calling Mariella a *Puerto Rican* wannabe. Because he really thinks Mariella is an inappropriate girlfriend for Jose because she isn't Puerto Rican *enough* (and she doesn't display the correct class performance), it would seem to make more sense to call her a *white* wannabe (a name sometimes given to Black and Puerto Rican "Valley Girls"). His use of the converse label emphasizes the centrality of Mariella's dating choice to her perceived racial claim.

Jose's commitment to Mariella, on the other hand, facilitates his middle-class aspirations, but it violates the notion that relationships with "white" girls (wannabes) shouldn't be taken too seriously, that white girls are to be exploited, not treated with respect. It is the seriousness of the relationship, and its romantic rather than sexual emphasis, that results in his harassment, rather than giving him status as a "stud." Jose seems genuinely fond of Mariella, but dating her also has tangible benefits: the educational opportunities and cultural capital her family provides him, as well as the academic credibility at their shared high school that her companionship extends to him. These benefits come with the cost of peer sanctions. The form and severity of the Puerto Rican response to the couple's relationship indicate its reception as a community betrayal. Because middle-classness is defined as white, his alliance with the middle class, cemented by his dating relationship with Mariella, forces Jose to privilege (white coded) middle-class behaviors over (Puerto Rican coded) working-class behaviors.

White working-class girls

Laughing, Lacey, a white working-class eleventh-grader, tells me, "Everybody's a Puerto Rican wannabe at one point. I was in eight grade, or seventh grade." But even though she sees wannabehood as a common "phase," she explains, "Some people don't grow out of it. They end up getting pregnant by a Puerto Rican guy or something and then they don't grow out of it." Jocelyn, a poor white ninth-grader, laughs too, "Puerto Rican wannabes? My brother always calls me that. I went through this stage where I was talking like Puerto Ricans."

White poor and working-class girls like Lacey and Jocelyn have a different relationship to Puerto Rican wannabes than do the other youth in this chapter. Because class is a central component of wannabehood, the class circumstances of these girls, including residential patterns and academic tracking, mean that they are more likely than white middle-class girls to have sustained relationships with girls identified as wannabes and with youth of color. Sometimes their interactions with wannabes are friendly, but they may also involve conflict. Wannabes "fight people," and so Jocelyn avoids the second floor by the stairs where the wannabes hang out. Sadie, a tenth-grader, reports being "jumped by white girls who were Puerto Rican wannabes."

For the white working-class girls I spoke with, identity management entails an ongoing dance with wannabehood. Although they may have to fight them, they are also likely to be identified as wannabes themselves. To try to sidestep this label, they engage in ongoing border work. Their experiences indicate the slipperiness of the wannabe label as well as its usefulness in disciplining girls for their violation of race, class, and gender norms. But they also indicate the difficulty of racial identity negotiations for white working-class girls in a context in which whiteness is defined as middle-class, working-classness is defined as Puerto Rican or Black, and racial identities are assumed to be biological.

For Lacey, the allure of Puerto Ricanness is not inexplicable, as it was for the white middle-class girls. Instead, it is an ongoing seduction, one she must constantly navigate in her own life. "I don't even know why white people want to be Puerto Rican," she tells me, but then she provides a list of possible reasons. First, Puerto Rican girls are heterosexually desirable. "I think girls want to be Puerto Rican because Puerto Rican girls are accepted. I mean, no guys don't like them. White guys, Black guys, Puerto Rican guys—they all like Puerto Rican girls." Second, wannabes get a lot of attention. "Maybe they act Puerto Rican just because they need attention. They're getting it. Yeah, either you're being hated on or liked." Third, whiteness doesn't provide a salient cultural identity: "You don't see too many Black people trying to be Puerto Rican. It's one of those pride things, I guess. Like you'll see Puerto Rican pride and Black pride but you don't see white pride. So I guess they want to have something to take pride in."

Wannabehood provides a solution to the invisibility and cultural nothingness of whiteness. Like the youth of color I spoke with, Lacey acknowledges that Puerto Ricans are seen as more interesting, more desirable, and more culture-ful than are white (working-class) youth. But wannabehood is a solution with significant social costs. Sadie tells me, "Well, they're not like real friends because Puerto Rican friends they have will talk shit about them but not to their faces. Because girls will try to do anything to please them. Make them steal for them—I've seen that. Friends, but not real friends." And Jocelyn says, "The homeys backstab the Puerto Rican wannabes—hang with them but talk about them behind their backs: 'They're trying to be like us, they're so stupid, they're nothing like us.'" Given the (presumed) exploitative character of wannabe relationships with youth of color, then, wannabehood does not seem like a good model for the pursuit of socially successful interracial relationships.

The challenge for these white working-class girls, then, is to establish a non-wannabe identity in racially mixed social networks (when thinking about this challenge remember that Carrie, the white middle-class girl, said she'd never seen a white girl date a Puerto Rican boy and not be a wannabe). For white middle-class girls, in contrast, Puerto Ricans and Blacks, with a few "token" exceptions, are so distant socially that their relationships to them are almost always symbolic. This social distance, in turn, allows the white middle-class girls to perform racial tolerance, because the tolerance is almost always abstract and rarely based on concrete interactions. For white working-class girls, these identity negotiations are far more complex. Shared class backgrounds means that white working-class girls and working-class/poor youth of color are likely to have common cultural frames. White working-class girls are unlikely to adopt the preppy look of the white middle-class girls (who Jocelyn calls "the Snot Squad"), and, among working-class/poor youth, it becomes difficult to tease out the line between "white" and "Puerto Rican" or "Black" fashion. As Lacey's brother told me, "Girls dress pretty much the same." Hence, working-class girls rely on more precise stylistic differences.

White working-class girls etch careful, nuanced distinctions to make it "clear," in Sadie's words, "who is and who isn't." For example, although she's dating a Puerto Rican boy and "hangs out with Puerto Ricans all the time," Sadie explains that she isn't a wannabe. "I don't have a Puerto Rican accent. I don't dress the way they do. I don't try to do my hair." To my eye, which has become better trained through my fieldwork than the eyes of most adults, but probably fails to see many of the nuances identified by her peers, Sadie's presentation of self, especially her carefully coiffed hair, are consistent with the wannabe look. But Sadie explains that her style is "white":

White girls act totally different. All I mean, how it's put … White people wear Abercrombie and Fitch, preppy clothes. Puerto Rican people usually wear more revealing clothing. Just like a stereotype. I don't wear Abercrombie and Fitch, but people say I dress white, I dress trendy. You've been to Rave and Deb … Puerto Rican girls wear bright colors, hoochie clothes. White people dress more conservatively, that's all.

Even though Sadie suggests that there is a clear distinction between "white" clothes and "Puerto Rican" clothes, she struggles to describe it, at first identifying white clothes in terms of the styles worn by white middle-class girls (Abercrombie and Fitch), but which are out of her economic reach. She never directly depicts her own style, instead describing it primarily in terms of what it is not: it's not Abercrombie and Fitch but it's also not revealing or "hoochie," like the clothes Puerto Rican girls wear. By locating herself in between, she claims a space for a white identity that is respectable ("more conservative") without being boring ("trendy").[11]

Lacey further illustrates the difficulties in distinguishing wannabe performances from the behavior of other white working-class girls:

Like Puerto Rican girls line their lips with black makeup but when white girls do it, it's just not cool. Everybody wants curly hair, everybody wants dark skin. They talk too, they talk weird. They try to get that accent in their voice. It's really annoying. You're not Puerto Rican. Stop talking like that. You can't just be born like that. It can rub off, though … when you're around them [Puerto Rican people], you start saying "yo" more. But it's not cool when white people start speaking Spanish. I mean you can learn it and stuff but when you start doing the "mira" thing.[12] They start to lie about it and stuff, like I'm half now. You'll meet their parents and they'll be like I'm Irish and he's French.

In this comment, Lacey provides a list of specific behaviors that aren't "cool" when adopted by white people, but she intersects that list with nods to the fuzziness of the boundary around racial crossover. It's not cool to wear dark lip liner, but everybody wants to look Puerto Rican. It's

---

11. Although she relies on sexualized images of Puerto Rican girls, Sadie's description is not angry or contemptuous, as the descriptions made by other youth were—a point I will return to.

12. Mira, which means "to look at" in Spanish, is often a loud and visible means of calling someone over, at least among local Puerto Ricans, and its use in this way is thus a symbol of Puerto Rican membership.

not cool to use Puerto Rican phrases or speak with an accent in ways that imply you're a cultural insider, but it's easy to fall into that habit if you hang out with Puerto Ricans.

In Lacey's comment, the detail that turns white girls into wannabes is their claim to Puerto Rican heritage. Sadie and Jocelyn both make the same point. "And somewhere along the line [wannabes] have some cousin or some relation to someone that's Puerto Rican" (Sadie). "Karen thinks she's Puerto Rican. Her mother was gay and her lover was Puerto Rican or Mexican or something" (Jocelyn). The middle-class youth I spoke with didn't make these comments; they focused exclusively on wannabes' cultural claims to Puerto Ricanness. It is likely that this difference reflects working-class girls' greater proximity to wannabes. But for these girls, shifting the focus from style to claims about ethnic heritage also makes sense. If the criteria for wannabehood centers on style, these girls are always at risk of being called wannabes. Defining wannabehood as a claim to biological and not just cultural membership better protects them from having the label applied to them as well. This strategy allows them to define white behavior to include participation in hip-hop culture as long as it doesn't also include a claim to nonwhite heritage.

In these descriptions, sexuality is not a primary indicator of wannabehood. This is a striking absence, given the stories told by all of the other youth in this chapter. Although Sadie called upon the image of the Puerto Rican "hoochie" to distinguish her clothes, she refuses to condemn the wannabes for their sexual behavior: "They're not sluts. I've known some for awhile. They're not slutty." Perhaps white working-class girls are more generous in their interpretations than are other youth, but I think it's more likely that they understand the slipperiness of the "slut" label. Condemning wannabes as sluts opens the door for scrutiny of their own behaviors—which include dating Puerto Rican boys.

As Tanenbaum (1999) documents, the slut label can be used to stigmatize girls for a wide variety of behavioral transgressions, including ones that have nothing to do with sex, and girls whose class or racial status deviates from the white middle-class norm are the ones most likely to be subject to the label. Jocelyn's experiences exemplify this. In a matter-of-fact tone, Jocelyn tells me:

> A lot of people don't like me in that school. I have a reputation, a bad one... there are rumors. Last year everyone thought I gave this guy a blow job and I didn't. The guy made it up. When he came into the cafeteria, all the guys stood

up and cheered for him.... I had a slutty personality. I'd flirt a lot and giggle in school. I had a boyfriend for two years. We didn't really do anything. It's the way other people see you. People call me a slut down the hallway. On the first day of school, all these guys grabbed my ass.

In Jocelyn's story, as in the stories told by many girls in Tanenbaum's study, she is labeled a slut after an incident of heterosexual victimization and the label, in turn, justified further victimization. What is striking about Jocelyn's story is that she expresses no outrage, but rather accepts her identification as a slut ("I had a slutty personality"),[13] and attempts to solve the problem by altering her own behavior. The result, she explains, is that "people think I'm gay now. People torture me.... They say I'm gay because I don't like guys. I don't have a boyfriend." Jocelyn has also been called a Puerto Rican wannabe. Her experiences suggest that the labels "slut," "gay," or "wannabe" can be used somewhat interchangeably to stigmatize a girl for her class outsidership. These labels call on different gender and race norms to ostracize Jocelyn, but they are united in their use of sexual deviance as the form of transgression. Stigmatized as a slut, Jocelyn had only one friend—a Black working-class girl—and that friendship fell apart over time because, as her friend explained to me, she was afraid that Jocelyn's reputation would rub off on her too.

Although white working-class girls are savvy identity navigators, the complexity of race, class, and gender rules mean that their strategies are vulnerable. Sadie seems to be the most successful at negotiating a middle ground but she has been jumped by girls she identifies as wannabes, and she "almost got into a fight—again. In gym. Not a Puerto Rican girl. A Black girl." Sadie explains that although she tried to keep her relationship with the Puerto Rican boy quiet, the relationship angered the girl who tried to pick the fight. Thus, Sadie's identity and the interracial relationships she attempts to forge do not go unchallenged.

For Lacey, interracial relationships have created other sorts of problems.

I used to only like Puerto Rican guys. I don't know why. I just thought they were cuter or something. Or I thought white guys didn't like me or something.

13. Jocelyn's self-labeling as slutty is distinct from the sexually proactive strategies used by goth women, because she voices shame over the label, rather than embracing it as a point of pride or empowerment.

It all depends on what you look like or dress like. Like if you're preppy, white
guys will like you or you have a bigger chance of white guys liking you.

Lacey's comment, although vague, acknowledges a heterosexual market
in which feminine desirability is attached to class performance. White
guys like the preppy girls. But Puerto Rican girls pose competition with
the Puerto Rican guys. "I like white guys now. Because Puerto Rican guys
are trash. They're not worth it. All they do is cheat on you—with a Puerto
Rican girl." Lacey attempts to navigate a heterosexual market in which
white working-class femininity does not seem to hold much value. She appropriates notions of an essential racial self to make sense of her decision
to gamble on white guys instead of Puerto Rican guys. "You can act like
yourself when you're with your own kind," she says, but adds that "white
guys...it seems like they care more." Lacey draws on the same racialized
assumptions as the white middle-class girls to explain her preference for
white boys (that white boys treat white girls better than do Puerto Rican
boys). Unfortunately, this gamble hasn't paid off for her. A few months
after this conversation, Lacey dropped out of high school and moved in
with a twenty-something white man in the next state. Although I have not
seen her since this happened, her family and friends have all expressed
concern to me about Lacey's relationship.

The white working class is often stereotyped and dismissed as "racist"
by color-blind middle-class whites. In contrast, Bonilla-Silva (2003) spec-
ulates that, among white people, working-class women are the most likely
to be racially progressive. He argues that the combination of shared experiences of "class vulnerability" and "social debasement," along with more
frequent experiences of meaningful cross-racial contact, facilitate the development of racially progressive attitudes among white working-class
women. The experiences of the girls in this section point to some of the
difficulties faced by white working-class girls as they try to navigate identities in cross-racial social networks. For these girls, the policing of racial
boundaries through the caricature of the wannabe requires that they
maintain a distinctive whiteness, and yet the conflation of class with race
makes it difficult for these girls to articulate a *white* working-class identity.

These girls map out different solutions to this problem, including
Lacey's invocation of language that suggests a "white superiority" perspective. For example, she tells me, "I have this friend who's half Puerto
Rican and she'd rather be white than Puerto Rican. She wasn't like that
freshman year but now she's got a white boyfriend. She probably realized
it's nothing to brag about." Another time, she says,

We should have a Caucasian festival. Because they have Puerto Rican festivals.
It would probably be called Ku Klux Klan festival or something. I told my history teacher that. She said everyday is a Caucasian festival. I don't really get that.

Lacey's race talk is jarring. It violates norms of tolerance and color-blind-
ness to which middle-class youth carefully adhere. And yet Lacey calls
upon the "psychological wages of whiteness" (Roediger 1991) in an effort
to regain dignity in a social setting in which she is failing. More, her use of
the rhetoric of white superiority solidifies her distinction from wannabehood, a distinction that is perhaps particularly important given the humiliation she experienced in her relationships with Puerto Rican boys.
Lacey's desire for a "Caucasian festival" is a stock symbol of white blindness to racial inequality, and yet its dismissal by Lacey's teacher (with
what is also a stock liberal response) seems truly bewildering to Lacey,
adding to her feelings of being beleaguered. While educated whites can
easily dismiss a "Caucasian festival" as ridiculous and racist, for Lacey,
racial pride, however inchoate, is the primary wage that whiteness pays.
Unfortunately, her use of whiteness blinds her to the inequities in her
relationships with white men.

Conclusion

The ways in which young people respond to the wannabe reveal both
the fragility and the resilience of their everyday understandings of race,
class, and gender. The wannabe is the subject of such scorn because she
violates those understandings—her violation both exposes assumptions
they would prefer remain unspoken *and* requires those assumptions to be
reworked to make sense of the wannabe. She is thus both an upset and
an opportunity: by sanctioning the wannabe, youth are also able to clarify
the rules for each other. These rules impose some limits on boys (e.g.,
that boys of color shouldn't take white girls seriously), but police girls'
behavior much more thoroughly.

Young people use the wannabe label to control each other in two ways.
First, by articulating what is wrong with the wannabe, they delineate their
expectations for each other. For example, the white middle-class boys'
rhetoric about the wannabes made clear that they expected that white
middle-class girls shouldn't be *too* confident. Second, the wannabe label can be used as a threat, much like the slut label, tossed at anyone
who violates behavioral expectations (as with Mariella and with the white

working-class girls). The use of this label underscores the importance of both class and gender to behavioral assumptions.

In contrast to what other studies have found (e.g., Perry 2002), then, boys in this study are able to engage in cross-racial friendships with fewer costs. The taken-for-grantedness of cross-racial friendships came up among all of the boys I spoke with, including among white working-class boys (who I chose not to include in this chapter). This is not to say that cross-racial friendships indicate some racial utopia, but rather that boys seem to experience fewer sanctions for their cross-racial friendships than do girls (of all racial backgrounds) for whom the threat of sexual impropriety is always looming. Boys' identities may also be more likely to be taken at face value because of the notion—common across race and gender groups—that girls are more likely to be insecure. This rhetoric invalidates wannabes' identity performances which can be dismissed as misguided cries for help, and validates the identity performances of other youth.

There is much at stake in these negotiations over racial membership. In the case of the Puerto Rican wannabe, the salience of racial language makes race the category of acknowledged negotiation. But the explicit transgression of racial categories does not mean that they are the only ones at stake. Indeed, profound class anxiety pervades the youth's stories but is displaced onto race; outrage over racial violations almost always expresses alarm about what the wannabe's strategy means for long-term class mobility.

Gender operates differently from either race or class. The wannabe manipulates her gender performance as a means of crossing racial boundaries. White youth and youth of color use her performance and its interpretations to shuffle raced femininities. However, this shuffling of gender meanings operates within an unacknowledged (and thus unchallenged) system of dichotomous, heterosexual gender identities, and thus reinforces gender boundaries. Moreover, even the struggles over gender meanings involve differently racialized girls laying claim to conventional notions of privileged femininity, rather than challenges to femininity's narrow and restrictive definition.[14] Among these youth, sexual restraint is the primary criterion for evaluating feminine performance.

14. Das Gupta (1997), Espiritu (2001), and Nagel (2003) all similarly discuss the centrality of restrained feminine sexuality to define ethnic group membership against the unrestrained feminine sexuality of the other.

In *Gender Trouble,* Butler (1990) theorizes that cross-gender performances destabilize dichotomous gender categories by exposing the performativity of gender. Like the drag queen, the Puerto Rican wannabe exposes the performativity of categories through her spectacle. As Butler's argument suggests, her performance destabilizes racial categories, adding elasticity to their boundaries and molding their content. Here, however, it is racial categories that are most clearly being destabilized. But even while the wannabes' performance challenges the clear alignment of assigned race with cultural performance, other youth interpret her performance in ways that realign them. Moreover, they use their interpretations to fortify hierarchical gender categories.

CHAPTER SEVEN

The Gendered Limits of Racial Crossover

The caricature of the wannabe elaborated in the last chapter suggests that she is a clear, knowable type—that one could walk down the street and easily pick out a wannabe, just as one can pick out a goth. I wondered why I hadn't noticed them before, and realized that part of the reason is that wannabes are often not immediately evident to outsiders. Wannabes sometimes look like "authentic" Puerto Rican young women; their style and comportment are racially ambiguous, distinguishable only to insiders. But I did, in fact, start to notice wannabes more as I became aware of them as a social type. I saw them at indoor playgrounds, gossiping with each other while their children played. I saw them at basketball games and at weddings. I saw them at clubs.

My initial observations suggested that wannabes are often successful at crossing racial borders, but the more I learned about the wannabes, the more I realized that "success" couldn't be distilled to a single moment. Instead, "success" was always in flux, contingent, insecure. The difference depended not only on the particulars of the performance but also on what was at stake in each interaction. But more, I came to realize that the question of success, as measured by the ability to "pass" or to be accepted as a legitimate, authentic member of a cross-racial community, only scratched the surface of the dynamics the wannabe puts into play.

In addition, focusing too much on cross-*racial* success distracted me from what else was going on. As I argued in the last chapter, cross-racial performances are not just about race. To her audiences, the wannabe's racial inauthenticity—her failure to "act like who she really is"—exposes a range of anxieties about not just race but also gender and class, but for the wannabe herself, racial crossover is a means of managing the limitations of gender and class.

White youth have long been fascinated with Blackness (Mailer 1959, Hebdige 1979), as Roediger's (2002) interpretation of Fiedler's observation that "white American males spend their early years as imaginary Indians and their teens as imaginary Blacks before settling into a white adulthood" reminds us (227). Fiedler's comment is informative on a number of levels. First, it suggests that wannabes are a contemporary example of a longstanding cultural relationship between whites and nonwhite "others." Wannabes, then, might be shocking, but the historical continuity between their behavior and the behavior of previous generations of white boys dispels any notion of racial radicalism. Second, Fiedler postulates a life course trajectory in which youthful cultural experiments don't impact adult structural positions: cross-racial play, he suggests, is just that—play. Third, invoking "white American males" locates this kind of racial experimentation as boy play, not girl play.

Puerto Rican wannabes differ from the "white American males" of Fiedler's observation in two significant ways: they are young women, and they are cut off from the middle class. Both differences complicate the structural safety implied in Fiedler's comment. As with other unconventional identities, white boys and men have greater freedom to, and incur fewer costs for, cross-racial experiments than white girls and women (Roediger 2002, Wald 1996). As these suggest, the gender and class contours of wannabes' racial transgressions make the implications of cross-racial experimentation much more complex.

Wannabes, race, class, and gender

Consciously or not, wannabes manipulate contemporary race reconfigurations to solve a variety of problems. They do this by inhabiting an identity labeled "wannabe" and marked as racially transgressive. Importantly, wannabehood is situational; it draws on the local racial order for its meanings. Here, the label is usually specified as *Puerto Rican,* but the women are also sometimes called *Black* wannabes. In the geographical area in which these women live, there is significant (but not complete) overlap between the two populations, particularly within the context of hip-hop culture. The more common *Puerto Rican* label does not imply a particular affinity to Puerto Rican culture over Black culture. The draw is hip-hop culture, and Puerto Ricanness is the more accessible entrance (both in terms of phenotypic considerations and in terms of relationship commitments). For the women in this chapter, it often seems that Blackness is the more desired category. For example, all but one of these women considered or chose names for their children that evoked Black, rather than Latino/a, naming patterns, even though the children all had Latino paternity. This implied privileging of Blackness is consistent with the greater status of Blackness within hip-hop in general (Rivera 2001).

As Puerto Rican wannabes, these women explicitly challenge the boundaries of whiteness. But the challenges enacted by wannabehood are also classed and gendered. Wannabehood gives these women an inhabitable, if stereotyped and degraded, persona in which to experiment with behaviors off-limits to good white middle-class girls and women. Breines (1992) argues that young white women in the fifties were able to violate restrictions on white feminine comportment through sexual liaisons with Black men. For the women in this chapter, wannabehood not only opens up access to taboo sexual desires and behaviors, it also provides experiences of toughness, courage, and coolness. The perception of racial transgression, then, masks the degree to which the wannabes are also gender transgressors. Wannabes, however, do not all interpret or enact their gender performances in the same ways.

The relationship between class and wannabehood is more complex yet. Because race and class, in practice, are read as "isomorphic," class behavior is often interpreted as race behavior (Ortner 1998). The equation of race with class pervades the wannabes' stories, but not in consistent ways. Importantly, and perhaps predictably, the project of racial transgression does not involve an attempt to cross into the Black or Puerto Rican middle classes, but into *working-class or poor* Black and Puerto Rican communities. For women without middle-class cultural capital, wannabehood provides a behavioral and identity alternative to the "white trash" label. But some wannabes grew up in the middle class, and abdicate middle-class resources in favor of working-class or poor Blackness/Puerto Ricanness. Moreover, class is more nuanced than these two patterns suggest. More finely carved class distinctions allow us to see more textured status hierarchies, including differential concern for and access to respectability. The differences in wannabes' attempted class negotiations expose the status impact of sex with Black and Latino working-class or poor men; regardless of other elements of their race/class performances, none of these women is able to fully achieve respectability from the perspective of outsiders.

Wannabes are caricatured and often ridiculed by outsiders, but these women are not simply dupes, cultural frauds, or women who are "insecure" with who they "really are." They are women who are constrained in different ways by their intersecting race, class, and gender identities, and who use wannabehood to manipulate those constraints. Although these women all employ a strategy of racial crossover, wannabehood does not address the same problems for all of them, nor do they perform wannabehood in the same ways. Instead, they draw on a range of transgressive symbolism to enact their identities. Despite these differences, in the end, their projects are limited by the same set of problems.

In this chapter, I tell three stories about individual wannabes. These are not the only wannabes I spoke with, but I have chosen to foreground their stories because they are the most richly detailed and, more importantly, because each woman represents a different way of doing wannabehood. Each woman in this chapter is white, in her mid-twenties, and the single mother of at least one child with Latino[1] paternity. Each woman engages in a range of cross-racial practices that result in her being labeled a wannabe by outsiders: in different ways, these women incorporate hip-hop style and hip-hop talk and locate themselves in predominantly Latino/a and Black spaces. But the common strategies among them are exclusive romantic and sexual involvement with Latino or Black men, and the cementing of this romantic/sexual commitment through the birth of a multiracial child.

Unlike the goths and the Unity Christians, wannabes do not share a formal space. Effective racial crossover requires that networks with other white women be minimized; wannabes hope to highlight their cross-racial ties, not their ties to whiteness. The wannabes' identity does not draw strength from numbers. Wannabe identity formation, then, is more complicated than for the goths or the Christians, as they do not have community resources to draw on. Moreover, the centrality of heterosexual ties with Black and Latino men to this identity project undercuts the development of sustained relationships with other women, both white and of color.

Instead of sharing a bounded space, the women in this chapter occupy a shared terrain that brings them into the same bars and the same neighborhoods, but does not bring them to identify with each other. The context

---

1. When I use the term Latino, I am not referring to people, groups, or spaces exclusively comprised of Puerto Ricans. Although Puerto Ricans are the predominant Latino group in the area, they are not the only one. Jamaicans, Dominicans, and South Americans all also sometimes play a role in these spaces.

provides a common set of local race and class symbols and circumstances, including the availability of Puerto Rican, other Caribbean, and American Black men.

The stories I tell here all emerge out of multiple interactions, and, in the cases of Jaclyn and Laurie, intimate immersion in their daily lives. I have known both Jaclyn and Laurie for about six years, and have shared countless hours, as well as critical life events, with each of them. In addition, I have spent a good deal of time with other important people in these women's lives. I spent less extensive time with Monica, but I also combined interviews with interactions with other people in her networks.

Each woman in this chapter has a different class origin. Monica is a graduate student from the upper-middle class. Jaclyn is working-class, currently employed in a low-level secretarial position. She grew up in household that struggled economically and has difficulties supporting her own household today, but has college-educated family members who have moved into the lower middle class. Laurie is poor, her life characterized by a pattern of "unsettled" living. She is unemployed, but has periodically supported herself by selling drugs. Monica, Jaclyn, and Laurie illustrate the distinct patterns by which differently classed women come to engage in projects of racial crossover. Different class experiences and resources shape each woman's motivation for racial crossover, her experience in cross-race communities, and the possibilities for recuperating white privilege.

I open with Monica. The most class privileged woman in this chapter, Monica is also the most at risk of fitting the stereotype of "class dupe"—of being used by men of color for her access to economic resources. Among other things, she has had her car stolen not once, but twice, by men with whom she was involved. Monica's racial project emerged out of political work, and is motivated by her explicit desire to ameliorate the race and class inequalities in which she is implicated. But it allows her to resist the gendered expectations of her race and class location as well, making her life more exciting and more rebellious. Of these women, Monica's immersion in poor Black and Latino/a communities is the most extreme class transgression, but her class capital is also the most difficult to unseat. Thus, she simultaneously has the most to lose and is the most protected from long-term class costs.

I move next to Jaclyn. In contrast to Monica, Jaclyn explains her racial project as class allegiance. In Jaclyn's view, participation in Black and Latino/a networks is not an act of crossover at all, but a natural fit emerging out of shared experiences of poverty. But Jaclyn manipulates her social surroundings and her self to achieve this fit—a strategy that makes sense in a context of decreased white working-class visibility. Jaclyn's racial project provides her with an alternative class identity, one with more capital among the poor and working classes in mixed-race communities, but it risks being dismissed as inauthentic. In the face of this assault to her identity, Jaclyn uses a particular kind of femininity to prove her respectability and, thus, her authenticity.

Unlike Jaclyn, Laurie, the final case, doesn't claim a natural fit in poor Black and Latino/a communities. Her desperate poverty means that such a fit is less problematic. Despite the label, Laurie doesn't "wannabe"; in many ways, she already is. And still, Laurie uses race strategically to ameliorate some of the oppressive class and gender circumstances in which she lives. For Laurie, race authorizes her gender rebellion, allowing her to resist the putative security of similarly classed white men, the domestic expectations of settled white working-class femininity, and the gendered norms that foreclose nonsexual illicit economic opportunities. Laurie's racial transgressions also allow her to avoid being completely swallowed by the expectations of her family of origin. Laurie's story is by far the most tragic of these cases, but she in fact has the least to lose and the most to gain from race crossover. And still, as will be clear, the costs are real and painful.

Monica: "You date a hustler, you get hustled"

I first heard about Monica at a gathering of graduate students, both white and Black, most of whom were from Monica's department and not my own. Monica's cross-racial performance was the subject of uncomfortable laughter, which was particularly noteworthy because it came from a group of people who defined themselves and their work as progressive and centrally concerned with both racial and sexual justice. Even though their norms of tolerance and social justice tempered their reactions, they saw Monica as a spectacle. Monica's racial performance violated racial boundaries, but it also violated class boundaries, bringing her into intense relationships with poor men. Monica's story, which revolves around the abdication of her white upper-middle-class roots in favor of participation in an economically marginal Black and Latino/a community, is an example of deliberate, politicized race and class realignment.

I met Monica for the first time in a local coffee shop frequented by white, young adult customers dressed in an array of mildly eccentric outfits. It is a coffee shop where a kind of white, middle-class version of young adult weirdness is cool. Dressed in a light green, fashionable track suit accessorized with large hoop earrings, her light brown hair worn long, straight, and loose, Monica's outfit seemed more out of place in that environment than it would have in many other places. But Monica didn't have the carefully coiffed appearance associated with the wannabe caricature and embodied by Jaclyn, who we'll meet next. She is pretty but not flamboyant.

As we spoke, she engaged with me in earnest and in a manner that bespoke her expensive, liberal education. Our conversation contained few glimpses of the cold hardness that edged her phone voice, the voice that had reminded me of other wannabes I had spoken with and had successfully intimidated me. Yet in between her efforts to keep her four-year-old, Asian-looking daughter (whose father is Central American) from wreaking havoc in the quiet coffee shop, and her conversation with me, she interacted occasionally with people she knew. In those conversations, her vocabulary and her cadence switched, re-presenting her political, spatial, and cultural position. She moved effortlessly between the white, educated, middle-class identity she affected with me and the urban, hip-hop identity she performed with her friends and political colleagues.

"Folks will joke with me—you have some Black in there," Monica tells me proudly. The use of Blackness as a reference point for Monica's life occludes the degree to which her border crossing is also about class. While her life is organized around Black and Latino/a community, while she does date Black men, and while she does have a multiracial child, Monica's rejection of whiteness is as much a rejection of her upper-middle-class origins as it is of whiteness—a rejections she defines as politically motivated.

Monica, like Jaclyn and Laurie, frequents tough bars with bad, racialized reputations. These are bars that I am warned about, bars where people purportedly offer you drugs as soon as you pull into the parking lot, bars where people are shot. Monica portrays her presence in these bars as a sign of her courage, although she doesn't use the word itself. Monica's evocation of this quality seems fitting to me when I think about my own unease around these bars. I have spent enough time in places where I am the only white person to be, if not comfortable, at least not uncomfortable in most all-Black or Latino/a settings. But I experienced palpable discomfort, even fear, when I went to the bars Monica frequents. I did not feel that I had the skills to handle those bars competently. Moreover, because I could not get any of my middle-class or stable working-class Black friends to accompany me, my discomfort seems to be a class, and not racial, mismatch.

Monica, however, describes these bars in terms of race, explaining to me that her willingness to go to them fosters the respect of Black people. She says, "I mean, the fact that I've put myself in situations that white people don't is reflective to people that I'm not your average white person." Monica's occupation of these spaces—"where [she's] the only white person for about three blocks"—are important to her cross-race credentials. But these bars and neighborhoods are marked not just by nonwhite people but by particular kinds of behaviors, behaviors that are designated as Black and Latino/a but are participated in by a minority of those populations. The comfort Monica claims in these places gives her access to a kind of toughness, courage, and excitement that most white people don't have, but her descriptions elide the concomitant class transgression of her bar choices. They also, it seems unwittingly, reify the cultural construction of certain behaviors (behaviors that are seen as normatively undesirable) as "Black" (or "Latino/a").

Monica tells me that "class and race are so connected," but her stories almost always turn on race rather than on class. Indeed, this pattern of using racial difference as a stand-in for class difference appears to be more than discursive. Monica, at least partially, uses racial border crossing as a means of exploring her own relationship to class. Rather than positioning herself as an organic community member, she portrays herself as having crossed into the community in which she now claims membership, and measures her success in terms of her ability to maintain the sensibilities of that community. Like Jaclyn, Monica explains her fit in the community in terms of alliance, but unlike Jaclyn, she explains her fit as a conscious political choice, not as an indigenous socioeconomic location.

Describing herself as "white, middle-class," she tells me that her parents own a successful business and put her through a small, private liberal arts college in the west. She went to Central America with a college-sponsored co-op program. Her experiences there opened her eyes politically: "Seeing the effects of the IMF and the World Bank, seeing the farmers—all these links were made." She got pregnant while in Central America. Her pregnancy tied her to the people she was working with both biologically (through the baby's paternity) and culturally. As she explains it, when she got pregnant at twenty-four, she "was like, oh, I can do this. I'm twenty-four, my time is running out. It was a different context." Monica's baby enacted Monica's crossover.

Monica returned to the U.S. with her baby's father, settling in the area while she works on her masters in international development. She and her daughter's father subsequently broke up. Despite the "privilege" of being a graduate student, Monica worked a job doing "grassroots organizing" for a local nonprofit. This job took her into urban housing projects where she did door-to-door work on welfare and housing issues.

Monica's history suggests politically motivated downward mobility. Monica's own interpretation suggests that her investment in her political work compelled her to "go native." Her early (by white middle-class and regional standards), nonmarital pregnancy launched her own economic struggles, blurring her class location. On the surface, Monica abdicates her own race and class privileges. As a single mother, she is faced with an ongoing economic struggle that is unlikely to be easily ameliorated. But, although she has given up many of the accoutrements of her race and class background, her strategy is complex. Not only are all the pieces of the race/class habitus in which she was raised difficult to recognize and unseat, but her claims to a less privileged socioeconomic position are not always accepted by others.

Monica, like Jaclyn, uses race politics and class location as forms of style that legitimate her community membership. For Monica, class alliance is implicit and race politics are explicit (a reversal of Jaclyn's emphasis in the next section). These different emphases reflect the differences in their class backgrounds as well as Monica's formal immersion in race politics via her education and her employment. But despite Monica's greater training in race politics and her obvious commitment to race and class equality, her rhetoric, like Jaclyn's, is contradictory.

The way Monica talks about her own class location reveals this murkiness. She describes herself decisively as "white middle-class" but uses class in more complicated ways in her stories. In these stories, Monica's (marginal) economic security is less a product of privilege than a result of her own ingenuity and diligence. (She doesn't, for example, question why she, a white college-educated woman, had the job organizing communities of color, even if she was poorly paid and overworked.) In these stories, she almost portrays herself as a bootstrap type success story:

> I'm really nervous about going from hands-on work to going back to academia. I have to theorize—seems like such a privilege, lofty. I feel like I'm just trying

to survive, put food on the table, build community around me. I'm playing it by ear, hoping to keep part-time work so I can keep my daycare voucher.

And:

They'll [the guys she's dating] will be like so and so has said something, they're hating. People are haters, I think. (*A:* Because you're white?) Yeah, for the most part. And I support myself and my daughter. I make about $28,000 a year, have my own apartment.

By centering economic survival, the first comment implies an indigenous class location. In the second, Monica suggests that when anger at her economic position (a position which is not great by middle-class standards, but significantly above the poverty line that is out of reach for many of the people she's organizing) is expressed in racial terms, it is misguided. This comment masks the race and class privileges that facilitate her economic stability; more, by suggesting that her economic stability comes from her own initiative, she invalidates race and class structures as an arena of complaint.

On one hand, these tales locate her as one of them. She expresses the same concerns, and explains with some pride that she "takes care of [her] self and [her] daughter." These stories contain ambivalence about her possible mobility back up. Education implies privilege, and she has considered abandoning it in favor of "surviving." I am sympathetic to this position. As a graduate student and single mother, I too had thoughts of abandoning academia in favor of a job that might provide immediate economic support for my son. "Surviving" would also maintain Monica's integrity within the community with which she identifies. On the other hand, Monica masks her privileges by explaining her success in meritocratic terms. This explanation is at odds with her professed motivation for her boundary crossing and with the political organizing that legitimizes her spatial presence in poor neighborhoods of color.

Ambivalence about class enters other topics as well. For example, Monica equivocates about the drug trade associated with poor communities:

I was going through this whole rationalization thing about why I date hustlers (men who sell drugs). Like I have problems with people selling crack to pregnant women. At the same time, I wouldn't date a guy who's an international banker investing in Enron or exploiting the rain forests. If I consider myself a socially conscious person, I understand how hard it is. But it's high, high risk.

You're basically going to end up in jail or get shot. I don't want to deal with
that sadness.

Monica's position is complex. As a politically conscious person involved
in community activism, it is hard to discount the impact of drugs on the
local community. But Monica is uncomfortable critiquing "hustlers" both
because she wants to date them and because she is aware that poor men
of color have few other economic options.[2] Monica deflects the problem,
by focusing instead on the immorality of many high status jobs associated
with white men. This shift allows her to distance herself without offering
moral or cultural condemnation; it salvages her political self-understand-
ing, and it legitimates her continued romantic and sexual involvement
with hustlers. At the same time, it justifies, without ever acknowledging,
her attraction to a certain *kind* of Black man, discussed more below.

"Obviously, I'm not doing drugs," she says another time. I was struck
by this comment. First, it wasn't obvious to me that she didn't do drugs.
Drug use is distributed across a broad spectrum of people, and so I almost
never assume that people do or do not use drugs. The clarity of her assertion indicated that her abstention was a key aspect of her identity, while
the prefix of "obviously" indicated her own assumptions about which kind
of people use and don't use drugs. This comment was the single place in
our conversation where she staked out a clear boundary between herself
and (presumed practices of) the community she worked in. This boundary, moreover, is more than rhetorical. She experiences it as a disruption
in her romantic relationships because she is not economically useful as a
buyer or, she says, "a connect" (someone who can set up contact with a
buyer) to the hustlers she dates. Thus, while Monica will date drug dealers, she won't use drugs herself or facilitate drug deals—a position that
creates moral and political dilemmas.

Monica dates poor Black and Latino men because she both works and
hangs out in poor communities of color, where she meets them. Heterosexual relationships anchor her crossing by adding personal ties to professional ties. Once involved in crossover relationships, Monica's world
became ever more centered in the community across the lines.

Monica, like all of the other wannabes I've spoken with, doesn't talk
about social context, however. "I just find myself attracted to men of

2. Patillo-McCoy (1999) notes that poor and middle-class Blacks often have an ambivalent relationship to drug dealers; on the one hand, they don't want drugs destroying their
neighborhoods; on the other hand, drug dealers are people they know, like, and trust.

color," she says. Such statements turn interracial attraction into something essential, an erotic feeling that arises out of the body without cultural context. Given the weight of opposition to cross-racial relationships, these explanations make sense. But they don't fit with the other ways wannabes talk about their attractions. Monica, for example, says, "Where I'm from, it's white and Indians...Native Americans...I ran with Indian kids, dated Indian boys."[3] This statement helps to naturalize her dating pattern by making it continuous across time, but it also suggests a fascination with whatever group happens to be the local "exotic other." This demonstrates the situatedness of the wannabe identity, which takes its meaning from local racial demographics. It is likely that, back home, Monica would have been called an "Indian wannabe," rather than a Puerto Rican wannabe, as she is called now.

Monica adds a political layer:

> I would date a white fellow...I don't know....The past couple years I find myself, I've been involved in the whole hip-hop culture, I find myself attracted to thugs. I don't know, I think it's the whole lifestyle—a couple guys who hustle. They have this pretty right-on analysis of how the system works. I don't feel like I can have a relationship with a white man because of how the whole system is set up. I'm crazy attracted to guys who have an analysis and have been part of the struggle.

In explaining her attraction to "thugs," Monica also explains why she's *not* attracted to white middle-class men—the groups of men from whom she's "supposed" to draw her sexual and romantic partners. Like other women involved with the "wrong" kind of men, Monica explains her disinterest in the "right" kind of men. In Monica's explanation, the structural position of white men makes them unpalatable as possible romantic partners. What is unclear is whether the problem is the political and cultural sensibilities of white men or the power advantage over her that their structural position confers. Probably it is a combination of both. Thus, Monica's involvement with men of color could be interpreted as a means of flattening out power differences in heterosexual relationships: Monica's racial advantage in some ways compensates for her gender disadvantage. Of

3. To me, Monica's use of the term Indian, rather than the currently more acceptable Native American, suggested her self-perception (accurate or not) of closeness to the Indian community, who, in my experience, use the term Indian among themselves, rather than her unawareness that Indian is no longer the acceptable ethnic label.

course, power relationships aren't neatly mathematical. And it is clear that gender reenters the heterosexual equation for Monica in significant ways.

Monica isn't just attracted to men of color, she's attracted, more specifically, to "thugs." Most residents of poor Black communities are not, in fact, involved in the "street" lifestyle, but the lives of those residents are less glamorous and exciting than those of thugs (Patillo-McCoy 1999). Monica's attraction, described in terms of race, is both raced and classed. Moreover, it invokes a particular kind of masculine posturing. The thug that emerges out of this race/class/gender complex is feared, romanticized, imbued with coolness, and associated with a racialized notion of hypersexuality. This combination is attractive, and is perhaps the most salient form of power to which most of these men have access. Monica's explanations gloss over the cultural pull of the thug. Indeed, it would be contrary to her politics to make this element of her attraction explicit. Yet her attraction doesn't happen in a cultural vacuum. Nor is her political explanation adequately explanatory, since not all thugs "have an analysis" and thugs are not the exclusive purveyors of "analyses."

The "thug" is also different from the kind of Black man who Jaclyn, the woman I introduce next, finds attractive. Indeed, Jaclyn makes fun of Black men who wear the trappings of the thug. The thugs that Monica desires have status that is built on their performance of race and class marginality, and their success at performing an illicit version of masculinity. The Black (and Latino) men that Jaclyn desires, in contrast, have status through Black-coded, but legal, channels, such as athletics and DJ'ing. This distinction suggests differences in Monica and Jaclyn's own race/class projects, particularly Jaclyn's greater need (because of her less secure class roots) to demonstrate her own respectable performance of class. The capital that Monica brings to her identity project secures her respectability, as the following comment suggests:

> I think the fellows I've dated too have always been impressed that I have my head on straight, take care of myself and my daughter. I don't know if the girls they dated before [were really messed up]. "[Monica], you're doing your thing. I'm proud of you." I'm the good girl. I kinda play that.

This comment acknowledges her use of her race and class position as a romantic strategy, but Monica is otherwise inarticulate about the sexual currency she accrues in a culture that constructs white women as the exemplars of feminine beauty and morality. Instead, she seems perplexed at the antagonism she sometimes feels from women of color:

> Women of color friends sometimes get mad because we'll go out and fellows will want to talk to me all the time. And I don't know why that is. My friends all know my style and who I'm attracted to.

Another time, she says, "People are going to talk. Like if an ex-girlfriend comes by, it's always like the 'white bitch.' To me, that argument doesn't hold much weight." She explains:

> I think it can be an issue particularly for women of color. I know the whole argument about white women taking Black men. I think we're moving into a new period where people are more accepting of biracial relationships. I know you see more Black men with white women. I understand the whole history of master-slave relationships. I think I do.

As Monica realizes, many Black women experience Black men's involvement with white women as a personal and a political betrayal (see Hill Collins 2004, Chito Childs 2005). Her explanation, however, legitimizes her claim to Black men both by suggesting that the problem of "white women taking Black men" is becoming less salient as biracial dating becomes more common, and that her political understanding of the problem compensates for her structural position. As Monica talks, she pushes the problem back further in history to slavery, stripping contemporary cross-racial relationships of racialized power dynamics.

Monica's words are expedient, yet they also reflect the absence of a discourse with which to make sense of her experiences. She is a thoughtful woman whose cross-race and cross-class commitments demand long, poorly paid working days. Despite her immersion in political organizing, the model of injustice on which she draws does not adequately account for gender. She acknowledges gender (she knows about the problem of "white women taking Black men"), but never develops it. Instead, by centering the race and class oppression of Black men, her model reduces the sociopolitical complexity of her relationships with Black men, and their impact on her friendships with Black women, and thus undermines her ability to cross over in a meaningful way.

Monica's race and class locations bestow advantages in the heterosexual game. They also come, it seems, with costs. Or at least their benefits are not sufficient to overcome the gendered problems that pervade heterosexual relationships with most thugs. Indeed, Monica's story contains elements that most resemble the image of the wannabe as class dupe—the victim of exploitative men of color who can "get away with whatever they want." Recall from the opening that Monica has had her car stolen not once, but twice, by men with whom she was involved. Monica's rural, white, upper-middle-class upbringing, it seems, has left her ill-equipped for dealing with the "codes of the street" (Anderson 1999).

"You date a hustler, you get hustled," Monica sighs, but she doesn't paint herself as vulnerable to exploitation because of her race and class naiveté; instead, she attributes the problem to the perceived lifestyle of the hustler:

> If you hustle, you don't turn off your cell phone. All this move, move, move. Also, like women are throwing themselves at hustlers all the time. Hustlers have like nice cars, nice clothes, and jewelry. The whole lifestyle isn't conducive to monogamy or being in a relationship.

And another time:

> Not always knowing if he's monogamous. There's always this game. So many walls put up to protect the self. The game is really ugly. At one time I might have romanticized that Black urban culture, but I've come to realize that it's not a viable option for making yourself a better man. How dudes move—it's really suspect. . . . There's room to get played. Dudes will break plans, make plans, call you the next day, "oh, I got tied up."

In these comments, the problems with her relationships emerge out of the structures of Black urban poverty. These structures encourage a version of masculinity that discourages men's romantic or sexual commitment to women, and that reward them for their ability to "play" women (to reel them in and get them to believe in the relationship, while the man continues to have sex with other women and to prioritize his own immediate desires over hers or the interests of the relationship; Anderson 1999, Edin and Kefalas 2005). Monica connects "how dudes move" to the occupational demands of drug hustling, rather than the cultural validation of a version of masculinity.

Later, though, she suggests that thugs don't commit to her because she's white:

International guys seem to have less of a problem with Black-white because they don't have the history of slavery....I think, in my own experience, not making generalizations or anything, the West African guy and [her daughter's] father, those guys treated me more like a wife, more a long-term commitment. Whereas, opposed to, I dated (she counts)...six African American guys and it was more like a girlfriend, no long-term visions of commitment, might have been in the context of those relationships. No future.

Monica is aware that part of her appeal may be the perception that she has money. In a somewhat embarrassed tone, she tells me, "I used to be like that (paying my own way) but I'm not going to play myself out and pay for everything." The embarrassment in her confession suggests that she recognizes, like other gender-politicized middle-class women I know, that women's independence emerges, in part, from their willingness to assume some of the economic responsibility for heterosexual relationships. But this strategy has left Monica burned—exploited by men who assume that, because she is white, her financial resources are endless.

Monica's attraction to thugs is counterintuitive to both herself and to significant people in her life. She tells me that her mother, her friends, and her boss all think she's "selling herself short." She also tells me that "despite having this attraction to thugs and hustlers, it's not what I want long-term." What she does want is "some sort of economic lockdown....Somebody who works hard and is interested in the same things so we can pull our resources together." At the end of the conversation, she says, "I would like to get married. I know I'm not going to find that in the kind of guy I'm dating now, I'm not that stupid."

Perhaps, though, she hopes that she will be able to rescue one of these men and convince him to settle down with her. "I felt the guys I've dated have really been looking for some normalcy," she says, "they're a little bit older, need to get out of the hustler lifestyle."[4] Monica's cross-race and cross-class adventures end up as an unfulfilled quest for heterosexual commitment. Jaclyn and Laurie, as we will see, end up on the same quest, despite the differences in their projects of race crossover.

Monica uses race to distance herself from both her whiteness and her class privilege. Her class crossover is the most extreme of the women in this chapter: she frequents the toughest bars, dates the toughest men, and

4. In their study of relationships among the poor, Edin and Kefalas (2005) similarly argue that poor men eventually move out of the hustling lifestyle.

works in the poorest communities. But she is also the least equipped to navigate the class waters she has chosen to swim in, and thus takes real hits to her pocketbook and to her ego. At the same time, she brings the greatest class resources to her project. These resources, including education, work opportunities, and a sense of entitlement, allow her to be perceived in her cross-race and cross-class community as "having her head on right," and thus better protect her respectability. Her respectability, however, is contextual. As we saw at the beginning, Monica's graduate student peers do not see her as "having her head on right." Because Monica's choices and gumption are much less respectable in the white middle-class, she has an additional incentive not to return.

Jaclyn: "There's a lot of white girls [who] give some white girls a bad name"

Of the women I discuss here, Jaclyn most matches the caricature of the wannabe outlined in the last chapter. Jaclyn uses racial crossover to establish a visible and interesting working-class identity. Although she claims her cross-race fit is natural, she constantly navigates accusations of inauthenticity. In response, she works hard to establish legitimacy, presenting an intense, consistent cross-racial persona.

The first time I saw Jaclyn was at a local park. Women mingled on the sidelines of a pickup basketball game. Some were fixtures, always hanging out after work, snapping gum, trading insults with their men, reading novels, yelling at the dogs. Other women showed up occasionally or only once, usually interested in securing the attention of one or more of the men. Jaclyn was one of the occasional women. The first time she showed up at the park, I couldn't take my eyes off of her. Neither could any of the men. Jaclyn commands attention. A striking white woman, she presents herself in a style associated with hip-hop culture: tight, trendy clothes and a gelled-back hairstyle worn by many local Puerto Rican young women. It's more than her fashion sense, though. Jaclyn has *attitude*. She doesn't just look confident, she looks tough; not because she exudes physical strength but because her features are fused in an expression of hostility. She expresses in her carriage her comfort in the Black and Puerto Rican–dominated basketball subculture.

Six years later, Jaclyn continues to project the same image. I have spent countless hours with her, at clubs and birthday parties and baby showers, at informal dinners, at my home and hers. In all of these contexts, she has been coiffed in the manner in which I first saw her. Even at her baby shower, thirty-eight weeks pregnant, she held court in elegant maternity wear and high heels, her expression as chiseled as it was at the basketball game.

Jaclyn grew up in economic instability, which was likely accentuated by the affluence of the town in which Jaclyn's family lived. Jaclyn's mother struggled to get an education while raising Jaclyn and her sister on her own—a feat she accomplished largely through her access to credit. I am not sure when Jaclyn began her project of racial crossover, but family lore (and many amused stories about "MC Hammer pants" and overalls worn with one strap undone) place it in junior high. Jaclyn's high school boyfriend was, in any case, Black and Puerto Rican. Jaclyn dropped out of high school her senior year, earned her GED, and has worked on and off as a receptionist since then. When I first met her, she spoke often of college plans, but after giving birth to her own child, her imagined future shifted to the (im)possibility of staying home full-time. Jaclyn is currently working, but she is confined to low-income jobs, and her economic situation is perpetually precarious.

Jaclyn resents the label Puerto Rican wannabe. She is proud that she can pass as Puerto Rican, but her ability to pass is situational. Newcomers often see her as Puerto Rican, but insiders identify her as white, and call her a wannabe. The small local context and her visibility in the local culture, ironically, decrease her ability to be seen as Puerto Rican. Too many people know her. The differences in how she's perceived underscore the degree to which both wannabehood and racial ascription are contextual and negotiated. Jaclyn claims an authentic, non-wannabe identity by invariably performing a highly stylized, flamboyant "Puerto Rican" femininity. This project relies on a constantly replenished supply of inexpensive but stylish and sexy clothing, as well as detailed attention to hair (dyed black), makeup, and eyebrows.

Jaclyn is tough. She never smiles; her eyes and mouth radiate hostility. She maintains this body and facial language at work, when shopping, and at basketball games (but is often silly, though not relaxed, in private family situations). Jaclyn has a reputation for fighting. "That's how you prove yourself," she explains. Although she says she no longer engages in physical fights, I have seen her kicked out of a club for fighting. And even while her involvement in physical conflict may have subsided, she is still verbally confrontational. She says, "I always speak my mind, always." And in my experience, she does. Not only have I witnessed her anger at a variety of people (intimates and nonintimates alike), but I have had her "speak her mind" to me on more than one occasion.

Toughness is a quality that is also associated with white working-class girlhood (Bettie 2003), but Jaclyn links it to race. She explains, "secure women that carry themselves with security date Black men.... The majority of white men like submissive women." Jaclyn draws on the commonplace assumption that Black women are more aggressive and willing to stand up for themselves than are white women. She does not want to be one of the "suckers" that Rafi described in the last chapter. Her fieriness connects her symbolically to tough Black women, and moves her away from the passivity she associates with white women.[5]

Jaclyn also uses space to align herself with Blacks and Latino/as. Jaclyn tells me that she "feels comfortable anywhere," but over the years I've known her, her social life has revolved exclusively around Black and Latino/a dominated spaces. Despite a rent hike, she moved from a predominantly white area to a racially mixed urban environment; she now lives on the edges of a tough, drug-riddled neighborhood. To many onlookers, Jaclyn's move is counterintuitive, the opposite of "white flight," as she moved from a more desirable (e.g., safer and cleaner), cheaper locale to a less desirable, more expensive environment. Her current neighborhood's undesirability results from a combination of race and class, and like Monica's experiences, underscores the relevance of class to the spaces wannabes occupy. Jaclyn's move makes it easier to meet and date Black and Latino men. Where she lives now, she has daily contact with them. Before the move, she had found it harder to sustain a relationship if a boyfriend had to make the forty-five minute drive every time they wanted to get together at her home.

Jaclyn's stylized performance is coded "Puerto Rican," but it is as much a performance of class as a performance of race. Sometimes class is salient to her, as when she told me she had cut a few inches off of her long hair because she didn't want "to look like white trash" or when she made fun of men who wear "do rags"—hair coverings associated with the "ghetto." More often, class is implicit. In earlier versions of this chapter, I described Jaclyn as "elegant," but as I reread, I realized I needed to qualify that description. Jaclyn is indeed elegant, but her elegance would never allow her to be mistaken for a middle-class or elite woman. Rather, the kind of elegance Jaclyn achieves provides her with status *within* a group

5. Interestingly, Pyke and Johnson (2003, 42) find that Asian American women associate *white* femininity with "assertiveness, self-possession, confidence, and independence."

marked as low class. Jaclyn's elegance demonstrates the superiority of her skills and desirability within the class community with which she identifies.

Jaclyn is never more effusive than when she is imparting her skills to a relatively unskilled audience—sometimes me or Trisha (another white working-class woman who spent a good deal of time with us) and sometimes the younger, white working-class high school girls who Jaclyn took under her wing for several years. Jaclyn taught us what to wear, combing her own overstuffed closet for outfits, or directing our purchases at clothing stores. She did our hair, waxed our eyebrows, scrutinized our makeup, and even told us how to walk. These lessons made Jaclyn the expert, allowing her to demonstrate her own technical competency. But they were also aimed at turning us into a suitable entourage. Jaclyn wanted us to be desirable enough to make us noticeable as a group. She achieved this by not only molding our appearances, but also by monitoring our comportment in clubs. Jaclyn offered approval or disapproval of the men with whom we interacted, declared some men too unattractive to talk with, and let us know if we had danced too much with any given man. We were to be sufficiently desirable, but we were also not to be *too* desirable. Jaclyn wanted us to look good so that she would look exceptional.

On one occasion, Trisha and I accompanied Jaclyn to a predominantly Black-attended club outside of a nearby, larger metropolitan area. This venture was costly, as it required us to get a hotel room so as to avoid a long, tired drive back in the middle of the night. I was exhausted by the idea, but agreed to go because it was Jaclyn's birthday. The higher cost of this club marked it as exclusive, an image that was enhanced by the attendance of a professional basketball player with whom Jaclyn had briefly been involved (his attendance, I began to suspect, was the real motivation for our trip). Moreover, the club had a dress code designed to keep out "street wear." Men wore ties and jackets, women wore inexpensive evening wear. Like Jaclyn's elegance, however, this club was not elite or even upper-middle-class, but rather the high end of a lower end.

Jaclyn intended to be the most desired woman in that club. To that end, she chose black evening dresses from her closet for me and Trisha to wear, and a red dress for herself. She had Trisha and I walk in first, and then followed us. This staging, however premeditated, had the desired effect; although Jaclyn never reconnected with the basketball player, the evening's success was symbolized by the nickname ("Big Red," because of her red dress) she had earned by the end of the night—a story she recounted for many months after.

Jaclyn's racial crossover is enacted across a number of dimensions, but like outsiders, she focuses on its sexual dimension. She explains that she "dates interracially [as a] lifestyle." When I first spoke with her, she naturalized her attraction to Black men, arguing that people are just attracted to who they're attracted to. But later, she developed an explanation of her dating pattern that rests not only on shared interests, but also on shared experiences. In these later explanations, her sexual desires don't determine, but instead emerge from, who she is:

> I mean, dating Black men is not this fad that a lot of people think it is; you know a lot of people think it's about being cool and about being down and because hip-hop is considered cool that everybody wants to do it. It's not about that. At all. It's about experiences and understanding and having different perspective and really being able to passionately feel with somebody else because you have felt similar things.... Like poverty. Like prejudice—because I'm a woman.

Jaclyn justifies her involvement with Black men by claiming a shared experience of oppression. In this way, she replicates distinctions between authentic and inauthentic participation in Black culture made by the youth of color in the last chapter. Jaclyn knows that white women have to account for their involvement with Black men. White men, especially, "have big issues with it." In the last section, Monica defended her interest in Black men by explaining why she wasn't interested in white men; Jaclyn's solution is a bit different. She uses her class disadvantage to establish an indigenous location in the community. Her assumption of class solidarity provides the scaffolding for many of her tales:

> There was this girl Christy (who was having sex with Jaclyn's then-boy-friend).... She was in the preppy group, "like, Oh my God." I was like, you know, I had been with Mikey for two years and I didn't really understand the whole concept. We had been through the same things together. My mother at the time was poor. I was poor. I mean, they [Christy's family] had money. She was rich. She did things for him. In all actuality, I understood what it was about, but I just didn't understand how he could betray me when I was trying to feel things the same way he was.

Jaclyn's implicit argument is this: her experience of poverty makes dating Black and Latino men both a *logical* choice and her *right*. By positioning herself as an organic member of the community from which she draws her sexual and romantic partners, Jaclyn challenges the assumption that white women's interest in Black men arises out of prurient fascination with the other. In doing this, she sidesteps political critiques of her behavior *and* establishes her claim to Black (and Latino) men as both more legitimate than the claims made by other white women and equally legitimate to the claims made by Black and Latina women.

Key to this strategy is Jaclyn's practice of distancing herself from other "embarrassing" white women. Like the non-wannabe girls in the next chapter, she uses the trope, but not the label, of the wannabe as a foil against which she positions herself as authentic and deserving: Unlike other white women who date Black men just to be "rebellious," she is genuinely concerned with racial oppression and Black culture. Unlike other white women who "try too hard," exaggerating symbols of hip-hop culture, and come across as "fake," she only exhibits those aspects of hip-hop culture that come naturally to her. And unlike other white women who date and sleep with any Black men that come their way, she's "not easy," shelving her sexual desire until she feels she has earned the respect of her partner.

Jaclyn's stories are contemptuous—similar in tone to the stories told by the middle-class white girls and the girls of color in the last chapter, but they are more intimate. These are stories told about women who are ostensibly her friends. These are stories told, not about the "other," but about women who are like her, about women she tries to turn into the "other" as a means of erasing her own otherness.

At our first, six-hour meeting, Jaclyn gossiped about Kelli, with whom she and I had just had dinner, and with whom she has an on-again, off-again friendship. The two women interacted with warmth and humor. Indeed, Jaclyn had invited Kelli to join us for dinner on the basis of their similarities. As soon as we were alone, however, Jaclyn indicated that she perceives these similarities to be superficial. Kelli is "fake," Jaclyn explains. As the three of us were talking, Jaclyn pointed out to me how Kelli's accent shifted when she began talking on the phone to her Black friends. Kelli "tries too hard." To further illustrate this point, Jaclyn told a story about a recent dinner the women had had with two semiprofessional basketball players:

And Andrew goes, "where are you from?" and she goes, "[College Town]." He goes, "oh, no, before that," and he said, "like from the south somewhere," and she's like—you know she got really offended because you could tell it was so fake and he was trying to tell her it was fake without saying it—you know, just blunt and right out, "hey, you're really fake," and uh, it was just really bothering me.

Kelli's behavior calls attention to her position as a racial outsider, as a white woman in a Black social world, and thus, by extension, to Jaclyn's whiteness. In addition, Kelli's exaggerated identity work is "embarrassing," as the youth of color in the last chapter made explicit, because it ties an undesirable class performance to Blackness.

Jaclyn is also embarrassed by Kelli's too-open display of sexual desire. She explains, "There's a lot of white girls [who] give some white girls a bad name, and it's true. Because Black men think that white girls are easy.... The way Kelli carries herself if she drinks too much in a club is extremely humiliating. And they all look at her like that horny, easy white girl. And I'm there with her. And I'm there *with* her, you know." Jaclyn claims (cross-) racial legitimacy by separating herself from the improper sexuality associated with white women. She appropriates the language of the youth of color to dismiss the white women "who give some white girls a bad name."

Despite her efforts, Jaclyn is dissatisfied with her heterosexual relationships. Poor treatment seems pervasive. Of one man, she says:

> And I just loved him, really, deeply, intimately loved him. And he would stand me up all the time.... For that to be the only thing wrong compared to other relationships I had, I said I'll take it, you know, but I would break down when he stood me up. I would lay on my bed and cry for days.

And another, "And he beat me up. And he spit in my face. And he cheated on me with everybody, and I never did shit." She suggested, ambivalently, that this ex-boyfriend treated her badly because she was white:

> He wouldn't go anywhere with me because I was white.... I guess it wasn't because I was white. He went out places with [another girl] and she was Puerto Rican, but I don't know, it's hard to say because all of his friends were white too... There were times when he called me a white bitch and I was (paused sadly) his girlfriend.

In line with this story, Jaclyn proposed that whiteness cripples her romantic quest: "A lot of Black men don't take white women seriously. They'll date them, they'll get intimate with them, but they won't further a relationship with them." Jaclyn illustrated her point with a long, painful story about her relationship with a man who had suggested that he would marry her but had eventually left her to marry a "mixed race," Black-identified woman with whom he had been simultaneously involved (although neither woman knew this at the time). Jaclyn responded to the romantic challenge by confronting her competition at the woman's workplace. According to Jaclyn, the other woman (Jen) didn't believe that Jaclyn had had a relationship with the man because Jaclyn is white:

> And she goes, "no, no, no [the boyfriend] tells me he wouldn't be with a white woman," and I'm looking at the woman like, "you're white," and I said, "what are you talking about?" and she goes, "well, my mother is white, my father is Black," but she was lighter than me . . . .

Racial authenticity is central to Jaclyn's heterosexual struggle. By invoking self-presentation over biology, Jaclyn shrinks the racial distance between herself and Jen, equalizing their claims to the Black boyfriend. Jen married the man sometime later, but Jaclyn maintained, "It's just so weird 'cause he loves me and he can't handle it." She reinvokes biological racial categories to make sense of her romantic loss: the boyfriend chose Jen because she was multiracial (and thus, "Black") and not because he loved her.

By explaining the competition between Jen and herself in terms of (her own) racial disadvantage as a white woman, Jaclyn inverts a powerful arena of critique by Black women, who frequently (and often vocally) perceive white women as using their racial status to gain access to Black men. Jaclyn is not only familiar with this perspective but appropriates it as her own. She explains:

> The people who suffer the most in the world are Black women because they're women and they're Black. They face more adversity than anyone else. So, um, for a Black man to take a white woman, and say a Black man makes money, like [the NBA player that Jaclyn had briefly been involved with], and he makes money, and then he marries a white woman, they feel like he should have taken them out of poverty and all that stuff that they face right now, all the adversity.

But then Jaclyn reverses her position: "There are a lot of Black women who get past it and they don't live their lives being jealous and bitter and racist."

Jaclyn's comments draw on contradictory racial analyses. Structural and individualistic explanations intertwine. Jaclyn's use of these seemingly incompatible analytical lenses is, in practice, seamless. She either doesn't see or doesn't acknowledge her rhetorical contradictions.[6]

As with Monica, Jaclyn's ability to shift between contradictory frameworks is useful to her. On one hand, she positions herself as someone who is familiar with and sympathetic to the racial inequalities faced by Blacks. Structural language aligns her politically with the Black and Latino/a community, adding to her cross-race credentials. At the same time, notions of individual stereotyping or discrimination defuse her own political responsibilities, transferring the political and interpersonal onus to Black women. This strategy reduces objections to Black men's relationships with white women to unenlightened discrimination. As such, her claim to Black men is not only politically acceptable, but more enlightened than the claims of Black women.

Like Monica's, Jaclyn's rhetorical contradictions are convenient, while also revealing the paucity of available racial discourses. The framework of structural inequality that Jaclyn employs, while sensitive to the "multiple jeopardies" (King 1988) of race, class, and gender, privileges race as the locus of inequality. The focus on race undercuts her own strategy of class alignment, invalidating her claim to Black men and to community membership. But Jaclyn cannot rely on "color blindness," so central to middle-class whiteness, either. Her racial transgressions force her to constantly acknowledge race. Jaclyn doesn't have access to a discourse that makes sense of the complexity of her own location as a white woman in a predominantly Black and Latino/a community. Instead, she frequently relies on an individualist framework to explain her own experiences. She uses this framework to her advantage, but it inevitably undermines her claims. This happens for two reasons. First, individualism is incompatible with the structural discourse she uses to claim political allegiance to the Black community. Second, individualism blinds her to racialized heterosexual competition as it is practiced (rather than as rhetoric) and prevents her from developing alliances with Black or Latina women. Monica, recall, ran into the same problems.

In the contemporary United States, race is a salient category of identity, while class is "hidden." Instead, racial identities are read as classed

---

6. Bonilla-Silva (2003) argues that incoherence and contradictions are central features of contemporary race talk among whites.

identities, and vice versa (Ortner 1998). Thus, to be Black is to be working-class/poor, and to be middle-class is to be white. When white people can't be folded neatly into the middle class, they are marked as classed others through derogatory labels like "redneck," "hillbilly," and "white trash." As Hartigan (2003) argues, middle-class whites use these labels to project undesirable aspects of whiteness (including economic instability and racism) onto poor whites, and thus to maintain the class and moral integrity of whiteness. These marked identities are not equivalent; both "redneck" and "hillbilly" can be rehabilitated as "identit[ies] that can be invested with valor" (Hartigan 2003, 97). "White trash," however, one of the few remaining categories of acceptable public denigration, is unequivocally undesirable. As Hartigan further argues, the designation "white trash" is typically reserved for whites whose lives are spatially and culturally closest to those of Blacks.

Working-class and poor whites, especially those living in urban or near-urban areas, lack a valorized cultural identity. Because the "redneck" and "hillbilly" identities are associated with rural (and often southern) lifestyles, they don't make sense in non-rural contexts; moreover, the overt racism frequently attributed to the redneck identity is undesirable to many whites who share space with Blacks and Latino/as. These whites can opt to identify with middle-class white culture, but this option can be demeaning since structural disparities make working-class whites less competitive at the middle-class game. Participation in poor Black and Latino/a (hip-hop) cultures, which are visible, thriving, and hip, provides another option.

Jaclyn's strategy is a sensible response to limited mobility. Without the educational opportunities and the cultural capital of the white middle class, Jaclyn has little chance of being a successful participant in white middle-class culture. Skilled in the Black and Puerto Rican culture she grew up around, she uses her personal resources (intelligence, self-presentation, assertiveness) to claim a place in it. Her efforts provide her with the status of notoriety, of desirability, of coolness, but also incur costs.

For example, while Jaclyn prides herself on being secure and on not backing down, her aggressiveness creates problems. She attributes her decision to get a GED rather than a high school diploma to the escalation of physical conflict in her high school, which culminated in an incident in which she accidentally hit a teacher. She has been fired at least once for "attitude." One of her ex-boyfriends told me that he broke up with her because he couldn't take the constant conflict. Conflict also attenuates her friendships with women. Women in general are penalized for the display of anger and aggression (see Brown 1998), and middle-class emotional standards expect women especially to avoid conflict (Stearns 1994, Kenny 2000), but the breadth of Jaclyn's problems seem to arise not from the display of anger, per se, but from the pervasiveness of her "attitude." Although it is tempting to suggest a psychological explanation for Jaclyn's amplified attitude or to suggest that hip-hop "attitude" in general would benefit from restraint, I think it is equally possible that Jaclyn's problems arise because she overperforms the crossover identity. In her effort to prove the consistency of her identity, she doesn't tailor her performance to context (for contrast, see my discussion of Laurie's "attitude" in the next section). In this case, Jaclyn is the white woman she denigrates, the one who "tries too hard."

Jaclyn's strategy is complex. Rather than collapsing the boundaries between racial categories, Jaclyn uses her class background to naturalize her location on the Black and Latino/a side of the boundary. She also implicitly suggests that she has earned her status as a racial insider through her properly gendered class performance. These concurrent strategies allow her to at once claim class alliance and class status. But to claim respectability, Jaclyn distances herself from the "humiliating" behavior of other white women—a strategy that re-marks the boundary between whiteness and Blackness or Puerto Ricanness. In her telling, she is an exceptional case, allowed to cross racial boundaries because of her exemplary (and thus, authentic) behavior; she thus leaves racial criteria intact.

Jaclyn's rhetoric of restraint, however, does not always match the perceptions of outsiders, as the last chapter made clear. Moreover, both because she claims status within the group through her heterosexual desirability and because she aims to secure the commitment of a Black or Latino man, her strategies exacerbate conflict and jealousy, particularly with other women, and thus reduce her acceptance.

Laurie: Improper femininity and unsettled living

Laurie is a different kind of wannabe. She doesn't decorate her body, but instead decorates her car, outfitting it with rims, tinted windows, and other custom features. She doesn't date hustlers, she is one. She doesn't try to protect her sexual reputation; she tries, often unsuccessfully, to be sexually ruthless like the men she knows. And while she has children, her relationship with them is akin to the parental relationships of noncustodial fathers: she does not live with them, but buys them things and takes them on occasional outings.

The differences between Laurie and the other women demonstrate the flexibility of the wannabe label, which we saw in the last chapter, and which can be used to punish women for a range of violations. The differences also expose an alternative position for women in hip-hop culture. As with other subcultures, men are seen as the legitimate carriers of hip-hop in a way that women are not (e.g., Rose 1994). Some women resist the hypersexualized representation of women in hip-hop by embracing more masculine personas: dressing in men's hip-hop styles, claiming sexual autonomy, and participating in gangs as dealers rather than sidekicks (Schalet, Hunt, and Joe-Laidler 2003). Laurie's identity better matches this autonomous version of femininity, although she too seeks to secure a man. Ironically, while the youth in the last chapter mentioned this version of wannabehood, they spent much less time deriding it. Nonetheless, Laurie is fiercely penalized—by herself and others—for her performance of racialized gender.

Like Jaclyn, Laurie is from a racially integrated poor and working-class community in which a visible white working culture is fading. For a while, the two lived in nearby neighborhoods. Laurie is located at the bottom of that community, however, while Jaclyn is at the top. As I said in the introduction, Laurie doesn't "wannabe" in the same ways—she, in many ways, already "is." For Laurie, a white woman in her mid-twenties, a lifetime of desperate poverty has been punctuated only sporadically by brief influxes of cash earned from selling drugs. Laurie lacks the familial, psychological, and economic resources of either Monica or Jaclyn. She comes from a poor white, openly racist family, and grew up tossed between foster homes. Because her class location is so oppressive, Laurie seems to have less to lose, but, as with the other women, her strategies bring both losses and gains.

The strategies of both Laurie and Jaclyn allow them to sidestep degraded white class identities by embracing a thriving and much hipper racialized working-class culture, but Jaclyn's cross-racial participation is more deliberately cultivated than is Laurie's. Laurie, whose experience of poverty and instability is much more extreme than Jaclyn's, is also less self-conscious about her strategies. Indeed, it is not clear that Laurie imagines racial crossover as a deliberate strategy. I attribute this difference, in part, to a distinct way of talking about identity choices. Laurie does not have access to middle-class ways of talking about one's self. Outside of her relationship with me, Laurie has limited contact with anyone who is middle-class. Moreover, Laurie's life is saturated with immediate problems: drug use, parenting crises, homelessness, and so forth. These problems take precedence in her talk. Engaged in the pattern of unsettled living that characterizes the lives of the very poor, Laurie's class allegiance to men of color is unambiguous. Laurie only dreams of reaching the kind of class-bounded respectability that Jaclyn works so hard to sustain.

The first time I met Laurie, she barely acknowledged me. She had no reason to trust me, and she later told me that my "teacher" (i.e., middle-class) demeanor intimidated her; she assumed I would think she was stupid or "bad" because her life wasn't like mine. The intimidation went both ways. I was unsettled by her hardness. Laurie lived up to none of the middle-class norms of polite friendliness and feminine warmth (regardless of its sincerity) that I had taken for granted up to that point. She was, at first, even more unapproachable than Jaclyn. While Jaclyn's icy, uncompromising elegance invited spectatorship, Laurie's hardness shut down any observation at all.

There are other differences in the "attitudes" of the two women. In contrast to Jaclyn's relentless, in-your-face attitude, Laurie's "attitude" is situational, and those situations are clearly defined by class boundaries. In situations in which she is the only non-middle-class person, Laurie's meekness made her appear standoffish and rude. On those occasions, Laurie barely looked up when spoken to, and made her exit as quickly as possible—often simply disappearing without saying good-bye. This demeanor is at odds with Laurie's aggressive, sometimes violent behavior with members of her family and with her class peers. Laurie's attitude is a survival strategy.

Unlike Jaclyn, Laurie can not pass for Puerto Rican, nor does she try. Instead, she incorporates elements of working-class white womanhood into her self-presentation. At a time when bangs were "out," she wore her dark, wavy hair long with teased bangs—in a hairstyle that Jaclyn ridiculed behind her back. Her clothes blend urban hip-hop symbols with white working-class stylistic staples. She wears baggy men's-style hip-hop jeans with oversized T-shirts, sports gold necklaces with large urban-style pendants, and alternates between unstylish Reeboks or super-stylish Timberlands. Laurie's look isn't androgynous—she sometimes has her nails done in the airbrushed style associated with urban working-class women, and once she bragged to her brother about having her eyebrows "done"—but her look eschews Jaclyn's tight, sexy look. Laurie's style is a better match with the athletic style worn by rappers like Brat and Missy Elliott, who claim their power more on men's terms than on women's.

Consistent with this style, Laurie is uncomfortable with being a spectacle. On one occasion, for example, Laurie and I were at my house getting ready for a party. While I was in a frenzy of pre-party energy, trying on different outfits and doing my hair, Laurie sat slumped over on the bed. She also had outfits to try on but didn't have any of the enthusiasm for the process that I did. She finally settled on the easiest outfit she could find—one that was suitable for the party but that did not emphasize her body. Laurie's lack of enthusiasm wasn't because she didn't care about her appearance, wasn't interested in the possibility of heterosexual interactions (in contrast, she asked a number of questions about the potential pool of men), or was objecting to the criteria for heterosexual attractiveness. Instead, she expressed considerable insecurity about her ability to determine the proper presentation of self. Moreover, she seemed unclear on the rules of this aspect of "girl culture"; I'm not sure she had ever engaged in this kind of pre-party ritual before, whereas it was like breathing to Jaclyn. On another occasion, I met Laurie at a local bar that caters to a slightly older, typically subdued crowd of Black patrons. Irritated with her boyfriend Paul's philandering, she eyed the crowd for potential pickups. But Laurie's pickup skills are nothing like Jaclyn's. Rather than working the patrons, she sat hunched over on her bar stool, dressed in jeans and a baggy sweater, despite the warmth of the bar. Laurie's sexual performance may contrast with Jaclyn's and Monica's confident cross-racial sexualities, but it does not impede her ability to meet men.

Nor does Laurie need to change her lifestyle to meet men of color; she encounters them regularly. Nonetheless, her choice to date and have sex with men of color is deliberate and consequential: it comes with both economic and physical reprisals. For Laurie, dating men of color violates the expectations of her family, who comprise her most enduring social network. Her brothers sometimes try to set her up with "appropriate" white men, who she rejects out of hand. Like Monica and Jaclyn, she explains that she tries to find white men attractive, but can't. She doesn't know what to say to them and she finds them boring.

Like the white boys in the previous chapter, the white men Laurie knows—her brothers and some family friends—believe that a white (working-class) boyfriend would save her. Her brother Kurt refuses to talk to her while she is involved with a Latino or Black man. Her brother Billy says Black and Latino men "screw his sister over." Billy has significant social and economic relationships with Black and Puerto Rican men, but he doesn't extend that racial flexibility to his sister. He is troubled both by her violations of "proper" femininity and by her romantic and sexual commitments to men of color. He sees these things as inextricable. Billy recalls his (white) friend's interest in her as if it was a salvation she had refused to accept (even though, knowing both Laurie and the friend, romance between them is inconceivable). The friend is also perplexed at Laurie's rejection. Attributing Laurie's drug use to her involvement with Black and Latino men, he's sure that she would be fine is only she'd chosen him. These savior fantasies misrepresent Laurie's life, though. For one thing, she was involved with men of color well before she began using drugs. And Laurie pulled Paul into the drug economy, not the other way around.

When I met her, Laurie spent most of her time in a (now closed) hole-in-the-wall bar with a reputation for drug distribution. The clientele in this bar were working-class to poor, Black and white. The bar had a violent, seedy reputation. I was warned repeatedly, and by an array of people (but not by Laurie, who often wanted me to go there with her), about going there. Although "girls like [me]" don't belong in places like that, Laurie *did* belong there. Not only was the bar the space in which she spent her leisure time, but it was also her workplace: she worked there first tending bar, and later selling drugs. The bar was so much a part of her everyday life that even her baby shower was held there.

I have heard the story of how Laurie's life came to revolve around "the bar" many times. I have heard this story from a range of narrators with different investments in Laurie's life, but the tale always has the same dimensions. Laurie grew up in and out of foster care, finally returning to live with her physically and emotionally abusive mother. Despite pervasive transience and instability, Laurie graduated from vocational high school—an accomplishment unmatched by any of her six siblings. Soon after, she set up house with her Puerto Rican high school boyfriend and had two children with him. This is the part of the story that is always her high point: she successfully cared for her children, kept a clean and homey house, and, she proudly proclaims, "didn't even smoke!" But Laurie's boyfriend beat her, and she eventually couldn't take it anymore.

This is where she falls. Unable to balance two kids and full-time work in a poorly paid job, Laurie began to rely more and more on her mother's help with childcare. Eventually her mother (the one whose abusive behavior had led to the loss of custody of Laurie and her brothers) took custody of her kids. Exhausted and ashamed, Laurie began to hang out at the bar that eventually became so central to her life. She began to smoke (cigarettes). She began to use drugs. She began to use a lot of drugs, and then she began to sell.[7]

Although Laurie is ashamed of her drug use (and as I write this has just completed a stint in rehab), the bar was a space in which she found reprieve from her profound social, cultural, and economic marginalization. As for other marginalized people, drug selling, even near the bottom of the distribution totem pole, made her life interesting, gave her unprecedented disposable income, and allowed her to avoid the sex work that is often the only viable economic option for women in Laurie's situation (see Maher 1997). In the periods in which she was actively selling drugs, the uncertainty and discontent that plagued Laurie were at least mitigated by activity. The daily rhythm of drug distribution meant her cell phone was always ringing. It also meant that she was able to buy clothing for herself, drive a newish SUV, take her children out to eat, buy presents for her boyfriend, and pay for a range of expenses. Her lifestyle was not opulent, but it allowed her to conduct economic activities that made her feel like a member of society. Moreover, it made her the one in charge, at least in a limited way; she wasn't dependent on her man's ability to hustle—or his forthrightness about how much money he made. Laurie's demeanor and daily patterns when she wasn't selling drugs bespoke the significance of economic participation to her daily life. During her "off" periods, Laurie disappeared, spending her days sleeping in her home, waiting for her man. When I was able to see her, I realized that she was nonfunctionally depressed.

The respite the drug economy provided was continually undercut by gendered surveillance. Laurie's drug use was destructive to her, but its social costs were much greater because she is a woman and because she is a mother. Laurie's surveillance was internal as well as external. After a drug binge, or even her perception that I might suspect a drug binge, she would avoid me for long periods of time. When she did reemerge, she

7. Despite the stereotype about the wannabes' use of drugs that was articulated in the last chapter, Laurie is the only woman in this chapter who uses drugs at all. Jaclyn also abstains from alcohol. In addition, the timing of Laurie's drug initiation indicate that drug use arose out of her life circumstances, rather than being a symbol she used to look "hard," as the stereotypes suggest.

talked endlessly about her feelings of shame and failure as a mother. Laurie, too, judged her drug use in gendered ways.

Maher (1997, 111) finds a "double standard" in interpretations of drug users in which women are perceived to be even more "erratic and unreliable" than male drug users. The men Laurie (and I) know who sell and use drugs are not subject to the same scorn; instead, they are accepted as functional members of the community and as competent parents. For these men, the drug world provides an outlet for their disenfranchisement and, even more, can bolster their masculinities. The contrast between the way Laurie revealed her involvement with drugs to me (in bits, accompanied by palpable shame, and always followed by temporarily disappearing), and the men's open boasting,[8] underscores the ways in which gender shades interpretations of drug use.[9]

The transgressions of the other women in this chapter are interpreted through a lens that foregrounds racial transgression, but Laurie's transgressions are refracted through a lens that foregrounds gender. Laurie herself portrays her problems as less economic and more about her inability to enact proper femininity. This perspective is reinforced from many directions. The story of her fall locates her demise at the moment when she stopped taking care of the home. Her problems are not portrayed by her or by others as stemming from her teenage maternity, her boyfriend's abuse, or her difficulties supporting her children on her own. When she was pregnant with her youngest child, her friends staged a baby shower (although this gesture contained symbolic contradictions since the party took place at "the bar"), at which she received an elaborate array of gifts. By celebrating the impending birth, this party seemed to symbolize the hope that maternity would save Laurie by directing her energies toward proper feminine pursuits.

Laurie negotiates her gender transgressions ambivalently. Sometimes she embraces a fantasy of successful domesticity, spinning white picket fence stories in which she cares for her children and is drug-free. At these

8. One man showed me a special spot in his truck where he had added a mirror to lay out lines of cocaine. A number of men used their ability to procure drugs as attempted sexual bait, hoping to prove their desirability through the size of their stash. The most frequent (and typically inaccurate) boast was that he "would never get caught." Moreover, the men I met all had children with whom they were regularly involved, but they were not criticized in the same ways as Laurie was for their simultaneous positions as parents and drug users/sellers. One time, when I criticized a man's relationship with his children, his friend told me that the man was a good father *because* his drug selling provided for his children economically.

9. See also Roberts 1997

times, she would go on a cleaning binge or prepare elaborate Caribbean meals. She worked hard to establish co-residence and what Monica would call "economic lockdown" with Paul, the father of her youngest child, but after finally achieving it, warned me to "be careful what you wish for," as co-residence not only failed to solve any of her problems, but also did not alter Paul's patterns of extrarelational sex and coming and going when he pleased. Eventually Paul left without saying good-bye, leaving Laurie and their daughter without money and on the eve of eviction. Each time these racialized strategies of proper working-class feminine display failed to change Laurie's life circumstances, she was shocked. She expected, she explained, that if she could just be a "good woman," everything would work out.

Maternity telescopes Laurie's gender transgressions. Rather than being a status from which she can garner self-worth or develop relationships with other single mothers, maternity increases the gender surveillance in her life and escalates her feelings of shame. Although multiracial children may serve as symbols of cross-racial allegiances, Laurie's children do not facilitate her membership in a cross-racial community. Instead, her children are constant reminders, to her and to others, of her failure as a woman. Laurie is the prototypical "bad mother," and she is judged as such by herself and by others.

I was in the third trimester of my pregnancy when Laurie was in the first trimester of hers. Our overlapping pregnancies set me up as the perfect foil. Laurie teased me about my behavior—in particular, she and others members of her family would rib me for not smoking during my pregnancy (I didn't smoke prior to the pregnancy either, so this wasn't a remarkable achievement on my part). On the surface, the jokes were on me. But the point of the jokes was to articulate proper womanhood, and I was clearly the proper woman against whom Laurie defined herself. After my son was born, Laurie would wistfully remark about "what a good job [I was] doing with [my son]," "what a good cook [I was]," etc. But her remarks were not confined to the domestic realm. Her compliments also included how I "had my shit together" and how I "was going somewhere."[10] (Recall that Monica used similar language to claim respectability for herself.) To Laurie, I was the superwoman-other compared to whom she always came up short.

10. Laurie and I had many conversations about the structural differences between us that made it easier for me to "go somewhere" with my life. Her recognition of these, though, didn't stop her from judging herself a failure.

Laurie expresses contradictory feelings about her children. She is periodically angry (and alternatively, concerned) that her mother is raising her children. She has told me more than once, "I know I could do a better job of raising them if I just had the chance." She imagines what life would be like if she got them back. In the fantasy she spins, she is always drug-free. At other times, Laurie portrayed herself as an impediment to her children. Despairing that her children witness her drug abuse, she suggests that her children might be better off if she killed herself. She begs me to take them. She asks her brother to take them.

Even when Laurie laments the loss of her children, the sadness of her lament seems to speak another sadness as well—Laurie's recognition that not only is she unable to care for her children in the way she is supposed to, but that she also does not feel about her children the way a mother is supposed to. Laurie's shame at being an unsuccessful mother (in contemporary cultural terms) is exacerbated by her inability to even maintain the "proper" feelings about her children. Thus, when she does express distance from her children, it is couched as maternal concern: "they would be better off without me." Never does she utter the culturally unthinkable, "I would be better off without them." She is unable to articulate her dissatisfaction with the exhausting expectations of motherhood because domesticity, and thus motherhood, is central to her vision of the proper embodiment of femininity. In this way, though, she is not different from most mothers, who cannot risk exposing ambivalence or distaste for mothering because of its profound implications for their value as women. Because she does not have access to a model of femininity that does not center domesticity, Laurie does not have any way to feel good about herself. In this way, she is strikingly different from both Monica and Jaclyn, and from me as well, for whom mothering provides a sense of competence and self-respect.[11]

Over and over, Laurie is betrayed by the rules of femininity. Laurie's attempts to live up to the feminine expectations of the old marital bargain are not rewarded with male loyalty, yet she is still held accountable to their rules. She is more comfortable in the street culture, but is ushered home because of her gender. Laurie desires the emotional edge to enact proactive sexual agency in a way that is typically reserved for men.

11. She is also different from the low-income unmarried mothers in Edin and Kefalas' (2005) study, whose lives and relationships are much like Laurie's. For the women in their study, motherhood is a source of accomplishment and competence.

When Paul cheated on her, she wanted to be able to cheat on him too. Occasionally, she was successful, but was undermined by her feelings for Paul. She wanted to be "hard" enough to not care. She admired women who had no-strings-attached sex with lots of men, and warned them not to trust men if they attached themselves to one. Once, she kissed a man whose girlfriend had recently given birth. In a scenario that reversed typical gendered scripts, she boasted about her conquest and her pleasure, but expressed scorn for the man's insincerity toward his girlfriend. In this atypical example, the man became the stigmatized slut and Laurie became the "player."

In poor communities of color, autonomy from men is an alternative route to respect (Rose 1994, Schalet, Hunt, and Joe-Laidler 2003). The "discourse of sexual autonomy," in contrast to the "discourse of sexual respectability," "revolves around asserting agency, lack of attachment to one's sexual partner, and control over self and others" (Schalet, Hunt, and Joe-Laidler 2003, 130). This path requires women to separate their sexual and emotional needs, abdicating "relational attachment." Perhaps because respectability is out of reach, Laurie wants to be autonomous, but she is undermined by both her feelings for Paul and by her continued judgment of herself according to more conventional gendered standards.

Laurie has been treated poorly by all the men in her life. Laurie's unsurprising mistrust toward men in general butts heads with her deep hope that a heterosexual relationship will some day save her. Ironically, Laurie's distrust of men impedes her ability to forge alliances with women. Her belief in the salvation of domesticity increases her investment in overcoming the odds with an individual man; for five years she fought bitterly, to focus Paul's affections on her, through periodic bouts of hyperdomesticity but more often by directing her anger at the other women in Paul's life. While she was Paul's "mistress," she had frequent verbal conflicts with the woman with whom Paul was cohabiting. After she moved into the position of domestic partner, she exerted an enormous amount of energy toward preventing and tracking down any infidelity. Once, for example, she gave me a list of numbers Paul had called and asked me to call them to find out who they were. For a period of time, she also accompanied Paul cross-country while he drove trucks, with the explicit purpose of preventing him from stopping to see other women. Her methods might seem desperate, yet they underscore both the paucity of imagined alternatives in Laurie's life and the powerful hold of the romantic notion that women will be saved by their prince.

Laurie is understandably bitter. She sees her brother's access to a steady wage of ten dollars an hour as an inexplicable and undeserved bounty, but she does not see the way in which gender differences have laid out their different paths. Gender and class interweave in Laurie's life in complex ways. Together, they limit her economic possibilities (in the legal marketplace, in the underground economy, and in the heterosexual market). Yet the gendered class structures in her life are invisible. Instead, her personal problems are blamed on her failed gender performance. Race is one way in which Laurie navigates these constraints. She claims Black and Latino men—the men who are considered more desirable, hipper, more interesting—and she uses her immersion in a predominantly Black social network to engage in drug distribution, and to invest more energy in pleasure and less in domesticity. In turn, Laurie's use of race to push against the limits of femininity is tabulated as another gender violation. To be sure, Laurie's strategies don't ultimately work, but they should not be dismissed as complete failures either. For Laurie, they provide some alleviation of deadening, impoverished domestic femininity.

Laurie's strategies are in some ways stickier than those of the other wannabes. Monica and Jaclyn use class-specific cross-race femininities to push against the limits of whiteness; in other words, they claim another *kind of femininity,* one where the rules seem to suit them better. But Laurie longs for the freedoms of the men she knows: to be sexually callous, to sell drugs, to be independent from maternal obligations. Perhaps Laurie's endeavors leave her so bankrupt because she has so few resources (economic, familial, or psychological) to begin with, or perhaps because she is more ambivalent about her efforts than are Monica and Jaclyn, constrained as she is by gendered expectations, or perhaps because her gender violations are more severe. Probably, her desperate situation comes from a combination of all three.

Monica and Jaclyn often use race as a language to talk about class, but Laurie's crossover performances *are* raced but not classed. Class operates differently for her because she already occupies a class-derided position. In her world, race and class are braided together in such a way that it's not clear which strand is on top. Like many members of the white working class, Laurie's family and some network members see whiteness as their trump card, as paying wages in terms of status (Roediger 1991). But whiteness is not so obviously higher status to Laurie, who loathes that she's seen as "white trash." For her, then, racial crossover offers at least the possible respectability of a real "cultural" identity (e.g., Caribbean).

Finally, by embracing Puerto Ricanness and Blackness, Laurie rejects her family's tenuous racial standing. The families of Monica and Jaclyn provide them with ongoing support, regardless of their racial performances, but Laurie's family is abusive and manipulative. Laurie constantly struggles to stand up to her family, yet almost always acquiesces to them. By bearing three nonwhite children, she sullies the only status her family has. This resistance is bold indeed.

Racial crossing and presentation of self

On the surface, the wannabes' racial transgressions are communicated through the consumption and incorporation of hip-hop culture, but the infiltration of hip-hop culture into even otherwise insular suburban spaces dilutes its communicative power. Hip-hop has been commodified and sold to young, white, trendy audiences (Kelley 1997), as any appraisal of the "Juniors" section of suburban department stores clearly indicates. Simply wearing hip-hop-inspired clothing does not adequately communicate a racially transgressive identity. Jaclyn notes the changing meaning of hip-hop symbols:

> Before if you were wearing bell-bottoms and platforms you were trying to be something you're not, and now everybody and their Barbie clones wears them. Barbie, Puerto Ricans, Black people all wear bell-bottoms. It's the style. Now it's okay for it to be the style, but before I couldn't wear shit?

Without indicators beyond style, wannabes risk being mistaken for the contemptible ordinary white hip-hoppers. This risk also adds to their own border policing, increasing their investment in a clear demarcation between themselves and whites for whom experimentation with hip-hop culture is merely superficial.

To distinguish themselves, some wannabes incorporate hip-hop symbols in spectacular ways. Some wear flamboyant clothing and elaborate hairstyles, for example, while others speak in thick Puerto Rican accents. Their bodies shout their racial allegiances, their self-identifications, and their heterosexual desires. Often they also signal racial ambiguity. But wannabes do more than just mold their self-presentations, they also shape their emotions, their political narratives, their leisure/residential/work locations, and their desires. Wannabes display hip-hop toughness and incorporate race and class narratives about urban poverty in different ways, but they all occupy racialized spaces and direct their romantic and sexual desires at Black and Latino men.

Despite different symbolic combinations, then, wannabes all integrate components of hip-hop culture that are typically off-limits to white people, and they all engage in racial realignments that go well beyond style. Their strategies make clear that racial crossing is not accomplished superficially, but rather requires the melding of cultural adjustments and structural accommodations. Wannabes attempt to position themselves into a class and race community by forfeiting the race privilege accorded to white women through their relationships with white men. They also forego the economic advantages promised by middle-class behavior. For Laurie, this loss is the smallest, for Monica, the largest, but for all these women, their structural realignments mean that the privileges of class and race are not easily recuperated.

The long-term effects of the wannabes' project occur at the intersection of race, class, and gender. Wannabehood provides a means of pushing against the strictures of white middle-class femininity, but it does not burst apart the seams of gendered constraints. Gendered norms constrain their navigation of race and class and are re-encoded in their racially transgressive heterosexual relations.

"A lot of Black men don't take white women seriously"

Cross-racial heterosexual relationships are wannabe's central identity strategy. For white women, these relations allow them to snub their noses at the race and class payoff white men offer in exchange for heterosexual inequity. White women's visible desire for sexual and romantic relations with Black and Latino men is a profound rejection of the "protection" white men historically have offered white women from the advances of Black men.

Sexual and romantic liaisons across the color line offer wannabes an alternative set of resources—the coolness, excitement, and danger associated with Black urban masculinity. For white working-class and poor women, for whom enduring relationships with white middle-class men are often unattainable, these relationships trade race privilege for cultural cool but within a bounded class location. But middle-class white women also use wannabehood to resist the suffocating expectations of white middle-class femininity. Further, crossing race and class lines may alleviate some of the guilt that accompanies awareness of one's unearned privilege.

But this sexual strategy is fraught with difficulties. First, wannabes still need men's approval, even if those men are Black and Latino instead of white. Wannabes need men not only to establish "economic lockdown," but to authenticate their racial crossover identities. Second, this strategy undermines wannabes' ability to develop satisfactory or supportive relationships with white women or women of color, which, in turn, increases their dependence on men. Third, it resuscitates the gendered constraints of domesticity in their lives. The wannabes' strategy mires them in hierarchical, isolated gender relations.

Muddy race and class navigations aggravate this process. Because of the culturally predominant notion of "natural" identities and the privileging of race over class (Ortner 1998), outsiders view wannabes as race transgressors; their class negotiations are submerged. Relationships between Black men and white women are emotionally and politically charged. Black women, and to a lesser extent, men, often perceive Black men's involvement with white women as evidence that Black men have internalized racialized hierarchies of beauty and are abandoning Black women, and that white women are exercising privilege in a way that undermines solidarity in the Black community (Chito Childs 2005, Dalmage 2000, Romano 2003). Thus, the wannabes' attempts to use cross-racial sexuality to establish membership can also be challenged as an act of cultural domination, racial naiveté, or "jungle fever"[12] (the notion that white desire for Black bodies emerges out of a fascination with racial difference), tipping their efforts upside down.

Wannabes also use race to explain their relationship problems.[13] "A lot of Black men don't take white women seriously," Jaclyn says. But the problems wannabes face, which include physical violence, infidelity, and marginal paternal commitment, are faced by women across heterosexual

12. This term was popularized by a Spike Lee film of the same name.

13. The wannabes' racial crossover occurs in a male-dominated arena. The wannabes' racial crossover is enacted through cultural (hip-hop) and, to a much lesser extent, political channels. A male-dominated cultural form, commercial hip-hop centers the perspectives of poor urban Black (and to a lesser extent, Latino) men, and marginalizes the concerns of Black and Latina women. In neither of these spaces, which sometimes overlap, is there a significant voice for the concerns of women. Indeed, as a number of feminists have complained about much of the antiracist movement, the concerns of women are understood to be subsidiary to the "real" problems of race (Carbado 1998).

relationships.[14] The focus on race in the wannabes' accounts creates an interpretive paradox. On one hand, by suggesting that their problems with men arise out of the particulars of interracial relationships, Monica and Jaclyn absolve men in general and men of color in particular of responsibility for their sexist behavior. Perhaps inadvertently, their explanations feed a cultural image of Black and Latino men as being less reliable and more violent, less capable partners.

These explanations also, ironically, intensify the commitment to achieving satisfactory domestic "lockdown," and thus divert energy from homosocial relationships and foster competition between women. As for other women, these outcomes are socially isolating, decrease the possibility of gender alliances, and increase the dependence of individual women on their heterosexual relationships, adding to the cultural power men hold in their heterosexual negotiations. For wannabes, these problems are magnified by the racial contours of their desires, which heighten and racialize heterosexual competition.

Wannabes' interpretation of this competition reveals the limits of their racial politics, underscores the centrality of sexuality to their identity strategy, and exposes the contradictions embedded in their cross-racial tactics. They defuse racialized competition over men by invalidating the political and cultural claims of Black women. At the same time, they draw on their race (and sometimes class) capital to jockey for a better position in the competition. Both techniques limit their political realignment, and thus undermine their project of racial crossover.

Finally, the wannabes' sexual strategy transposes traditional heterosexual gender relations onto cross-racial relationships. It thus relies on the achievement of the "ideology of domesticity" (Stombler and Padavic 1997). Indeed, at least for the middle-class women, the project of racial crossover seems to justify their reinvestment in more conservative models of femininity in which they pull back from their own career ambitions in favor of "economic lockdown."[15] But the dream of domesticity is elusive.

14. Edin and Kefalas (2005) argue that these problems are endemic in poor communities, but note that they occur in all racial groups.

15. Although I have chosen to focus on three cases in this chapter, I found this pattern among other middle-class wannabes as well. This is also interesting in juxtaposition to Sidel's (1990) finding that many young women are now growing up believing that they must be able to take care of themselves, rather than investing in dreams of domesticity, and Stombler and Padavic's (1997) finding that belief in women's economic independence is more common among Black women than among white women.

Multiracial babies and racial crossover

For these women, as for many poor women (Edin and Kefalas 2005), do-mestic fantasies that pregnancies would solidify their heterosexual unions are unrealized. Rather than compelling their boyfriends to settle down with them, the wannabes' pregnancies set them up as single mothers shoul-dering disproportionate economic, physical, and social responsibility for their children. Moreover, their position as mothers of multiracial babies solidifies their race and class transgressions, foreclosing at least some of the privileges of white middle-classness.

For wannabes, multiracial children raise complicated political and practical issues. These children challenge the notion that these women's involvement with Black and Latino men is a "phase" or a "rebellion" by committing them to a lifetime of involvement through their biracial chil-dren. But although children may seem to be a potent symbol of racial au-thentication, they do not confer automatic cross-racial legitimacy to their mothers, and may actually increase the criteria for membership by adding culturally specific expectations for mothering (Winddance Twine 1999). They thus don't decrease wannabes' dependence on men of color for their racial crossover identities.

Multiracial children potentially provide community membership in three ways. First, under the cultural legacy of hypodescent, multiracial ba-bies can be seen as automatic members of communities of color; they are (usually) understood to be "of color" themselves. Second, Black or Latino paternity gives the multiracial child biological ties to members of the Black or Latino communities. Third, the experience of mothering, particularly under circumstances that do not correspond with the white middle-class script (none of these women are married and they all rely on some sort of state economic assistance), provides them a point of commonality with other women in poor communities of color. In combination, these factors bring these mothers more directly in contact with some of the issues of ra-cial stereotypes and discrimination both through the experiences of their children and through their own involvement with social services—an arena in which their multiracial children make their transgressions conspicu-ous.[16] Accordingly, these children complicate these women's economic

16. In some communities, white middle-class parents of adopted Black children are in-creasingly visible. Wannabes are easily distinguishable from these more respectable parents because of their race, class, and gender performances. Additionally, birthing a multiracial

mobility—at the least making upward mobility more difficult. In many ways, then, these children solidify the race and class transgressions of their mothers.

As for other women, motherhood deepens the requirements for good gendered behavior. The pervasive "ideology of intensive mothering" holds all mothers, regardless of race or class, accountable to a set of increasingly time- and emotion-consuming standards for maternal behavior (Hays 1996). For mothers of children of color, the responsibilities can be even more intense, as they need to be able to teach their children to navigate racism with their dignity intact (Hill Collins 1994). Preliminary studies of white mothers of multiracial children suggest that they face additional expectations within communities of color to prove their abilities to mother nonwhite children: to pass on the cultural traditions of the father's family, as well as to teach racial navigation (e.g., Winddance Twine 1999). These mothers also face the possibility of having their children perceived as "trophy" children, increasing, rather than decreasing, disdain for their racial transgressions. Remember Nia's dismissal in the last chapter: "I see someone and I know they're just struggling to be anything but white. Like they have a kid with a Black guy or something. It's just gross." Thus, multiracial babies may not confer automatic membership in communities of color, even while they increase the gendered constraints on the behavior of the mothers.

When women become mothers, expectations of conventional gender performances increase. For these reasons, Sikes (1997) finds, maternity is the one circumstance that legitimates young women's exit from gang participation. Thus, even for women whose prematernity behavior did not conform to conventional notions of proper femininity, motherhood can usher in an intensification of gender policing. Children, then, can deflate the gendered space (even if it was small to begin with) garnered by wannabes' cross-racial projects (even when the experience of mothering is in itself satisfying or a source of esteem). As Laurie's experiences with motherhood illustrate, children can actually work to invalidate community membership by creating a new and emotionally powerful arena for improper gender performances.

Multiracial babies, then, do not undo wannabes' reliance on heterosexual bonds with Black and Latino men for community authentication.

baby is stigmatized, while adopting a Black baby may be seen as humanitarian (see Dalmage 2000).

This situation is perhaps best exemplified by Jaclyn, whose enactment of motherhood includes the integration of elements of Puerto Rican culture into her child's life. But Jaclyn has a divisive relationship with her child's father and has been rejected by the Puerto Rican community who initially embraced her. Her identity continues to be centered on her quest for an enduring relationship with a Black or Latino man.

Conclusion

The three women in this study do not match the pictures drawn of wanna-bes by the youth in the last chapter. Although they may have some of the same contours (Jaclyn more so than the others), their cultural projects are more multifaceted and less superficial than their stereotypes suggest. These are not just women hoping to be cool, though they are often also that, but women who use the possibilities of racial crossover to solve a wide array of problems posed by the contradictions of narrowly defined race, class, and gender identities. These are not just insecure women searching for a visible identity, but women who consciously use cultural resources to redefine their own relationships to race, class, and gender.

Women "wannabe" for a range of reasons. Resisting the limitations of whiteness, they engage a strategy of racial crossover that gives them access to coolness, toughness, and excitement, and that allows them to avoid expectations that they be "nice." In each of these cases, racial crossover is a class strategy, but one that is shaped by different class resources. For Monica, the upper-middle-class woman, wannabehood is a means of ab-negating race and class privilege. Her strategy involves class crossover in a way that Jaclyn's and Laurie's do not, but is ensnared by her fail-ure to fully give up the cultural capital that maintains her relative privi-leges. Jaclyn's working-class strategy claims class allegiance, rather than class crossover. Jaclyn uses race to make her class identity more interest-ing, and to open up an identity path on which she can hope to achieve some success. Key to this project is maintaining a respectable working-class identity. She is tripped up, however, by the challenges to her au-thenticity that arise out of racial identity politics. Finally, for Laurie, suf-focated by the conditions of her desperate poverty, wannabehood is a means of accessing disreputable feminine behaviors, of throwing off the limitations that come with white femininity, even if that whiteness is "low class." Her strategy eases the constraints in her life, but because it also increases surveillance of her gender performance, is always on the verge of coming undone.

Although their racial transgressions follow different patterns and employ different cultural resources, what these women have in common is their desire for Black and Latino men. Indeed, it is this desire that marks them as "wannabes." Constrained by the expectations of a white middle-class femininity that is undesirable, insufficiently rewarding, or out of reach, wannabes use racial transgressions to breach the attendant sexual rules. By embodying and acting upon their desire for Black and Latino men, wannabes violate expectations for intraracial sexuality, expectations that are leveled much more heavily at women than at men. The wannabes' project expands the bounds of heterosexual desire, but it does not easily throw off all of the confines of white middle-class feminine performances. Instead, it draws upon and reinstates normative expectations for other aspects of feminine sexual behavior. Aimed at domesticity, wannabes' sexual strategies perpetuate competitive and hierarchical relations between women, and thus legitimate heterosexual double standards that privilege men's sexuality over women's. Thus, their racial transgressions only partially transform the meaning of gender in their own lives, and do not undo hierarchical gender relations more generally. Indeed, their racial and, for some, class transgressions are enabled by their invocation of a more conventional sexuality, albeit aimed at the wrong kind of men.

Even when wannabes perform sexuality differently, they face similar constraints. Jaclyn works to command heterosexual attention, posturing herself as a heterosexually savvy, sexually desirable woman, but Laurie is uncomfortable with such a role. Jaclyn claims sexual restraint; Laurie struggles to abandon her own feelings of sexual obligation in order to enact unrestrained sexuality. Despite these distinctions in their performances of sexuality, both are seen as sexually deviant. Their sexuality is marked as nonnormative because they desire Black and Latino men.

Roediger (2002) argues that one limitation of experiences of racial cross-pollination is that they are largely "mediated by commodities." Cross-racial engagement through commodities is typically time-limited, occurring among youth, and ultimately undermined by the "possessive [material] investments" of white adults. This process makes cultural cross-racial engagement superficial by locating them solely in the realm of culture, and not engaging issues of economic or political power. The women in this chapter, however, are situated differently. First, as we've seen, their racial crossover is not limited to commodity consumption. Indeed, it is enacted more powerfully though romantic and sexual realignment. Second, it is not ephemeral. Not only have these women been participating in racial crossover projects for many years, but what may have started as youth projects have spilled over, perhaps irrevocably, into adult commitments. For white women, the long-term rejection of white men as heterosexual partners is a disinvestment in white property. Their racial crossover limits their ability to enact white power and privilege through material investments. For Monica, some white middle-class privileges might be recoverable, but for both Jaclyn and Laurie, multiracial babies in combination with other class markers severely limit upward mobility.

Yet the wannabes' projects are neither personally nor collectively transformative, even when they explicitly embrace simultaneous projects of antiracism, as Monica does. These women's lives are caged in by their almost singular investment in heterosexuality. While the use of sexuality to achieve racial crossover mounts a more significant challenge to racial boundaries than consumption alone, it reworks inequalities of race, class, and gender in their lives. Their sexual strategy enmeshes them in disempowering gender relations, limits their class resources, and, by not directly confronting issues of gender inequity, stunts their racial project as well.

CHAPTER EIGHT

Conclusions, Contradictions, and Collisions

G oths, University Unity Christians, and Puerto Rican wannabes are all examples of local subcultural identities claimed by contemporary young adults. Although these identity projects are visibly marked, and are often inexplicable to outsiders, they have much in common with other identities young adults deploy as they navigate the advent of adulthood. Indeed, in some ways these identity projects are as much a part of the ritual and folklore of the contemporary process of coming of age as learning how to drive and being able to buy alcohol legally. But despite their pervasiveness, subcultures continue to alarm. This alarm, in part, arises from the personal instability and cultural uncertainty of adolescence and young adulthood. Identity projects may be part of adulthood, but they also have the potential to go wrong, to fail to be transitory, or to bring permanent costs. This alarm probably expresses real intergenerational anxieties, but it is also a useful smokescreen; moral panic about the putative immorality and apathy of contemporary youth deflects political and cultural attention from other social problems (see Males 1996).

Subcultures are an important site of investigation, then, simply because they can shed some light on this cultural hand-wringing. In investigating subcultures, we get a closer view of the role they play in the lives of contemporary youth, and thus gain insights into the paradoxes faced by contemporary young adults—subcultural participants or not. This scrutiny can also address the question of potential danger. But while subcultures are often implicated in the youth crisis, their role in reproducing the adult culture, even while providing temporary relief from it, is well established by subcultural theory (e.g., Willis 1977, Bettie 2003).

My analyses of goths, Unity Christians, and wannabes are consistent with this theoretical tradition. Depending on one's perspective, the subcultural stories I have told might provide relief: none of these participants is as weird, volatile, or disruptive as she initially seems. For those whose perspective is more like my own, these stories are probably discouraging, reminding us that even audacious, spectacular cultural experiments, the kind of projects some of us might wish we could have tried, are hemmed in by the intractability of race, class, and gender.

This conclusion, however, is merely the tip of the iceberg. These subcultures are useful analytical sites for a number of specific and more general reasons. First, because they offer spectacular, if explicable, solutions to the problems posed by young adulthood, they provide an exceptional vantage on the contemporary experience of coming of age. Second, subcultures are sites of marked identity production. They thus add to our understanding of how identities are constructed and deployed. In particular, these examples illustrate the centrality of sexuality to the process of identity construction and marking.

Third, the dilemmas these youth face—social marginalization, the navigation of the dichotomy between cool and mobile/respectable, compulsory dating—are bound up in and produced out of extralocal and local changes in the meaning of race, class, and gender categories. Their negotiations thus illustrate the processes by which these categories are activated, manipulated, and pinned in place; in other words, they illustrate how identities are shaped by inequalities. They also expose how the contradictions posed by the need to navigate bounded categories are played out in daily lives. Moreover, they show us how alterations to the content of race, class, and gender categories can be consolidated into existing hierarchies of meaning. Finally, these subcultures demonstrate how race, class, and gender are woven together, exposing the ways in which these systems of inequality are not just experienced as intersected but are in fact mutually reinforcing systems.

Becoming authentic

The variations in the goth, Unity Christian, and wannabe projects emerge out of particularities in their relationships to the web of young adult dilemmas: their own race and class locations, their skills and experiences, their personal histories. Even within projects, individual differences and shifting contexts lead to different strategic emphases. These projects draw on an arsenal of accoutrements that includes clothing, music, language, emotions, politics, and sexuality. But although they draw from similar arsenals, there are variable formulas for identity construction.

Wannabes, goths, and Unity Christians pick and choose from this arsenal, piecing together novel and situationally variable combinations with the aim of achieving authenticity. Although this process allows for individual creativity, it is by no means a free-for-all. Authenticity is an ongoing achievement that relies on the display of the race, class, and gender meanings assigned to the identity. These projects manipulate race, class, and gender expectations, yet authentic membership also relies on identities achieved through the "proper" performance of race, class, and gender. Thus, "authentic" identities allow some shifts in race, class, and gender meanings, while hardening other dimensions.

The goths, the Unity Christians, and the wannabes also show us that authentic membership cannot be superficially achieved. Debates about "posers" make this clear. When individuals perform identities thinly— by manipulating only their physical presentations or their musical tastes, for example—they are not accorded authenticity. Instead, authenticity requires an alignment of "inner" selves with outer performances.[1]

Goths, University Unity participants, and wannabes tell stories to establish authenticity. Their stories rely on similar narrative formulations claiming a core, coherent, and stable self. By becoming goth, wannabe, or Christian (with Jesus's help), they found their real selves. As with other identities, mastery of the (sub)cultural narrative signals successful membership.

Within subcultures and outside of them, fashion is an important medium for the communication of group and individual boundaries. By demarcating boundaries between groups, fashion communicates both inclusion and exclusion, while also allowing for individual differentiation (Simmel 1972). Fashion thus allows participants to demonstrate membership as well as to claim status within the group. Fashion is also used to create hierarchies between groups and to communicate information about the group. Eckert (1989) argues:

---

1. Goffman (1959, 58) notes that we often assess authenticity by giving "special attention to features of the performance that cannot be readily manipulated, thus enabling us to judge the reliability of the more misrepresentable cues in the performance." In keeping with this analysis, inner lives seem less "readily manipulated" than do outer identity markers, even while we have seen the ways in which they too are molded.

As a social marker of group membership, clothing style is closely associated with social and cultural characteristics of groups and can elicit powerful emotional reactions. Style is interpreted as not just as an indication of social affiliation but as a direct and intentional expression of group values, a marker of group boundaries, and thus a rejection of alternative values (62).

The projects in this study all illustrate this relationship between style and group values. Dark goth outfits reject mainstream fashion rules and dominant emotional expectations. Conservative Christian attire communicates commitment to order and restraint. Wannabes' hip-hop outfits signal cross-racial allegiances.

For youth, whose insatiable consumption of fashion has been exploited by marketers for several generations, fashion is a particularly dynamic arena of identity production. At once, fashion can induce anxiety *and* be fun, allowing young people to play with "looks" and styles. Moreover, while commentators often lament teen use of fashion to "fit in," youth also use fashion to differentiate themselves—from each other and, crucially, from their parents. Hippies, for example, are legendary for their use of loose, androgynous clothing and hairstyles to communicate their rejection of uptight "bourgeois" adulthood. The symbolic efficacy of style resides in its visibility: fashion has great shock value and its message is communicated to all onlookers. But it is also useful because it is transitory. Identity accoutrements are, for the most part, easily put on and taken off, allowing individuals to slip out of confrontational identities if necessary. Moreover, entire styles can be abandoned over time. Thus, hippies again are noted for their eventual assimilation into the adult middle-class mainstream. For (middle-class) youth part of the strategic appeal of fashion is its impermanence. Indeed, for middle-class youth, stylistic rebellion from the parent culture is almost an expected aspect of the growing up process. Fashion is a safe and expected arena for middle-class youth rebellion.

Despite, or because of, these attributes, style is a variable signifier. Because audiences vary (by cohorts, for example) in their assumptions and knowledge about fashion, its communication of group values can be "opaque" (McCracken 1998). A parent may be alarmed about his or her child's new look (although we have seen that many parents are not), while peers may interpret the same look as inauthentic. Thus, style needs to be combined with other components of identity to ensure accurate communication. Moreover, as my examples demonstrate, while style is a key part of the identity arsenal and helps shape the identity ideal type, it isn't mandatory. Some goths wore non-goth ensembles for work or other obligations. Wannabes put together variable fashion combinations. And even some Unity Christians talk about the growing acceptance of deviant stylistic markers like piercings and dyed hair. These subcultural identities, then, are not fully reliant on fashion.

Emotional orientations are another important, but much less explicitly visible, arena for the expression of subcultural norms. Although the mass popularity of psychotherapy (and of mood-altering drugs) suggests that emotions can be changed, emotions are typically viewed as innate, and are thus seen as signaling something about a person's core self (Irvine 1999). Goths, Unity Christians, and wannabes all use emotional distinctions to position themselves vis-à-vis "mainstream" emotional expectations. The goths are "dark." Unity Christians are "happy." Wannabes have "attitude." These emotional orientations work much like fashion: they establish group boundaries and communicate the group's values. For the goths, darkness is a visible rejection of the "fetishized happiness" of the middle class. For the Christians, happiness proves that they are good people. And for the wannabes, attitude is a means of establishing cross-racial and sometime cross-class allegiances. Subcultural emotional patterns thus establish the authenticity of a participant's identity and the superiority of the subculture.

Emotional styles are also solutions. Each offers a different way of managing dominant emotional expectations. The goth's darkness allows them to express pain and sadness typically seen as socially undesirable. Unity Christians' happiness anchors their goodness, but also "proves" the rightness of their identity path. Attitude allows wannabes emotional expression outside the bounds of white middle-class feminine passivity. These examples show that emotions are used to mark group boundaries *and* to make identity expectations more manageable. They thus point to both the importance of emotions in the bounding and navigation of race, class, and gender identities, and the difficulties posed by emotional expectations that are often unmarked and assumed to be "appropriate."

Much like fashion, however, emotional performances are uneven. Unity Christians, more than the other groups, demand emotional conformity, although their expectations are higher for women than they are for men. "Attitude" varies among wannabes. Jaclyn has attitude all the time, Laurie's attitude is situational, and Shari (whose story I chose not to tell) laughs at the notion that she has attitude at all. Goths expect that intense preoccupation with darkness will be transitory, while also jokingly pointing to a subgenre of membership they call the "perky goth." Thus, emotional performances are an important component of identities, but their use is elastic.

In contrast to both fashion and emotions, however, in this study, sub-cultural performances of sexuality were inflexible. Goths solidify their freakiness as well as their claim to emotional, moral, and political supe-riority through their rejection of normative sexual practices like monogamy, strict heterosexuality, and "vanilla" sex. Unity Christians require a com-mitment to nonmarital sexual abstinence. The wannabes are wannabes, and not just trendy hip-hoppers, because they consistently claim Black and Latino men as their rightful sexual partners. The role of sexuality in these projects reveals its centrality to race, class, and gender meanings.

As a cultural resource, sexuality works differently from other forms of style. As I noted in the introduction, contemporary understandings of sex-uality locate it as something intrinsic to a person; thus, although it might in experience be experimental, temporary, or transitional, sexuality isn't culturally understood as something that someone can try on and take off in the way that clothes and other commodity markers are. But it is not just interiority that makes sexuality such a powerful identity marker—emotion, after all, is also seen as interior.

In the next sections, I look more closely at the role of sexuality in these young people's negotiations, first, of race, and then of gender. In the first section, I revisit the dilemmas posed by the cultural opposition of cool-ness and mobility, considering the roles of race and class in both shaping and solving these dilemmas. In the second, I foreground gender, analyz-ing the links between femininity, sexuality, romance, and respectability. Finally, I turn to the ways in which each subculture's sexual strategies, in combination with its other social logics, shape friendships among women and across other social boundaries.

Dilemmas of whiteness and class location: coolness and mobility

The tension between cool and mobility is a common dilemma of young adulthood. Being cool brings excitement, fun, infamy. It provides an anti-dote to experiences of unbendable structure or sterility. It puts you on the social map. But it also comes with social costs—not just through the potential fallout associated with discrete behaviors but also because it is ani-mated by an explicitly racialized and implicitly classed cultural dichotomy.

For middle-class white people, whiteness is a taken-for-granted identity, one that is powerful because it is unmarked. The normalcy that gives middle-class whiteness its social power also renders it boring and unhip. Cool, in contrast, evokes race and class anxiety, even when race and class are invisible. The goth, Unity Christian, and wannabe projects provide different solutions to this dilemma. For all three of these projects, mediating the relationship between cool and mobility also mediates their relationships to whiteness and to class.

The wannabes are the only group that make race explicit, but the subcultures in this study are all racial projects. Populated almost entirely by white participants, each subculture provides a different contemporary, local way of doing whiteness. These subcultures solve personal dilemmas for the participants, allowing them to stake out meaningful identities in a historical period in which whiteness has come to mean cultural emptiness. These projects also offer collective solutions to the question of white identity by providing diverse ways of being white. If nothing else, each of these subcultures provides an alternative to the vacuousness and conformity they associate with the white middle-class mainstream—the preps who become frat kids.

In the case of the wannabes, the relationship between race and coolness is most explicit. Wannabes claim coolness through the performance of a lower-class, Puerto Rican–associated femininity, and through their relationships with Black and Puerto Rican men, who are culturally designated as the ultimate embodiment of cool. Their claims are anchored by their sexuality. For some of the wannabes, this claim makes sense, since their access to mobility was already limited by their class location. For other wannabes, the claim to coolness allays the dissatisfactory payoff for women of seeking mobility. In either case, the challenge to their claim by youth of color exposes its race and class dimensions. Youth of color make clear that coolness is a raced characteristic off-limits to whites. Although they implicitly add a class dimension to coolness, class membership alone is not a sufficient criterion for claiming cool (Eminem's phenomenal success as a poor white hip-hopper notwithstanding).

The goths attempt to stake out a middle ground, combining elements of cool with elements of mobility, and moderating their claims to cool by adding safety valves. This strategy sidesteps the long-term pitfalls of the wannabes' approach, but it doesn't provide an unsullied claim to cool either. The abandon and freedom of cool, the stance of "not giving a fuck" (Boyd 1997), is undermined by the goth strategy of limited liability. But while the goth claim to cool is partial, it nevertheless expands the territory of whiteness, and of middle-classness, to include spectacular cultural play. Thus, it provides an interesting and fun cultural identity for white, middle-class youth.

The University Unity Christian strategy, in contrast, denies the validity of cool altogether. Instead, Unity Christians focus on conventional aspects of mobility: hard work, discipline, and restraint. For some, this strategy dismisses the cultural value of an arena in which they were never competitive. For others, the rejection of cool can be more ambivalent; the abandonment of any claim to cool may come at the cost of social pain. The Unity Christian strategy updates a conservative cultural tradition, while also creating a safe and meaningful alternative for some white middle-class youth.

These three projects offer different resolutions to the same problems: How do I reconcile my short-term desire to be cool with my long-term desire to be successful? How do I establish a meaningful cultural identity when whiteness seems to have no culture? The identities these subcultural projects offer provide individual solutions to these dilemmas, helping participants steer through the pain, anxiety, and unsettledness of young adulthood. But, in doing so, they also recreate many of the cultural distinctions— between cool and mobility, white and nonwhite, moral and immoral—that shape their dilemmas in the first place.

The dichotomy posed between cool and mobile is a principal cultural script through which young people read race. This script is complicated, as it does not provide an unequivocal condemnation of Black and Puerto Rican culture. Instead, it mixes contempt with longing into a thick and steamy brew. This murky mix dissolves race and class, and thus young people can avoid acknowledging them at all (consciously or not). But despite this (real or feigned, deep or surface) "color blindness," young people are savvy cultural navigators. They know the costs and associations of the cool-mobility mix, and choose their strategies accordingly. This is made transparent by the reactions to the wannabes, whose claim to cool is challenged on racial grounds by the youth of color.

Moreover, although young adulthood reshuffles the status hierarchies of later adulthood, this shuffling is ambivalent. Despite the valorized invocation of cool, both wannabes and youth of color are also aware of their costs (see also Carter 2005). Cool provides a "badge of dignity" (Bettie 2003), but this badge does not ameliorate its costs to stability and respectability. Wannabes' claim to coolness via alternative race performances

ultimately precludes their access to mobility. Responses to the wannabes
expose the racial costs of cool, in addition to the costs to mobility. Cool
is equated with a social darkening. The symbolic opposition of these concepts perpetuates race and class hierarchies.

To be clear, I am not suggesting that white people can never be seen
as cool or popular (these aren't necessarily the same social positions).
In most white-dominated high schools (such as the ones most goths and
Unity Christians attended), white youth top the social hierarchy. Accordingly, the symbolic boundaries that goths and Unity Christians draw are
often (but not always) against other *white* youth. This is not altogether
surprising; Stuber (2006) finds that college students draw symbolic class
boundaries against the groups positioned *above* them, rather than below.
This process, she suggests, maintains their privilege in two ways. First, it
keeps those who are less privileged invisible. Second, it allows groups to
deny their own privilege (because they compare themselves to *more* privileged students).

For the goths and the Unity Christians, self-marginalization aids this
process; by focusing their attention on their own experiences of outsidership, self-marginalization blinds them to their own structural privileges *and*
to the experiences of those who are less privileged than they. Race and
class are visible to the wannabes in ways that they are not to either the
goths or the Unity Christians, and yet, in their attempts to achieve race
neutrality, wannabes also fail to apprehend some of the ways in which
they are privileged as white women (or, in Monica's case, by class). Self-
marginalization is abetted by race status, moreover, as a privilege of
whiteness is that it can be displaced by a presumably raceless, subcultural
identity (this is not the case of the wannabes, for whom race is ever visible; Nayak 2003). Note that hip-hop is ubiquitously referred to as "Black,"
while goth is *not* described as "white."

As these projects show, whiteness is flexible. The multiplicity of whiteness, and its ability to shift course, allow it to flow over and past potentially damming challenges to its meaning and taken-for-granted superiority. Variations in whiteness are accompanied by variations in class.
Although there is some range within each project, the goths could be
roughly characterized as upper-middle-class in comparison to the less stable middle-class locations shared by most of the Unity Christians. These
gradations within the generic category "middle-class" may help shape the
choices of cultural project made by the participants. The goth project is
not only enabled by material resources, it also activates more bourgeois

values, particularly the emphases on creativity and self-expression. It is also riskier in its attempts to combine cool with mobility. The Unity Christian project, in contrast, shores up its middle-class location by emphasizing qualities associated with mobility. Notably, in both projects, although participants use consumption in their identity performances, they disdain conspicuous consumption.

Wannabes, who have more complicated class origins, are also white. They are both more aware of and more ambivalent about their whiteness than the participants in the other groups. Rather than expanding the territory of whiteness to include access to cool through Black and Puerto Rican cultural forms (which may be what white, suburban hip-hoppers are doing), Wannabes attempt to gain cool by crossing racial lines: in other words, they do not try to pull cool into whiteness, but rather to propel their own white bodies into Black and Puerto Rican cool. In doing this, they are also exiled from whiteness by their white peers. The wannabes' project of racial crossover abandons them in a racial Neverland: they are neither welcome as fellow white travelers, nor are they fully welcomed into Blackness and Puerto Ricanness. This liminal position, seemingly contradictorily, unsettles *and* reactivates fixed racial categories. It also exposes the boundaries of those categories, and the ways in which they are also shaped by gender and sexuality.

"Bad boys" and "bad girls" are not cultural equivalents. When men and boys are "bad," they do not violate assumptions about their essential masculinity, whereas when women and girls are "bad," they are judged unfeminine. For women, raced and classed femininity relies as much, or more, on "good girl" behavior, on being respectable, than it does on the performance or acquisition of skills associated with socioeconomic mobility through paid labor force participation.

Sexuality animates these gender dilemmas. Unconstrained and successful heterosexuality is central to cool, while restrained sexuality is central to femininity. In addition, judgments about sexual restraint position women in race and class hierarchies, with each group using feminine sexual restraint to claim superiority (Nagel 2003, Wilkins 2004a). Wannabes attempt to resolve this dilemma by combining nonsexual components of cool (attitude, style, spatial occupation) with sexual liaisons with cool men. They thus hope to retain respectability while also accessing cool. But the narrow range of respectable feminine sexual behavior, regardless of race or class location, means that wannabes' desire for the "wrong" men closes the doors on either side of the race divide, shutting them out of whiteness, while preventing their full access to Blackness and Puerto Ricanness. The experience of the wannabes suggests that the centrality of sexuality to divisions of gender *and* divisions of race and class makes racial status less stable for women.

Dilemmas of femininity: Romance and respectability

Goth, Unity Christianity, and wannabehood each provide young women with a distinctive solution to the paradoxes posed by contemporary expectations for femininity, and particularly feminine sexuality. The goth, Unity Christian, and wannabe projects differently reject the demands of the young adult sexual and romantic marketplace. Goths explode the behavioral constraints of feminine sexuality by claiming desire, experimental sexuality, and the right to have multiple partners. They also expand dominant notions of sexual attractiveness to include presentations of feminine sexuality at which they are skilled. Unity Christians sidestep the ubiquitous college marketplace by postponing sexuality and romance altogether. Wannabes dismiss the mandate that they be available exclusively (or at all) for sexual and romantic relationships with white men.

These responses are all distinct assertions of young women's right to define their own sexual choices—to decide with whom, how, or when they will be sexually engaged. They emerge from and reiterate the feminist declaration that women have the right to write their own lives. Moreover, they are responses that, in exposing and challenging assumptions about gendered sexual behavior, nudge open—if only slightly—the possibilities for feminine sexuality, and thus also for femininity. Each project, differently, provides young women with agency, with alternative choices, with pleasures and experiences unavailable in the conventional sexual marketplace. These projects importantly remind us that feminist struggles can be found in the most unlikely places, even when they are not claimed as such.

But each project, as I've shown, is also limited. Viewed together, these limitations, which are also often specific to the assumptions and strategies of each subculture, tell us something more generally about the reproduction of gender despite attempts to push open its constraints. What these projects have in common is the use of romance as a solution to threats of respectability. In each subculture, establishing a romantic commitment with a man is the key to securing gender, race, and class membership. Goth, Christian, and wannabe women each invoke romance as an important personal goal. In each case, romance is a strategy of redemption, tempering the costs of their various sexual violations.

The use of romance comes with costs. Despite, or because of, their challenges to sexual rules, none of these groups of women challenges the inequities embedded in cultural scripts of romance. Because sexuality and romance are entangled, the failure to critique romance confines each of their sexual strategies. Romance remains the primary frame through which young women's sexuality is made acceptable. Romance is not only seen as a feminine concern, interest, and responsibility, but it is also animated by different and unequal gender roles (Montemurro 2006). Romance is thus a principle axis of gender difference, recreating gendered experiences, responsibilities, and vulnerabilities.

By investing in romance, these very different young women hinder their attempts to carve out sexual space. Instead, they maintain their dependence on men for their identities and self-worth. In this sense, the Unity Christian strategy is in some ways, and unexpectedly, powerful, as it at least pushes back the pull of romance altogether. But this too is temporary.

Moreover, as these three projects make vivid, romance isn't just an axis of gender inequality. Romance binds gender projects to race and class concerns. Romance is the gendered filter activated by young women to mitigate the race and class costs of their sexual transgressions, however small. Through its link to, for example, the wedding industry, romance also generates consumption and ever more opulent class displays.[2] This use for romance goes beyond these three examples, as the "love knows no bounds" discourse behind the current movement to legalize gay marriage exemplifies (see, e.g., Fields 2004). Romance makes deviant sexual appetites respectable.

But romance doesn't work equally well in all of these projects. The wannabes also long for romantic heterosexual relationships, but this longing does not make them respectable. The wannabes' sexuality is in many ways more conventional than that of the goths (they are typically monogamous, they do not embrace bisexuality or other forms of experimental sex), yet they are less able than the goths to recuperate from their sexual transgressions. In part, this distinction illustrates the different sorts of protections afforded to middle and upper-middle-class sexual experiments.

2. Between 1984 and 1994, average wedding costs increased from $4,000 to $16,000 (Otnes and Pleck 2003; see also Ingraham 1999, Montemurro 2006).

But this difference also suggests that sexual desire across the color line (especially if it also across the class line) is more threatening than sexual desire that upsets intraracial and intraclass gender boundaries. The experience of the wannabe Monica, whose privileged class background is similar to the backgrounds of most of the goths, adds weight to this suggestion. Monica was not seen as respectable, despite her upper-middle-class cultural capital. Instead, the birth of a "mixed" baby and her continued liaisons with the "wrong" men tarnished her. The raced and classed dimensions of romance undermine the wannabes' use of romance as a gender strategy. Indeed, their desire for romance, rather than just sex, with poor Black and Puerto Rican men may be the factor that permanently undermines their respectability. Sex across the color line, while transgressive, could be rehabilitated as a perhaps understandable, although unfeminine, desire to experience the exotic other. Romance across the color line evokes permanence, suggests that there is more to the desire than just the erotic exploration of the other, and makes wannabes unavailable for intraracial family formation. For wannabes like Monica, it also propels them across the class line.

Romance draws on essentialized notions of love that resonate with cultural discourses that "love is blind," that people can and should find their "soul mates," and that love should therefore not be subject to social control. These ideas can be used to push against boundaries of love, such as in the quest for gay marriage, but their assumptions occlude the many ways in which love is, in fact, socially organized. This social organization not only shapes its gendered expression but also, significantly, shapes its race and class expression. Although the legal restrictions on interracial marriage have been stricken down for almost forty years, and rates of intermarriage have risen accordingly, race and class homophily in marriage continues to be a central means of bounding access to social, cultural, and economic capital (e.g., Romano 2003).

Responses to different sexual violations also point to the importance of the relationship between (raced and classed) femininity and (raced and classed) masculinity: the acceptability of women's sexual strategies is shaped by its impact on masculinity. The goth women's use of sexuality to push against the bounds of femininity, while it does challenge the ideas that men should control the terms of sexuality and that men have the right to exclusive sexual ownership of the women with whom they are involved, also benefits the masculinity of goth men. It provides them with access to successful sexuality, it reduces the labor involved in the sexual chase, and, more insidiously, it allows them to see themselves as nicer and more "evolved" than other men. As long as proactive feminine sexuality does not deny white, middle-class men sexual access to women, it can bolster their political and moral position by allowing them to see themselves (or be seen) as more progressive than "Neanderthal" men who presumably objectify or otherwise mistreat women (Wilkins forthcoming). The wannabes, in contrast, deny white, middle-class men access, providing an ideological victory of sorts to Black and Puerto Rican men.

Sexuality is a powerful system of regulation, in part because it ties together systems of inequality. It marks gender difference, class difference, and racial difference, dividing women from men, bad women from good women. Despite dramatic changes in women's sexual behavior, the performance of feminine restraint retains a powerful hold. Even within the diverse sexual cultures in this book, each group of women uses romance and commitment to claim sexual respectability. Men's ability to project some sexual competence is also valuable, but it is given more latitude; it is women's sexual restraint that matters most for group status (Das Gupta 1997, Espiritu 2001). Thus, for women, deviating from the narrowly prescribed sexual role threatens both gender and racial status. This double jeopardy undercuts women's attempts to maneuver along either dimension, reigning in their struggles on the gender boundary and on the race (and class) boundary. Sexuality is the trap from which they cannot be sprung.

Friendship

Each cultural project structures not just relations between women and men, but also relations among women. Both goth and University Unity Christianity lay the foundation for intensive friendships with others inside their group. In both subcultures, participants spend substantial time together. For goths, weekly get-togethers at the Sanctuary are supplemented by ongoing online exchanges. Both goths and Unity Christians are expected to emotionally disclose to each other—an expectation that intensifies their bonds. For Unity Christians, these bonds are more stable.

Differences in stability emerge out of differences in their sexual cultures. Because Unity Christians don't date, their energy and time is not diverted into heterosexual relationships. In addition, sexual intrigue doesn't threaten existing bonds, as it can with the goths. The goth norms of polyamory and women's bisexuality endorse multiple emotional commitments, but these norms can bring unintended costs. Because it entails multiple relationships that need to be nurtured, polyamory is often more draining of time and emotion than is monogamy. Moreover, the possibility of sexuality between women expands women's sexual options, but also creates new expectations that potentially undermine their friendships with other women. First, for goth women, the possibility of sexual relationships with women friends often means that such relationships are expected. As Beth recounts, she has been pressured (often by men with whom the women were also involved) to begin or resume sexual relationships with women friends. In practice, then, a norm of bisexuality among women can reduce their options to have nonsexual friendships with other women. And, sexual relationships are often more tenuous than nonsexual relationships (although I have been impressed with the ways in which some goth women maintain friendships with women with whom they had been sexually involved, so this outcome is not inevitable). Finally, goth participation in live journals provides an additional avenue to friendship fallouts.

While Unity Christian friendships are more stable, however, they are also more constraining. University Unity women describe their friendships with other women as emotionally sustaining. This emotional sustenance, however, depends on, and lays the groundwork for, internal monitoring of behavior and feelings. Community norms not only allow, but demand, that they intervene when others seem to be straying. Thus, in University Unity, friendships are an important mechanism of regulation. Goths also regulate each other's behavior and feelings, but their community norms are more flexible than are those of the Unity Christians. This flexibility arises, in part, out of the goths' more permeable group boundaries, as well as their more (but not, as I've shown, endlessly) flexible definitions of moral behavior.

Both goths and Unity Christians draw boundaries around their subculture, but these boundaries have different implications for friendships with people outside the group. Unity Christians repeatedly describe being frustrated by their inability to sustain close friendships with non-Christians. In part, this inability comes from the degree to which University Unity saturates their daily lives, draining time from other people and interests. It also comes from the degree to which they come to identify talking about God as central to their emotional well-being. This conversational topic does not play well in all contexts, and leads non-Christians or less devoted Christians to see them as abnormal or cultish. It is important to note, moreover, that the particularities of the Unity Christian identity foreclose meaningful relationships with Christians who practice Christianity differently, and thus limit the possibility of community networks with differently raced or classed Christians who participate in other organizations.[3]

Goth boundaries are more porous than University Unity boundaries. In part, this is because goth demands less time than does Unity Christianity—goth devotion to Internet communities notwithstanding. Thus, both sexual and nonsexual relationships may develop across community lines. Nevertheless, the non-goth spaces in which they circulate are also race and class homogenous. In addition, goths define "freak" broadly enough to include other unconventional sorts, rather than just goths. Still, the people who they define as fellow freaks are likely to share their class assumptions and race privileges. In contrast, goths derisively dismiss participants in Black popular culture, for example, as "sheep," "conformists," or "repulsive."

Puerto Rican wannabes, as I've shown, are different from both goths and Unity Christians in significant ways. Wannabes do not share a closely bounded group from which they can draw friends. Instead, the primacy of heterosexual relationships and the racial implications of their cross-racial pairings attenuate their friendships with other women. Wannabes, for the most part, do not maintain enduring relationships with either white women, who often call attention to their strategy of race neutrality, or with women of color, who are often disenchanted both by the wannabes' claims on Black and Puerto Rican men and by their inability (or unwillingness) to fully grasp the dynamics of race in their lives. Instead, for these women, jealousy and conflict are endemic features of their relationships with other women.

Intersectionality and cultural projects

The often invisible intersection of gender, race, and class constrains each project in this book. Specifically, for each, expansion along one boundary relies on the stability of another boundary. This process happens in both directions: in each project, stability on one boundary legitimates the challenge to another boundary, and each project's boundary challenge is blunted by its dependence on the stability of other boundaries. So even

---

3. On another predominantly white campus, Lassiter (2007) found that white Christians are more socially distant from Blacks than are other white students.

while wannabes launch a challenge to racial categories, their limited success recreates conventional, hierarchical gender relations. Similarly, the
partial success of the goth challenge to the gendered organization of heterosexuality relies on the stability of their privileged race and class location, while race and class anxiety, in turn, limits their gender challenge.
And the Unity Christian use of conservative sexuality to create gendered
space for their academic and psychological concerns is both enabled and
constrained by their more conventional race and class reproduction. Thus,
even while wannabes, goths, and Unity Christians use these identities to
elbow more space for themselves, in order to alter the gender, race, and
class rules to which they are held accountable, new gender, race, and class
rules snap into place, or old rules are resurrected. These insights point to
the benefits of trying to see social patterns from shifting perspectives.

This book, in part, is intended as an alternative to univocal portrayals of cultural projects. In the analysis and the writing, I moved between
analytical lenses deliberately, attempting to treat each group as raced,
classed, *and* gendered. This strategy, I admit, was easier said than done.
For me, it was much easier to see the ways in which each project was gendered than to see the race and class elements, particularly of the goths
and Unity Christians. I also found it difficult to think about the projects
as *simultaneously* gendered, raced, and classed without privileging gender (or getting hopelessly tangled). The notion that white middle-class
people are also raced and classed is not new, but few sociological studies have mapped out *how* such work should be done.[4] We simply have
too little practice treating white middle-class people as classed and raced,
particularly when race and class are unspoken among them (as they often
are). Despite these difficulties, the approach I took in this book yielded a
more complete picture of the successes and limitations of each project and
provided insight into how systems of inequality are woven together. More
specifically, the findings provide a window into the ways in which gender,
race, and class intersect in everyday lives, not just as statuses that people
carry and manipulate, but as ideological systems that organize inequality.

These findings, in turn, have implications for how we think about the
political potential of cultural movements and about social change. These
projects are limited precisely because they don't see, or don't see well
enough, the ways in which their lives are shaped by gender, race, *and* class.
The problems these projects face are not confined to youth or young adult

4. See Frankeberg 1993, Kenny 2000, and Perry 2002 for some exceptions.

projects, but are also faced by organizations with more explicit political goals. A more complete understanding would help cultural projects to better do what they aim to do: provide collective solutions to personal problems. At the same time, it would move us closer to significant social change.

Works Cited

Alumkal, Antony W. 2004. "American Evangelicalism in the Post–Civil Rights Era: A Racial Formation Analysis." *Sociology of Religion* 65.3:195–213.

Ammerman, Nancy. 1987. *Bible Believers: Fundamentalists in the Modern World.* New Brunswick, NJ: Rutgers University Press.

Anderson, Elijah. 1990. *Streetwise: Race, Class, and Change in an Urban Community.* Chicago: University of Chicago Press.

———. 1999. *Code of the Street: Decency, Violence, and the Moral Life of the Inner City.* New York: WW Norton.

Anderson, Margaret L. 2005. "Thinking About Women: A Quarter Century's View." *Gender & Society* 19.4 (August): 437–55.

Barton, Bernadette. 2002. "Dancing on the Moebius Strip: Challenging the Sex War Paradigm." *Gender & Society* 16:585–602.

Bearman, Peter S., and Hannah Bruckner. 2001. "Promising the Future: Virginity Pledges and First Intercourse." *American Journal of Sociology* 106:859–912.

Bellah, Robert N., Richard Madsen, William M. Sullivan, Ann Swidler, and Steven M. Tipton. 1985. *Habits of the Heart: Individualism and Commitment in American Life.* Berkeley: University of California Press.

Bettie, Julie. 2003. *Women without Class: Girls, Race, and Identity.* Berkeley: University of California Press.

Blumer, Herbert. 1958. "Race Prejudice as a Sense of Group Position." *Pacific Sociological Review* 1.1 (Spring): 3–7.

Bobo, Lawrence, James R. Kluegel, and Ryan A. Smith. 1997. "Laissez-faire Racism: The Crystallization of a Kinder, Gentler Antiblack Ideology." In *Racial Attitudes in the 1990s: Continuity and Change.* Edited by Steven Tuch and Jack Martin. Westport, CT: Praeger.

Bonilla-Silva, Eduardo. 2003. *Racism without Racists: Color-Blind Racism and the Persistence of Racial Inequality in the United States.* New York: Rowman and Littlefield.

Booth, Karen M. 2000. "'Just Testing': Race, Sex, and the Media in New York's 'Baby AIDS' Debate." *Gender & Society* 14.5 (October): 644–61.

Bourdieu, Pierre. 1984. *Distinction: A Social Critique of the Judgment of Taste.* Cambridge, MA: Harvard University Press.

Bourgois, Phillipe. 1995. *In Search of Respect: Selling Crack in El Barrio.* New York: Cambridge University Press.

Boyd, Todd. 1997. *Am I Black Enough for You? Popular Culture from the Hood and Beyond.* Bloomington: Indiana University Press.

Breines, Wini. 1992. *Young, White, and Miserable: Growing up Female in the Fifties.* Boston: Beacon Books.

Brodkin, Karen. 1999. *How Jews Became White Folks and What that Says About Race in America.* New Brunswick, NJ: Rutgers University Press.

Brown, Lyn Mikel. 1998. *Raising their Voices: The Politics of Girls' Anger.* Cambridge, MA: Harvard University Press.

Brumberg, Joan Jacobs. 1997. *The Body Project: An Intimate History of American Girls.* New York: Random House.

Brunson, Rod K., and Jody Miller. 2006. "Gender, Race, and Urban Policing: The Experience of African American Youths." *Gender & Society* 20.4 (August): 531–52.

Butler, Judith. 1990. *Gender Trouble: Feminism and the Subversion of Identity.* New York: Routledge.

Carbado, Devon W. 1998. "Black Male Racial Victimhood." *Callaloo*, special issue, 21.2 (Spring): 337–61.

Carpenter, Laura. 2005. *Virginity Lost: An Intimate Portrait of First Sexual Experiences.* New York: New York University Press.

Carter, Prudence. 2003. "'Black' Cultural Capital, Status Positioning, and Schooling Conflicts for Low-Income African-American Youth." *Social Problems* 50.1:136–55.

———. 2005. *Keepin' It Real: School Success Beyond Black and White.* New York: Oxford University Press.

Chancer, Lynn S. 1998. *Reconcilable Differences: Confronting Beauty, Pornography, and the Future of Feminism.* Berkeley: University of California Press.

Chito Childs, Erica. 2005. "Looking Behind the Stereotypes of the 'Angry Black Woman': An Exploration of Black Women's Responses to Interracial Relationships." *Gender & Society* 19.4 (August): 544–61.

Chong, Kelly H. 2006. "Negotiating Patriarchy: South Korean Evangelical Women and the Politics of Gender." *Gender & Society* 20.6 (December): 697–724.

Conley, Dalton. 2000. *Honky.* New York: Vintage Books.

Connell, R. W. 1987. *Gender and Power.* Stanford, CA: Stanford University Press.

Coontz, Stephanie. 1992. *The Way We Never Were: American Families and the Nostalgia Trap.* New York: Basic Books.

———. 1997. *The Way We Really Are: Coming to Terms with America's Changing Families.* New York: Basic Books.

———. 2005. *Marriage, a History: From Obedience to Intimacy, or How Love Conquered Marriage.* New York: Viking.

Cooper, Marianne. 2000. "Being the 'Go-to Guy': Fatherhood, Masculinity, and the Organization of Work in the Silicone Valley." *Qualitative Sociology* 23.4:379–405.

D'Emilio, John, and Estelle B. Freedman. 1988. *Intimate Matters: A History of Sexuality in America.* New York: Harper and Row.

Dalmage, Heather M. 2000. *Tripping on the Color Line: Black-White Multiracial Families in a Racially Divided World.* New Brunswick, NJ: Rutgers University Press.

Danius, Sara, and Stefan Jonsson. 1993. "An Interview with Gayatri Chakravorty Spivak." *boundary* 2.20:24–50.

Das Gupta, Monisha. 1997. "What is Indian about You? A Gendered, Transnational Approach to Ethnicity." *Gender & Society* 11.5:572–96.

Davidman, Lynn. 1991. *Tradition in a Rootless World: Women Turn to Orthodox Judaism.* Berkeley: University of California Press.

Davis, Angela. 1981. *Women, Race, and Class.* New York: Random House.

Donovan, Brian. 1998. "Political Consequences of Private Authority: Promise Keepers and the Transformation of Hegemonic Masculinity." *Theory & Society* 27:817–43.

Eckert, Penelope. 1989. *Jocks and Burnouts: Social Categories and Identity in the High School.* New York: Teachers College Press.

Edin, Kathryn, and Maria Kefalas. 2005. *Promises I Can Keep: Why Poor Women Put Motherhood Before Marriage.* Berkeley: University of California Press.

Ehrenreich, Barbara. 1989. *Fear of Falling: The Inner Life of the Middle Class.* New York: Pantheon Books.

Emerson, Michael, and Christian Smith. 2000. *Divided by Faith: Evangelical religion and the Problem of Race in America.* New York: Oxford University Press.

Espiritu, Yen Le. 2001. "'We Don't Sleep Around Like White Girls Do': Family, Culture, and Gender in Filipina American Lives." *Signs: Journal of Women in Culture and Society* 26.2:415–40.

Esterberg, Kristin. 1997. *Lesbian and Bisexual Identities: Constructing Community, Constructing Selves.* Philadelphia: Temple University Press.

Ferber, Abby L. 1998. *White Man Falling: Race, Gender, and White Supremacy.* New York: Rowman and Littlefield.

Ferguson, Ann Arnett. 2000. *Bad Boys: Public Schools in the Making of Black Masculinity.* Ann Arbor: University of Michigan Press.

Fields, Jessica. 2001. "Normal Queers: Straight Parents Respond to Their Children's 'Coming Out.'" *Symbolic Interaction* 24.2.

———. 2004. "Same Sex Marriage, Sodomy Laws, and the Sexual Lives of Young People." *Sexuality Research & Social Policy* 1.3 (September): 11–23.

———. 2005. "'Children Having Children': Race, Innocence, and Sexuality Education." *Social Problems* 52.4:549–70.

Fine, Michelle. 1988. "Sexuality, Schooling, and Adolescent Females: The Missing Discourse of Desire." *Harvard Educational Review* 58.1:29–53.

Fordham, Signithia. 1996. *Blacked Out: Dilemmas of Race, Identity, and Success at Capital High.* Chicago: University of Chicago Press.

Frankenberg, Ruth. 1993. *White Women, Race Matters: The Social Construction of Whiteness.* Minneapolis: University of Minnesota Press.

———, ed. 1997. *Displacing Whiteness: Essays in Social and Cultural Criticism.* Durham, NC: Duke University Press.

Fuchs Epstein, Cynthia. 1992. "Tinkerbells and Pinups: The Construction and Reconstruction of Gender Boundaries at Work." In *Cultivating Differences:*

Symbolic Boundaries and the Making of Inequality. Edited by Michele Lamont and Marcel Fournier. Chicago: University of Chicago Press.

Gaines, Donna. 1990. *Teenage Wasteland: Suburbia's Dead End Kids.* Chicago: University of Chicago Press.

Gallagher, Sally, and Christian Smith. 1999. "Symbolic Traditionalism and Pragmatic Egalitarianism: Contemporary Evangelicals, Families, and Gender." *Gender & Society* 13:211–33.

Gamson, Joshua, and Dawne Moon. 2004. "The Sociology of Sexualities: Queer and Beyond." *Annual Review of Sociology* 30:47–64.

Gans, Herbert J. 1979. "Symbolic Ethnicity: The Future of Ethnic Groups and Cultures in America." *Ethnic and Racial Studies* 2.1:1–20.

Gans, Herbet J. 1999. "The Possibility of a New Racial Hierarchy in the Twentieth-Century United States." In *The Cultural Territories of Race: Black and White Boundaries.* Edited by Michele Lamont. Chicago: University of Chicago Press.

Garfinkel, Harold. 1969. *Studies in Ethnomethodology.* New Jersey: Prentice Hall.

Glass, Jennifer, and Jerry Jacobs. 2005. "Childhood Religious Conservatism and Adult Attainment among Black and White Women." *Social Forces* 84.1 (September): 555–79.

Goffman, Erving. 1959. *The Presentation of Self in Everyday Life.* New York: Anchor.

Gordon, Hava. Forthcoming. "Gendered Paths to Teenage Political Participation: The Impact of Parental Constraint on Girls' Emergence into Community Politics."

Hackstaff, Karla B. 1999. *Marriage in a Culture of Divorce.* Philadelphia: Temple University Press.

Hall, Brian. 2006. "Social and Cultural Contexts in Conversion to Christianity among Chinese American College Students." *Sociology of Religion* 67.2:131–47.

Hall, John R. 1992. "The Capital(s) of Cultures: A Nonholistic Approach to Status Situations, Class, Gender, and Ethnicity." In *Cultivating Differences: Symbolic Boundaries and the Making of Inequality.* Edited by Michele Lamont and Marcel Fournier. Chicago: University of Chicago Press.

Harris, Anita. 2004. *Future Girl: Young Women in the Twenty-first Century.* New York: Routledge.

Hartigan, John, Jr. 2003. "Who Are These White People?' 'Rednecks,' 'Hillbillies,' and 'White Trash' as Marked Racial Subjects." In *White Out: The Continuing Significance of Racism.* Edited by Ashley Doane and Eduardo Bonilla-Silva. New York: Routledge.

Harvey, Paul. 1997. *Redeeming the South: Religious Cultures and Racial Identities among Southern Baptists 1865–1925.* Chapel Hill, NC: University of North Carolina Press.

Hays, Sharon. 1996. *The Cultural Contradictions of Motherhood.* New Haven, CT: Yale University Press.

———. 2003. *Flat Broke with Children: Women in the Age of Welfare Reform.* New York: Oxford University Press.

Heath, Melanie. 2003. "Soft-Boiled Masculinity: Renegotiating Gender and Racial Ideologies in the Promise Keepers Movement." *Gender & Society* 17.3 (June): 423–44.

Hebdige, Dick. 1979. *Subculture: The Meaning of Style.* London: Methuen.

Hennen, Peter. 2004. "Fae Spirits and Gender Trouble: Resistance and Compliance Among the Radical Faeries." *Journal of Contemporary Ethnography* 33.5 (October): 499–533.

———. 2005. "Bear Bodies, Bear Masculinity: Recuperation, Resistance, or Retreat?" *Gender & Society* 19.1 (February): 25–43.

Hertz, Rosanna. 2006. *Single by Chance, Mothers by Choice: How Women Are Choosing Parenthood without Marriage and Creating the New American Family.* New York: Oxford University Press.

Hewitt, John P. 1989. *Dilemmas of the American Self.* Philadelphia: Temple University Press.

Higginbotham, Evelyn Brooks. 1993. *Righteous Discontent: The Women's Movement in the Black Baptist Church 1880–1920.* Cambridge, MA: Harvard University Press.

Hill Collins, Patricia. 1991. *Black Feminist Thought: Knowledge, Consciousness, and the Politics of Empowerment.* New York: Routledge.

———. 1994. "Shifting the Center: Race, Class, and Feminist Theorizing About Motherhood." In *Mothering: Ideology, Experience, and Agency.* Edited by Evelyn Nakano Glenn, Grace Chang, and Linda Rennie Forcey. New York: Routledge.

———. 2004. *Black Sexual Politics: African Americans, Gender, and the New Racism.* New York: Routledge.

Hochschild, Arlie Russell. 1983. *The Managed Heart: Commercialization of Human Feeling.* Berkeley: University of California Press.

———. 1989. *The Second Shift: Working Parents and the Revolution at Home.* New York: Viking.

Holland, Dorothy C., and Margaret A. Eisenhart. 1990. *Educated in Romance: Women, Achievement, and College Culture.* Chicago: University of Chicago Press.

Hondagneu-Sotelo, Pierette, and Michael A. Messner. 1994. "Gender Displays and Men's Power: The 'New Man' and the Mexican Immigrant Man." In *Theorizing Masculinities.* Edited by Harry Brod and Michael Kaufman. Thousand Oaks, CA: Sage.

Ingraham, Chrys. 1999. *White Weddings: Romancing Heterosexuality in Popular Culture.* New York: Routledge.

Irvine, Janice M. 2002. *Talk about Sex: The Battle over Sex Education in the United States.* Berkeley: University of California Press.

Irvine, Leslie. 1999. *Codependent Forevermore: The Invention of Self in a Twelve Step Group.* Chicago: University of Chicago Press.

Jayson, Sharon. 2006. "Abstinence Message Goes Beyond Teens." *USA Today* (October 31).

Jewell, K. Sue. 1998. *From Mammy to Miss America and Beyond: Cultural Images in the Shaping of U.S. Social Policy.* New York: Routledge.

Katz, Jack. 1975. "Essences as Moral Identities: Verifiability and Responsibility in Imputations of Deviance and Charisma." *American Journal of Sociology* 80.6 (May): 1369–90.

Kelley, Robin D. G. 1997. *Yo' Mama's Dysfunctional! Fighting the Culture Wars in Urban America.* Boston: Beacon Press.

Kelly, Nathan J., and Jana Morgan Kelly. 2005. "Religion and Latino Partisanship in the United States." *Political Research Quarterly* 58.1 (March): 87–95.

Kenny, Lorraine Delia. 2000. *Daughters of Suburbia: Growing Up White, Middle Class, and Female.* New Brunswick, NJ: Rutgers University Press.

Kim, Rebecca Y. 2004. "Second-Generation Korean American Evangelicals: Ethnic, Multiethnic, or White Campus Ministries?" *Sociology of Religion* 65.1:19–34.

King, Deborah. 1988. "Multiple Jeopardy, Multiple Consciousness: The Context of a Black Feminist Ideology." *Signs: Journal of Women in Culture* 14:42–72.

Kleinman, Sherryl. 1996. *Opposing Ambitions: Gender and Identity in an Alternative Organization.* Chicago: University of Chicago.

Kotchemidova, Christina. 2005. "From Good Cheer to Drive-By Smiling: A Social History of Cheerfulness." *Journal of Social History* 39.1 (Fall): 5–37.

Lamont, Michele. 1992. *Money, Morals, and Manners: The Culture of the French and American Upper Middle Class.* Chicago: University of Chicago Press.

———. 1999. *The Cultural Territories of Race: Black and White Boundaries.* Chicago: University of Chicago Press.

———. 2000. *The Dignity of Working Men: Morality and the Boundaries of Race, Class, and Immigration.* Cambridge, MA: Harvard University Press.

Lamont, Michele, and Marcel Fournier. 1992. *Cultivating Differences: Symbolic Boundaries and the Making of Inequality.* Chicago: University of Chicago Press.

Landale, Nancy S., and R. S. Oropesa. 2002. "White, Black, or Puerto Rican? Racial Self-Identification among Mainland and Island Puerto Ricans." *Social Forces* 8.1 (September): 231–54.

Lao, Augustin. 1997. "Islands at the Crossroads: Puerto Ricanness Traveling Between the Translocal Nation and the Global City." In *Puerto Rican Jam: Essays on Culture and Politics.* Edited by Frances Negrón-Muntaner and Ramón Grosfoguel. Minneapolis: University of Minnesota.

Laqueur, Thomas. 1990. *Making Sex: Body and Gender from the Greeks to Freud.* Cambridge, MA: Harvard University Press.

Lareau, Annette. 2003. *Unequal Childhoods: Class, Race, and Family Life.* Berkeley: University of California Press.

Lassiter, David. 2007. Race Travesty: Studying the Negative State of Race Relations at the University of Colorado. Master's thesis, University of Colorado.

LeBlanc, Lauraine. 1999. *Pretty in Punk: Girls' Gender Resistance in a Boys' Subculture.* New Brunswick, NJ: Rutgers University Press.

Lee, Stacey J. 1994. "Behind the Model-Minority Stereotype: Voices of High- and Low-Achieving Asian American Students." *Anthropology and Education Quarterly* 25.4:413–29.

Lees, Sue. 1993. *Sugar and Spice: Sexuality and Adolescent Girls.* London: Penguin.

Levine, Judith. 2002. *Harmful to Minors: The Perils of Protecting Children from Sex.* Minneapolis: University of Minneapolis Press.

Loewen, James. 1971. *The Mississippi Chinese: Between Black and White.* Cambridge, MA: Harvard University Press.

Lorber, Judith. 1994. *Paradoxes of Gender*. New Haven, CT: Yale University Press.

Luker, Kristin. 1996. *Dubious Conceptions: The Politics of Teenage Pregnancy*. Cambridge, MA: Harvard University Press.

Luttrell, Wendy. 1993. "'The Teachers, They All Had Their Pets': Concepts of Gender, Knowledge, and Power." *Signs: Journal of Women in Culture and Society* 18.3 (Spring): 505–46.

Lynd, Helen M. 1958. *On Shame and the Search for Identity*. New York: Harcourt Brace.

Maher, Lisa. 1997. *Sexed Work: Gender, Race, and Resistance in a Brooklyn Drug Market*. Oxford: Clarendon Press.

Mailer, Norman. 1959. "The White Negro." In *Advertisements for Myself*. New York: Putnam.

Maira, Sunaina Marr. 2002. *Desis in the House: Indian American Youth Culture in New York City*. Philadelphia: Temple University Press.

Majors, Richard, and Janet Mancini Billson. 1992. *Cool Pose: The Dilemmas of Black Manhood in America*. New York: Lexington Books.

Males, Mike A. 1996. *The Scapegoat Generation: America's War on Adolescents*. Monroe, ME: Common Courage Press.

Mason-Schrock, Douglas. 1996. "Transsexuals' Narrative Construction of the 'True Self.'" *Social Psychology Quarterly* 59.3 (September): 176–92.

McCracken, Grant. 1998. *Culture and Consumption: New Approaches to the Symbolic Character of Consumer Goods*. Bloomington: Indiana University Press.

McRobbie, Angela. 1991. *Feminism and Youth Culture: From 'Jackie' to 'Just Seventeen.'* London: MacMillan.

McRobbie, Angela, and Jenny Garber. 1997. "Girls and Subcultures." In *The Subcultures Reader*. Edited by Ken Gelder and Sarah Thornton. New York: Routledge.

Mihelich, John and Debbie Storrs. 2003. "Higher Education and the Negotiated Process of Hegemony: Embedded Resistance among Mormon Women." *Gender & Society* 17.3 (June): 404–22.

Milner, Murray, Jr. 2004. *Freaks, Geeks, and Cool Kids: American Teenagers, Schools, and the Culture of Consumption*. New York: Routledge.

Mohanty, Chandra Talpade. 1991. "Cartographies of Struggle: Third World Women and the Politics of Feminism." In *Third World Women and the Politics of Feminism*. Edited by Chandra Mohanty, Ann Russo, and Lourdes Torres. Bloomington: Indiana University Press.

Montemurro, Beth. 2006. *Something Old, Something Bold: Bridal Showers and Bachelorette Parties*. New Brunswick, NJ: Rutgers University Press.

Moore, Joan, and Raquel Pinderhughes. 1993. *In the Barrios: Latinos and the Underclass Debate*. New York: Russell Sage Foundation.

Mullaney, Jamie. 2001. "Like a Virgin: Temptation, Resistance, and the Construction of Identities Based on 'Not-Doings.'" *Qualitative Sociology* 24.1:3–24.

Nagel, Joane. 1996. *American Indian Ethnic Renewal: Red Power and the Resurgence of Identity and Culture*. New York: Oxford University Press.

———. 2000. "Ethnicity and Sexuality." *Annual Review of Sociology* 26:107–33.

————. 2003. *Race, Ethnicity, and Sexuality: Intimate Intersections, Forbidden Frontiers*. New York: Oxford University Press.

Nayak, Anoop. 2003. *Race, Place, and Globalization: Youth Cultures in a Changing World*. New York: Berg.

Negrón-Muntaner, Frances. 1997. "English only Jamás but Spanish only Cuidado: Language and Nationalism in Contemporary Puerto Rico." In *Puerto Rican Jam: Rethinking Colonialism and Nationalism*. Edited by Frances Negrón-Muntaner and Ramón Grosfoguel. Minneapolis: University of Minnesota Press.

Odem, Mary E. 1995. *Delinquent Daughters: Protecting and Policing Adolescent Female Sexuality in the United States, 1885–1920*. Chapel Hill, NC: University of North Carolina Press.

Omi, Michael, and Howard Winant. 1986. *Racial Formations in the United States: From the 1960s to the 1980s*. New York: Routledge.

Orr, Catherine M. 1997. "Charting the Currents of the Third Wave." *Hypatia* 12.3 (Summer): 12–44.

Ortner, Sherry. 1998. "Identities: The Hidden Life of Class." *Journal of Anthropological Research* 55.1 (Spring): 1–17.

————. 2003. *New Jersey Dreaming: Capital, Culture, and the Class of '58*. Durham, NC: Duke University Press.

Otnes, Cele C., and Elizabeth H. Pleck. 2003. *Cinderella Dreams: The Allure of the Lavish Wedding*. Berkeley: University of California Press.

Pascoe, C. J. 2005. "'Dude, You're a Fag!' Adolescent Masculinity and the Fag Discourse." *Sexualities* 8.3:329–46.

Patillo-McCoy, Mary. 1999. *Black Picket Fences: Privilege and Peril Among the Black Middle Class*. Chicago: University of Chicago Press.

Patton, Cindy. 1996. *Fatal Advice: How Safe-Sex Education Went Wrong*. Durham, NC: Duke University Press.

Perry, Pamela. 2002. *Shades of White: White Kids and Racial Identities in High School*. Durham, NC: Duke University Press.

Peterson, Richard A., and Roger M. Kern. 1996. "Changing Highbrow Taste: From Snob to Omnivore." *American Sociological Review* 61.5 (October): 900–907.

Phillips, Lynn M. 2000. *Flirting with Danger: Young Women's Reflections on Sexuality and Domination*. New York: New York University Press.

Pipher, Mary B. 1994. *Reviving Ophelia: Saving the Selves of Adolescent Girls*. New York: Putnam.

Polhemus, Ted. 1994. *Streetstyle: From Sidewalk to Catwalk*. London: Thames and Hudson.

Pyke, Karen. 1996. "Class-Based Masculinities: The Interdependence of Gender, Class, and Interpersonal Power." *Gender & Society* 10.5 (October): 527–49.

Pyke, Karen D., and Denise L. Johnson. 2003. "Asian American Women and Racialized Femininities: 'Doing' Gender across Cultural Worlds." *Gender & Society* 17.1 (February): 33–53.

Quindlen, Anna. 1996. "And Now, Babe Feminism." In *Bad Girls/Good Girls: Women, Sex, and Power in the Nineties*. Edited by Nan Bauer Maglin and Donna Perry. New Brunswick, NJ: Rutgers University Press.

Read, Jen'nan Ghazal, and John P. Bartkowski. 2000. "To Veil or Not to Veil? A Case Study of Identity Negotiation among Muslim Women in Austin, Texas." *Gender & Society* 14.3 (June): 395–417.

Reich, Jennifer A. 2005. *Fixing Families: Parents, Power, and the Child Welfare System.* New York: Routledge.

Risman, Barbara, and Pepper Scwartz. 2007. "After the Sexual Revolution: Gender Politics in Teen Dating." In *Feminist Frontiers,* 7th edition. Edited by Verta Taylor, Nancy Whittier, and Leila J. Rupp. New York: McGraw-Hill.

Rivera, Raquel Z. 2001. "Hip-Hop, Puerto Ricans, and Ethnoracial Identities in New York." In *Mambo Montage: The Latinization of New York.* Edited by Augustin Lao-Montes and Arlene Davila. New York: Columbia University Press.

Roberts, Dorothy. 1997. *Killing the Black Body: Race, Reproduction, and the Meaning of Liberty.* New York: Pantheon Books.

Rodriguez, Clara E. 2000. *Changing Race: Latinos, the Census, and the History of Ethnicity in the United States.* New York: New York University Press.

Roediger, David R. 1991. *The Wages of Whiteness: Race and the Making of the American Working Class.* New York: Verso.

———. 2002. *Colored White: Transcending the Racial Past.* Berkeley: University of California Press.

Romano, Renee. 2003. *Race Mixing: Black-White Mixing in Postwar America.* Cambridge, MA: Harvard University Press.

Rose, Tricia. 1994. *Black Noise: Rap Music and Black Culture in Contemporary America.* Hanover, NH: Wesleyan University Press.

Rosenberg, Debra, and Pat Wingert. 2006. "First Comes Junior in a Baby Carriage: Four in Ten Kids are Now Born to Unmarried Moms" *Newsweek* (December 4).

Schalet, Amy, Geoffrey Hunt, and Karen Joe-Laidler. 2003. "Respectability and Autonomy: The Articulation and Meaning of Sexuality among the Girls in the Gang." *Journal of Contemporary Ethnography* 32.1 (February): 108–43.

Scheff, Thomas J. 2000. "Shame and the Social Bond: A Sociological Theory." *Sociological Theory* 18.1 (March): 84–99.

Schippers, Mimi. 2002. *Rockin' Out of the Box: Gender Maneuvering in Alternative Hard Rock.* New Brunswick, NJ: Rutgers University Press.

Schor, Juliet. 1998. *The Overspent American: Upscaling, Downshifting, and the New Consumer.* New York: Basic Books.

Schwalbe, Michael, and Douglas Mason-Schrock. 1996. "Identity Work as Group Process." In *Advances in Group Processes,* vol. 13. Edited by Barry Markovsky, Michael Lovaglia, and Robin Simon. Greenwich, CT: JAI Press.

Schweingruber, David, and Molly Meyer. 2007. What's Wrong with Dating? Critiques of "Dating" in Evangelical Romance Manuals. Presented at the Meeting of the Midwest Sociological Society, Chicago (April 4).

Sennett, Richard, and Jonathon Cobb. 1972. *The Hidden Injuries of Class.* New York: Knopf.

Shanahan, Michael. 2000. "Pathways to Adulthood in Changing Societies: Variability and Mechanisms in Life Course Perspective." *Annual Review of Sociology* 26:667–92.

Sheff, Elisabeth. 2005. "Polyamorous Women, Sexual Subjectivity and Power." *Journal of Contemporary Ethnography* 34 (June): 251–93.

Sidel, Ruth. 1990. *On Her Own: Growing up in the Shadow of the American Dream.* New York: Penguin.

Sikes, Gini. 1997. *8 Ball Chicks: A Year in the Violent World of Girl Gangs.* New York: Doubleday.

Simmel, Georg. 1972. *Georg Simmel on Individuality and Social Forms.* Edited by Donald N. Levine. Chicago: University of Chicago Press.

Skeggs, Beverly. 1997. *Formations of Class and Gender: Becoming Respectable.* London: Sage.

Smith, Christian. 2000. *Christian America: What Evangelicals Really Want.* Berkeley: University of California Press.

Smith, Christian, with Melinda Lundquist Denton. 2005. *Soul Searching: The Religious and Spiritual Lives of American Teenagers.* New York: Oxford University Press.

Solinger, Rickie. 1992. *Wake up Little Susie: Single Pregnancy and Race before Roe v. Wade.* New York: Routledge.

Stacey, Judith. 1990. *Brave New Families: Stories of Domestic Upheaval in Late Twentieth Century America.* New York: Basic Books.

Stearns, Peter. 1994. *American Cool: Constructing a Twentieth-Century Emotional Style.* New York: New York University Press.

Stein, Arlene. 1989. "Three Models of Sexuality: Drives, Identities and Practices." *Sociological Theory* 7.1 (Spring): 1–13.

———. 1997. *Sex and Sensibility: Stories of a Lesbian Generation.* Berkeley: University of California Press.

Stokes, Randall, and John P. Hewitt. 1976. "Aligning Actions." *American Sociological Review* 41 (October): 838–49.

Stombler, Mindy, and Irene Padavic. 1997. "Sister Acts: Resisting Men's Domination in Black and White Fraternity Little Sister Programs." *Social Problems* 44.2:257–75.

Stuber, Jenny M. 2006. "Talk of Class: The Discursive Repertoires of White Working-and Upper-Middle-Class College Students." *Journal of Contemporary Ethnography* 35.3 (June): 285–318.

Swidey, Neil. 2003. "God on the Quad." *Boston Globe Magazine* (November 30).

Tanenbaum, Leora. 1999. *Slut! Growing up Female with a Bad Reputation.* New York: Seven Stories Press.

Tapia, Andres T. 1997. "After the Hugs, What? Next Steps for Racial Reconciliation." *Christianity Today* 41.2 (February 3): 54.

Thompson, Sharon. 1995. *Going All the Way: Teenage Girls' Tales of Sex, Romance, and Pregnancy.* New York: Hill and Wang.

Thornton Dill, Bonnie. 1983. "Race, Class, and Gender: Prospects for an All-Inclusive Sisterhood." *Feminist Studies* 9.1 (Spring): 131–50.

Thornton, Sarah. 1996. *Club Cultures: Music, Media and Subcultural Capital.* Hanover, NH: Wesleyan University Press.

Tolman, Deborah. 1996. "Adolescent Girls' Sexuality: Debunking the Myth of the Urban Girl." In *Urban Girls: Resisting Stereotypes, Creating Identities.* Edited by Bonnie J. Ross Leadbeater and Niobe Way. New York: New York University Press.

Traber, Daniel S. 2001. "LA's 'White Minority': Punk and the Contradictions of Self-Marginalization." *Cultural Critique* 48.1:30–64.

Turner, Ralph H. 1976. "The Real Self: From Institution to Impulse." *American Journal of Sociology* 81.5 (March): 989–1016.

Wald, Gayle. 1996. "'A Most Disagreeable Mirror': Reflections on White Identity in *Black Like Me*." In *Passing and the Fictions of Identity*. Edited by Elaine Ginsburg. Durham, NC: Duke University Press.

Wartenberg, Thomas. 1988. "The Situated Concept of Social Power." *Social Theory and Practice* 14.

Waters, Mary C. 1990. *Ethnic Options: Choosing Identities in America.* Berkeley: University of California Press.

Wellman, David. 1997. "Minstrel Shows, Affirmative Action Talk, and Angry White Men: Marking Racial Otherness in the 1990s." In *Displacing Whiteness: Essays in Social and Cultural Criticism.* Edited by Ruth Frankenberg. Durham, NC: Duke University Press.

West, Candace, and Don H. Zimmerman. 1987. "Doing Gender." *Gender & Society* 1.2:125–51.

West, Candace, and Sarah Fenstermaker. 1995. "Doing Difference." *Gender & Society* 9.1:8–37.

White, E. Frances. 2001. *Dark Continent of Our Bodies: Black Feminism and the Politics of Respectability.* Philadelphia: Temple University Press.

Wilcox, William Bradford. 2004. *Soft Patriarchs, New Men: How Christianity Shapes Fathers and Husbands.* Chicago: University of Chicago Press.

Wilkins, Amy C. 2004a. "Puerto Rican Wannabes: Sexual Spectacle and the Marking of Race, Class, and Gender Boundaries." *Gender & Society* 18.1 (February): 103–21.

———. 2004b. "'So Full of Myself as a Chick': Goth Women, Sexual Independence, and Gender Egalitarianism." *Gender & Society* 18.3 (June): 328–49.

———. Forthcoming. "Unconventional Heterosexualities and Intimacy Talk: Recuperating Masculinity in Two Young Adult Subcultures." *Signs: A Journal of Women in Culture and Society.*

Willis, Paul. 1977. *Learning to Labor: How Working Class Kids Get Working Class Jobs.* New York: Columbia University Press.

Winddance Twine, France. 1997. "Brown-Skinned White Girls: Class, Culture, and the Construction of White Identity in Suburban Communities." In *Displacing Whiteness: Essays in Social and Cultural Criticism.* Edited by Ruth Frankenberg. Durham, NC: Duke University Press.

———. 1999. "Transracial Mothering and Antiracism: The Case of White Birth Mothers of 'Black' Children in Britain." *Feminist Studies* 25.3 (Fall): 729–46.

Wolf, Naomi. 1991. *The Beauty Myth: How Images of Beauty are Used Against Women.* New York: W. Morrow.

Wolkomir, Michelle. 2006. *Be Not Deceived: The Sacred and Sexual Struggles of Gay and Ex-Gay Christian Men.* New Brunswick, NJ: Rutgers University Press.

Films

8 Mile. 2002. Directed by Curtis Hanson. Imagine Entertainment.
"Education of Shelby Knox." 2005. Directed by Marion Lipschutz and Rose Ro-
    senblatt. Incite Pictures.
Saved! 2004. Directed by Brian Dannelly. United Artists.
Save the Last Dance. 2001. Directed by Thomas Carter. Cort/Madden Productions.

Index